INTERIBERICA, S.A. DE EDICIONES

DESERTS AND GRASSLANDS
The World's Open Spaces

Doubleday and Company Inc.,
Garden City, New York, 1977
A Windfall Book

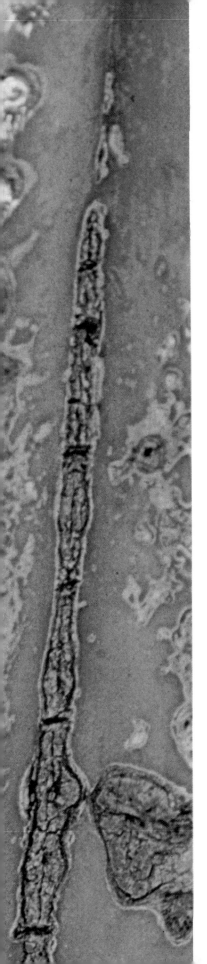

DESERTS
AND GRASSLANDS

Part 1
Desert Life

by John Cloudsley-Thompson

ISBN: 84-382-0016-8. Dep. Legal: S.S. 602-1975
Printed and bound in Spain by
T.O.N.S.A., and Roner S.A.,
Crta de Irun, Km.12,450, Madrid—34

Series Coordinator Geoffrey Rogers
Series Art Director Frank Fry
Design Consultant Guenther Radtke
Editorial Consultant Donald Berwick
Series Consultant Malcolm Ross-Macdonald
Art Editor Douglas Sneddon
Copy Editor Maureen Cartwright
Research Barbara Fraser
Art Assistant Michael Turner

Contents: Part 1

Editorial Advisers

DAVID ATTENBOROUGH Naturalist and Broadcaster.

MICHAEL BOORER, B.SC. Author, Lecturer, and Broadcaster.

MATTHEW BRENNAN, ED.D. Director, Brentree Environmental Center, Professor of Conservation Education, Pennsylvania State University.

PHYLLIS BUSCH, ED.D. Author, Science Teacher, and Consultant in Environmental Education.

JAMES OLIVER, PH.D. Director of the New York Aquarium, former Director of the American Museum of Natural History, former Director of the New York Zoological Park, formerly Professor of Zoology, University of Florida.

Foreword by David Attenborough

*T*he plains of the world provide a stage on which the most spectacular creatures on earth perform dramas in the open for all to see. The actors include the biggest, the tallest, and the swiftest of all the land animals as well as the largest living bird. The supporting cast parades in staggering numbers. A quarter of a million wildebeest migrate each year across the savannas of the Serengeti in East Africa. Buffalo grazed the prairies of America in herds so dense that they blackened the land for as far as the eye could see—until man hunted them to the point of extinction.

The fact that the plains are largely without cover has led some birds to develop extraordinary displays that depend for their effect upon being seen at a considerable distance. The result is theatrical spectacle on an unforgettable scale. In America, sage grouse cocks congregate on special display grounds, inflate themselves grotesquely, and quiveringly strut around one another. In Africa, crowned cranes assemble in the dawn and begin to dance, often throwing small objects such as feathers into the air, as though playing some skittish game.

Some 2 million years ago, one actor of special interest made its entry onto this stage. It was a small apelike creature with a taste for meat. In order to hunt on the open plain, it learned how to rise onto its hind legs and stand erect so that it could get a better view of its quarry, grazing in the distance. It was neither swift nor powerfully armed. But it overcame these handicaps by developing elaborate vocalizations so that members of a hunting band could communicate with one another; and it learned how to use tools. It was our ancestor.

Little wonder, therefore, that the study of life on the plains is of great fascination to us. And the more that biologists look at these stunning sights, the more they discover about the complexities and subtleties of the processes that have produced these creatures in such forms and led them to behave in such ways. Dr. Eric Duffey, in the pages that follow, unravels some of the tangled, intricate relationships between the vegetation of the plains, the creatures that browse on them, the great carnivores that prey upon the herds, and the scavengers that consume the remains of all.

The grasslands, as they extend into the tropical zones, become drier and hotter until they are transformed into deserts. The savannas of Africa merge northward into the Sahara, the American prairies are continuous with the deserts of Arizona and New Mexico. The transition brings huge changes to life in these open spaces. Some plants shrivel. Others become grossly bloated in order to store the maximum amount of water. Reptiles, which relish the heat to warm their cold blood, flourish. But most animals find the day so searingly hot that they are active only in the night or early morning. The methods that many creatures have developed to combat these conditions are intriguing. Professor Cloudsley-Thompson has specialized in the study of desert life and he gives an authoritative account of the ways in which creatures manage to conserve water, prevent over-heating, build up food stores, and even go into a form of suspended animation between one brief rainy period and another many months later.

Together, these two authors provide a detailed account of the many marvelous ways in which animals and plants have managed to colonize the plains where life can seem so lush and the deserts where it is so harsh—accounts that interlock to form a picture of the vast open spaces that are man's original home.

David Attenborough.

The Desert Environment

An astronaut looking at earth from space is bound to be struck by the huge areas of brown desert that he sees. Desert and semidesert lands make up 20 to 25 per cent of the total land surface. From the Atlantic Ocean, the largest desert in the world (which biologists call the Great Palaearctic Desert) stretches almost continuously across North Africa and Asia Minor to northern India and the heart of China. In addition, much of southern Africa and of North and South America, as well as most of Australia, can be classified as desert or semi-desert.

The desert presents a variety of forms. Sometimes it is a rocky plateau, sometimes a pebbly plain. In some places there are huge depressions with dunes of shifting sands; in others, mountainous escarpments. As an observer approaches the cores of the great desert regions, where the rainfall becomes less and less frequent, he reaches a stage where the landscape looks quite lunar because its erosion by wind has so long exceeded that by water. Even in such "dead" spots as the central Sahara, however, dried vegetation carried by the winds from the desert's edge supports a small population of insects preyed on by arachnids and reptiles. So, as we shall see, an amazing variety of living creatures inhabits these seemingly inhospitable regions.

Although it is not difficult to recognize a desert, opinions vary as to the physical features of the environment that should be used as criteria for defining a desert climate. Rainfall must obviously be taken into account, and desert conditions usually prevail in tropical regions when the average annual precipitation is under 5 inches, with semidesert conditions occurring when the average rainfall is over 5 but under 15 inches. But such figures can be only approximate, because what matters is not only the amount but the effectiveness of rain; and the effectiveness of rain depends on its seasonal occurrence, its rate of evaporation, and the nature of the soil. If we

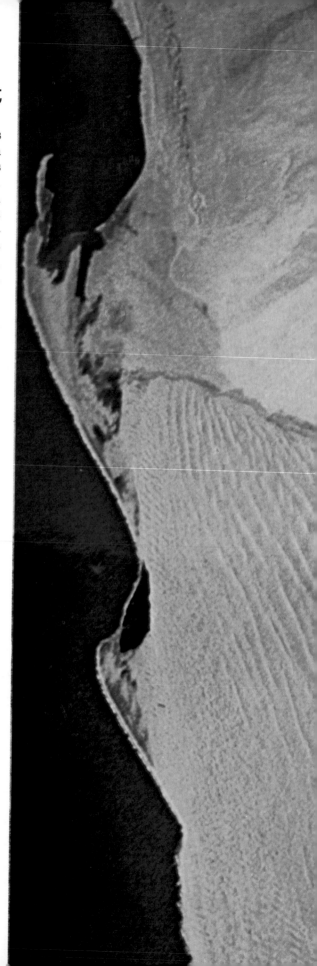

The Namib Desert of Southwest Africa—perhaps the oldest of all deserts—viewed from the newest of vantage points, an American space ship. Two types of desert terrain are visible: the massive parallel dunes of the central Namib at the bottom, and rocky flats at the top. The Kuiseb River clearly divides them.

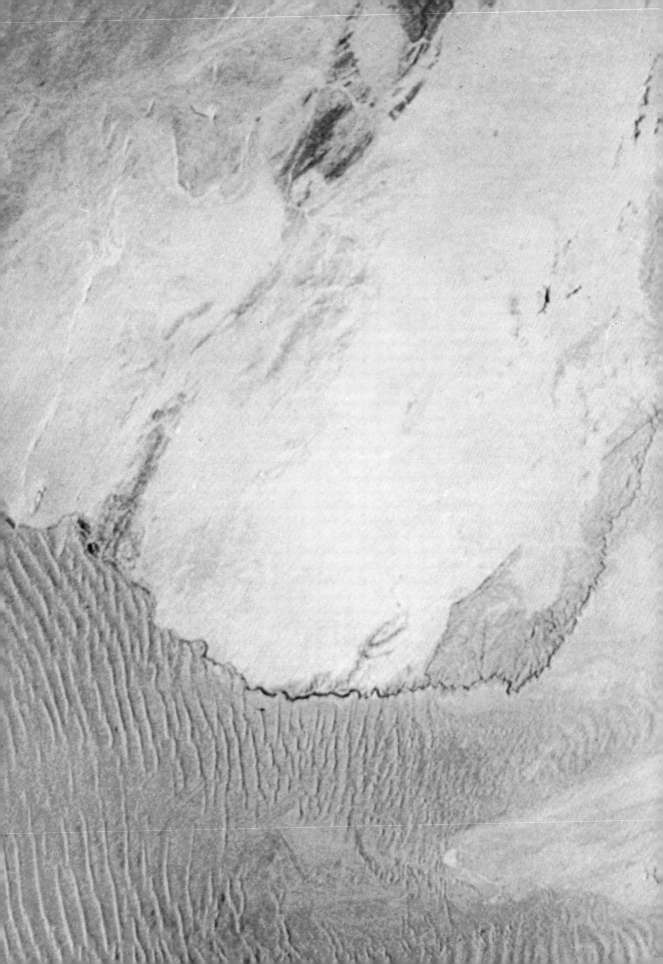

define deserts as areas that have high temperatures and less than 10 inches of rain annually, 14 per cent of the earth's 56 million square miles of land must be classified as desert; and another 14 per cent of steppe land, which has high daily and annual temperature ranges and a yearly rainfall of between 10 and 20 inches, contributes vastly to the total arid zone.

The aridity that results mainly from a lack of rain is often due to the way in which the atmosphere circulates, particularly in its lower layers, and this partly explains the geographical distribution of the world's deserts: near latitudes 30°N and s, the direction of the winds tends to vary, and the air sinks. When this happens, it is warmed by the hot ground, and clouds are dispersed. At the same time, high-pressure belts that separate the polar westerly winds and the tropical easterlies occur near these latitudes. Consequently, the disturbances associated with low pressure, which usually cause rain, are rare.

Then, too, there are local factors that sometimes result in low rainfall. These include the rain-shadow effects of mountain ranges, which cause the air to drop all its moisture as it crosses them. For example, much of the Australian desert behind the Queensland coast is caused by the rain-shadow of the mountains that block the path of the south-east winds; and the Cascade and Sierra Nevada mountains, which force Pacific winds to drop their rain, are responsible for most of the North American desert regions. Not mountains but sheer remoteness from oceanic moisture is responsible for the drought of the central Sahara and Gobi deserts. And— just as an illustration of the complexity of the question of what causes deserts—it is not remoteness from the ocean but *closeness* to the ocean that is responsible for the coastal deserts of Chile, Peru, and southwest Africa. In these regions, cold oceanic currents flowing from the poles to the equator bring with them cool winds that carry fog and mist but not rain. For though the humidity of the air is usually high, there is a lack of the atmospheric disturbances that normally cause rainfall.

To generalize, then, the major deserts of the world result primarily from global or hemispheric wind patterns, and they are characterized by low rainfall, which is usually associated with considerable exposure to the rays of the sun from a cloudless sky. Very few, if any, deserts are completely dry, but desert rainfall is always

unreliable. Although it sometimes tends to be seasonal, it is most erratic. One spot in the desert may experience heavy rain, while another, only a few miles away, is dry. Rainfall is extremely variable from one year to the next; and even when plentiful it may not be beneficial because, as there is little vegetation, most of the water runs quickly off the surface of the ground. Within a few minutes, dry watercourses may become roaring torrents, removing any vestige of topsoil and eroding deep gulleys.

My wife and I saw something of all this when driving across the Sahara in midsummer, a few years ago. One evening in northern Tchad, a devastating thunderstorm struck just as we began to prepare camp for the night. A sudden gale was followed by a torrential downpour. Within minutes, the entire landscape, brilliantly illuminated by the continual lightning, was inundated. Looking out from our jeep, we seemed to be floating in a vast sea, the ripples from the wind giving the effect of rapid currents. When the rain stopped abruptly at 1 A.M., we literally had to shout in order to be heard above the fantastic chorus of croaking toads and stridu-

lating insects. (Similar eruptions of sound follow flash floods in Arizona, New Mexico, Australia, and other desert places.) Yet all was quiet after sunrise, a few hours later. All was quiet—and, a few miles farther on, the ground was bone dry.

It will be clear, from these remarks, that average figures of rainfall are of little significance as far as the lives of desert plants and animals are concerned. The same is true for figures of mean temperatures. This is because cool, or even cold, nights may follow very warm days. Likewise, although the summer days can be extremely hot, the following winter may be really cold.

In nondesert regions, where the air is often laden with water vapor, either diffused or in the form of clouds, less of the sun's heat can penetrate to the ground during the day; and less is lost by radiation at night. Thus, in humid areas some 20 per cent of solar radiation may be deflected by clouds, 10 per cent by dust, and 30 per cent by water surfaces and vegetation. In clear desert air, on the other hand, only about 10 per cent of the solar radiation is deflected by dust particles and cloud. At night, the situation is reversed. Up to 90 per cent of accumulated heat

Above: the Colorado River winds its way through Arizona's Grand Canyon, one of the world's most spectacular examples of desert erosion caused by water. The river has cut a channel through soft sedimentary rock interspersed with harder layers. The sides are almost vertical because they are not eroded by rain.

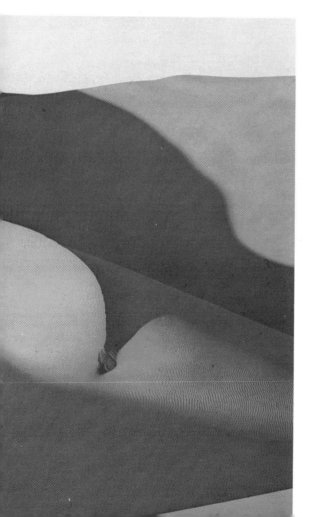

Left: in the Sahara Desert, where water in any form is scarce, wind shapes the great, shifting sand dunes, many of which reach heights of 700 feet and stretch for hundreds of miles.

To survive in their harsh environment, some desert plants have evolved ways of discouraging hungry animals from devouring them. The creosote bush (above) gets its name from its acrid odor, which is so unpleasant that few creatures will eat the blooms. And the sharp spines of the cholla (left) stay in the flesh.

In arid regions, animals may need extra defenses. The Gila monster of Arizona is one of the only two species of venomous lizard.

Above: the only defense of the South African springbok lies in its speed. These small antelopes used to migrate in vast herds, but hunting has greatly reduced their numbers.

escapes from the desert soil to the upper air, because there are no clouds to blanket the earth, whereas in humid regions only 50 per cent of the heat escapes, with the rest either reflected by clouds and dust or retained by soil, vegetation, and water. As a consequence, humid climates tend to have daily and seasonal stability; temperatures in humid equatorial areas, for instance, remain relatively constant, with comparatively cool days and warm nights. In contrast, most deserts are characterized by extremes of temperature and humidity. It is such extremes—high temperatures liable to reach lethal levels alternating with low temperatures that limit the growing season or even cause freezing—that affect living organisms most.

As I have indicated, winds are a constant feature of deserts. They tend to be strongest in spring and early summer and to blow hardest during the day, whereas the nights are relatively calm. Although their speeds seldom exceed 50 miles an hour, and average only about 10 miles an hour throughout the year, the effect of wind is enhanced by the drought, high temperatures and

lack of vegetation. For desert winds carry either small particles of dust and sand, which erode the rocks (sometimes producing weird and statuesque effects), or larger grains, which cause dunes as they are swept across the soil surface. As a result of the consequent erosion, desert sand consists of rounded grains, often frosted by the chemical action due to an unending alternation of wetting by dew and drying by the sun. These grains are so smooth that they are not painful when blown into a person's eye; and they are far less gritty than sea sand when they get into food.

Throughout large areas of desert, the distribution of plants and the way plants and animals live are determined chiefly by the presence or absence of certain kinds of wind. Desert winds are, indeed, so special in character that we have highly special names for them. There is, for instance, the North African *khamsin* (from the Arabic word for "50"), which is said to blow for 50 days at a stretch—a suffocating, dust-laden gale that cakes you with yellow mud, spoils your food, and reduces visibility to zero. I remember one night, in Libya, when I could not see a

13

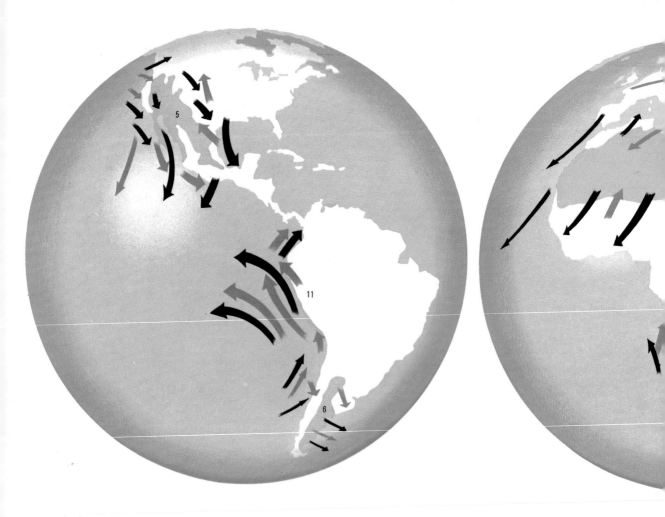

Major Deserts of the World

		Square miles
1	Sahara Desert	3,500,000
2	Australian Desert	1,300,000
3	Arabian Desert	1,000,000
4	Turkestan Desert	750,000
5	Great American Desert, including the Great Basin, Mojave, Sonora, and Chihuahua Deserts of southwestern North America	500,000
6	Patagonian Desert (Argentina)	260,000
7	Thar Desert (India)	230,000
8	Kalahari and Namib Deserts (Southwest Africa)	220,000
9	Takla Makan Desert, including the Gobi Desert (from Western China to Mongolia)	200,000
10	Iranian Desert	150,000
11	Atacama Desert (Peru and Chile)	140,000

These globes show the location of the major deserts listed at left and the direction of prevailing winds. Black arrows show January winds, brown arrows those that predominate in July. Direction of wind is of vital importance for rainfall. The northward-moving July winds, for example, bring monsoon-type summer rain to the southern and central Sahara and to the deserts of India and the Middle East. The main cause of aridity in the central Sahara, Arabia, Gobi, and Australian deserts is the fact that they are far from the sea and beyond the reach of rain-bearing winds. In contrast, the Namib Desert and the deserts of Chile and Peru lie in coastal regions, but cold oceanic currents from the Antarctic Ocean bring only fog and mist, not rain. Subtropical deserts, including the Kalahari and the southern part of the Sahara, may result from semipermanent belts of high pressure, whereas much of the North American and part of the Australian desert are deprived of rain by nearby mountains that drain the moisture out of the winds that blow over them from the Pacific Ocean.

lighted torch from a distance of five paces. In Algeria, the *khamsin* is known as the *sirocco*, in the central Sahara as the *shahali* (meaning "wind from the south"), and elsewhere as the *harmattan* or the *simoom*. The *haboobs* (dust storms) of the northern Sudan can also reduce visibility to a few feet and bring about almost complete darkness at noon. Even more spectacular are the *chubaseos* of the North American deserts, where wind speeds may reach 80 to 100 miles an hour.

Another familiar phenomenon, the whirlwind (known as a "dust devil" in India and an *ebliss* in the Sudan), results from a sudden upward rush of heated air on a still day. Such whirlwinds often carry sand and other objects from the soil to great heights. No doubt many small plants and animals are destroyed in this way, and others may be dispersed to new habitats far from their original homes. In general, however, desert plants tend to specialize in adaptations that prevent their seeds from being dispersed too

widely; and desert animals are adept at finding shelter from wind. Otherwise many species would long ago have lost the battle for survival.

As you can see, it is not easy for plants and animals to survive in this setting of climatic extremes, of drought and flood, of erratic rainfall, and of rapid change from intense heat during the day to extreme cold at night. It is not surprising that their adaptations should be correspondingly extreme. Desert animals usually run faster than their relatives in temperate regions. Venomous forms are more poisonous than their allies beyond the desert's fringe. Spiny plants are more prickly, and distasteful ones more unpleasant, than anywhere else.

Yet the desert exerts a strange fascination on every traveler, whether or not he is a naturalist. In the binding glare of the midday heat, when goats and camels huddle in the scanty shade of bare rock or sparse vegetation, and when the salty sweat stings one's eyes, the desert's appeal may seem less than impressive. But in the cool

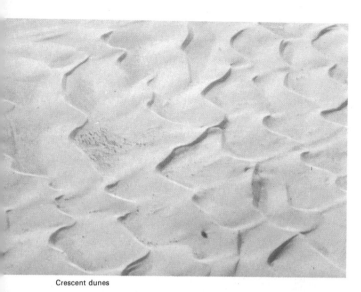

Crescent dunes

Longitudinal dunes

Above: a desert storm at the Australian oasis of Alice Springs. Storms of dust and sand, carried by strong winds, occur in arid regions where soil is not bound by vegetation.

Transverse dunes

The three photographs at left show different dune patterns. When wind blows from only one direction and sand is sparse, dunes tend to be crescent-shaped (top) because sand blows most readily over the dunes' low "horns," which advance faster than the central hump. Longitudinal dunes (center) are made by strong winds, which move both coarse and fine sand, leaving parallel troughs. Moderate winds moving only light sand form transverse dunes (bottom). Other shapes, such as star-shaped dunes, arise where wind blows from all directions.

of evening, as a crimson sun tints the western sky with indigo and splashes the scattered clouds with violet rays, the bizarre and barren landscape is often strikingly beautiful. Moreover, as the temperature falls, the human body recovers from its sense of extreme discomfort, for it is now able to replenish the liquid it has lost during the day. Under extreme conditions of heat and low humidity, we lose water, through the evaporation of sweat, more rapidly than we can absorb it by drinking; and so progressive desiccation is unavoidable throughout the day. During the night, this trend is reversed and all is

well—if there is plenty of drinking water at hand.

The Arabs have several words to describe the varying intensities of thirst. They range from the minor thirst that most of us have often experienced to the raging thirst of death. A man stranded in a hot desert may survive for about a day without water, provided he does not undertake heavy work. By nightfall his mouth will be dry and bitter, his lips, tongue, and uvula swollen. (The uvula is the fleshy lobe hanging down at the back of the throat.) He will live through the night and for perhaps an hour after daybreak. But as the sun relentlessly climbs in the sky, he

The expanse of water reflecting the hills in the distance is not real, but a mirage photographed in the Mauritanian region of the Sahara. The illusion of water—a frequent one in desert areas—is caused by rays of light above the horizon being refracted by a shimmering layer of hot air close to the ground. The effect is the same as if a pool of water lay on the desert, reflecting light from the sky.

will surely die unless he finds water. Death may come from choking as the uvula swells so much that it closes the throat, or it may take the form of "explosive heat death": as water is lost, the blood becomes gradually more viscous, and this puts an increasing strain upon the heart, until, with the blood unable to circulate fast enough to carry metabolic heat away to the skin, body temperature rises suddenly and death quickly occurs. As we shall see, camels, donkeys, and other desert creatures have evolved adaptations that enable them to overcome this problem.

For a man or woman well supplied with water, however, the desert is a stimulating environment, though uncomfortable at times. In it were born Judaism, Christianity, and Islam and in it have been fought some of history's most savage and significant battles. Speaking before the Battle of the Pyramids, in 1798, Napoleon Bonaparte said: "Soldiers, consider that from the summit of these pyramids 40 centuries look down upon you." He was not without a due sense of history. The modern ecologist must also be aware of history, as well as of evolution, of the habits and habitats of animals and plants, of soil and weather, of day and night, and of summer and winter. He cannot understand the community of life in the desert environment without an intelligent consideration of all these contributory factors.

Real desert beauty more than matches the splendor of a mirage. Here the Arizona sun sets behind an ocotillo bush. Leaves and crimson blossoms adorn the ocotillo only in rainy seasons. Most of the year its branches are bare to conserve moisture.

Life in the Soil

The popular idea of a desert as a vast region of drifting sand, devoid of vegetation except for an occasional oasis, may apply to certain areas, but it by no means applies to all. Indeed, deserts are as diverse as the climates and geological factors that have produced them, and this is why they have a richer flora and fauna than is generally realized. Even single-celled protozoans, which are essentially aquatic, can exist in deserts by encysting during the dry season. During times of rain, when the ground is moist, soil amoebas move actively and feed among the grains of sand. Then, as the moisture evaporates, these microscopic animals secrete a resistant outer covering (or *cyst*), within which they remain dormant for months, or even years, until rain falls again. In the desert around Cairo, for instance, the activity of such creatures is limited to a few days in the year. Yet 50 living species have been found after 8 months of drought.

In general, the protozoans that inhabit desert soil are no different from those to be found in fresh water. Even "ciliate" protozoans can—and do—live in places where temporary rain pools form, feeding on bacteria, unicellular algae, and other microorganisms. These unicellular organisms swim actively by means of hairlike projections, or *cilia*. Like amoebas they encyst when the water evaporates, but normally they are unquestionably aquatic. The fact that they exist at all in a desert shows not only that they are extraordinarily adaptable, but also that there is much more to the desert than at first meets the eye.

Earthworms, unlike protozoans, cannot live in deserts except in irrigated areas and oases, because they dry up too rapidly. Even in an oasis they can survive periods of drought only by burrowing very deeply. On the other hand, snails form a conspicuous element of the fauna of some arid regions. In parts of California, North Africa, and Arabia, for instance, the ground may be quite white with their shells. The activity of desert snails is confined to the winter months, however, and mating takes place during the rains. Most of the numerous shells that you can see at other times of year are empty, for the living snails aestivate—that is, they pass the dry summer in a torpid condition deep down in cracks

Desert soils are of three main kinds: top left, loose sand, as in the wind-formed dunes of the Namib; bottom left, rock or stone, as in parts of central Australia; and above, clay, illustrated by a photograph showing cracks spreading through a dry clay soil in California. Sand—which many people think of as typical of desert areas—is probably the least common throughout the world.

in the ground, or among rocks. While the desert snail is aestivating, the mouth of its shell is closed by a thick diaphragm, which reduces the loss of water by evaporation. The rate of water loss from dormant snails is so low, in fact, that the normal reserves of these animals are sufficient for several years' survival. And although their stores of fat and carbohydrate are small, the metabolic rate of aestivating snails is also so low that the body tissues can sustain an extremely low rate of oxygen consumption.

Naturalists have recorded many spectacular examples of such suspended animation. For example, a desert snail that had been glued to an appropriate support and exhibited in the British Museum of Natural History from March 1846 to March 1850 revived and began to feed after being placed in water. Two other snails that had been collected in Egypt in 1854 were still alive in 1859. And some members of another species, from a region of the Sahara where there had been no rain for 5 years, were kept dry in a bottle for another 3½ years—and then recovered when supplied with water!

Conditions within the desert soil, where such creatures as amoebas and snails can remain alive even if dormant, are very different from those outside. Soil animals are sheltered from the extremes of the desert climate. They are insulated from the sun's intense heat and the nighttime cold. On an autumn day, I once recorded a sand surface temperature of nearly 183°F in the Red Sea Hills; four hours later, it had dropped to about 100°F. Conditions became far less extreme only a short distance below the surface. At about 18 or 20 inches below ground, there is hardly any daily temperature variation in the sands of the Sahara; and at twice that depth, the *annual* variation is no more than about 18°F. Thus, with relatively moderate and constant temperatures, at a depth of only 2 or 3 feet, burrowing animals can avoid the killing extremes of heat and cold.

Another feature of major importance to the inhabitants of desert soil is the fact that it is comparatively damp. Even in summer, the air surrounding loose grains of dirt or sand at a depth of 20 inches will have a relative humidity of 50 per cent. Similarly, caves and rock fissures

A desert snail feeding on a saltbush in southern Tunisia. Snails of various species are found along the northern edge of the Sahara fringing the Mediterranean Sea and are also common in the Negev and other desert regions of the Middle East.

form the natural habitats of many desert animals, because conditions within them are relatively damp as well as mild and uniform. But it must be remembered that desert soils vary greatly from one locality to another, and some are less suitable for life than others. Before taking a look at the kind of life we all associate most naturally with the soil—vegetation—let us briefly examine some of the varieties of soil in the desert. And first let us consider how they got that way.

In arid regions, soil is formed almost entirely as a result of the fragmentation of rock by mechanical and chemical weathering. Chemical weathering is considerable even in arid climates, because its effect is increased by the high temperatures. And rainstorms, though rare, exert a profound effect on bare rock and soil unprotected by vegetation. Furthermore, rocks tend to flake and crumble when they are constantly heated and cooled. Finally, they are occasionally ground against one another in torrential desert-stream flows, and they are constantly being abraded by windblown sand. One of the more striking results of such wind action is the carving of rock faces, such as the pink towers of Bryce Canyon in Utah and the rock columns of New Mexico and the Sahara. On a smaller scale, wind action often shapes stones so that one or more sides are flattened. This usually produces pebbles with three facets on the upper side, known as *Dreikanter* (related to the German word for "three").

The towers of Bryce Canyon, Utah, are a particularly striking result of ancient rivers that cut through the softer rocks of a limestone plateau, leaving the more durable spires behind.

Most desert soils possess almost no humus—decomposed organic material—for they contain very little material of vegetable origin and are not much more than fragmented rock. They are of three main types: rocky, stony, and sandy. The first of these, rocky desert, is known as *hammada* in the Sahara and is composed of denuded rocky plateaus smoothed and polished through abrasion by the wind. Libya's great Selima sand sheet, which stretches over some 3000 square miles of the country, consists of a thin layer of sand covering such eroded bedrock. The rocks of the coastal deserts of Chile, Peru, and southwest Africa have lichen growing on their seaward side only. This is because these deserts are caused by cold oceanic currents, which bring cool winds that carry fog and mist, but not rain. Therefore the sheltered landward side of the rock has no growth on it. Anyone lost in one of these deserts could find his way to the sea just by the lichen!

When desert *wadis*—water courses that are dry throughout most of the year—terminate in alluvial basins, the sediments they carry become stratified and gradually extend until they fill the whole internal drainage basin. Thus they tend to form immense level plains. And such plains always include patches of the second main type of desert soil: stony desert, with a mosaic surface of gravel or pebbles. In western America, alluvial plains are called *playas*, after the Spanish word meaning "a beach," and temporary lakes often form in them after rain. When dry, however, such areas are usually covered with glistening salt, whose whiteness reflects the dazzling sunshine. Similar saline crusts, covering large areas in enclosed basins, can also be found in the western desert of Egypt, in the so-called *shotts* of Algeria and Tunisia, in the salt pans of the Kalahari in southwest Africa, and in many other alluvial plains. Some of them, such as the salt flats of Utah and of Lake Eyre in Australia, are so thick and sturdy that racing cars have made speed records on them. In contrast, the North African *shotts* are treacherously thin, and cover bogs in which whole vehicles can easily be swallowed.

When irrigated, large parts of alluvial basins can be very fertile. Rocky and stony soil cannot be made fertile, however; and neither—or, at any rate, seldom—can the third main type: sand. Many deserts consist in part of *ergs*—vast sandy wastes occupied by masses of dunes. The Libyan erg is as large as France, and the two Algerian ergs (the Grand Erg Oriental and the Grand Erg Occidental) each measure at least 100 to 200

Left: looking south along a stretch of the Namib Desert that fringes the southwestern coast of Africa for a distance of 1000 miles. To the north the massive dunes give way to gravel plains occasionally interrupted by flat-topped hills. In such coastal deserts, lichens, of which two types are shown above, generally grow on the seaward side of rocks, where moisture condenses at night.

miles across. Desert dunes may grow to an enormous height: 700 feet or more in the central Sahara, for example. They are formed, of course, by the strong desert winds; and few regions on earth might seem to be so utterly inhospitable to living organisms as these hot, windy, dry, barren mounds of sand.

Yet, in spite of all the drawbacks, most desert and semidesert regions support some degree of vegetation. The smallest amount of plant life exists in areas of rocky *hammada* and cracking clay; but plants can grow even in such soil whenever it is traversed by wadis. And sandy desert usually supports a flora of some kind, except on the dunes, which tend to stay quite bare. Several species of acacia, in fact, require only two thirds as much rainfall in sandy soils as they do when growing on clay. Then, too, many plants, such as annual grasses and other small herbs, evade the more extreme desert conditions by completing their life cycle during the short rainy season and passing the remainder of the year lying dormant as fruits or seeds in the soil. Dry seeds can often survive high temperatures without losing their ability to germinate later under more favorable conditions.

Evasion of the rigors of summer does not depend only on the ability of seeds and fruits to withstand prolonged drought and heat. In addition, the whole life cycle is compressed into a few weeks. Because of this, such plants are sometimes termed *ephemerals*. They have few leaves, and may even flower while the embryonic cotyledons (the seed leaves) are still on the plant. Flowering herbs have been found near Khartoum in the Sudan within less than 25 days of a heavy shower. In California, the grama grass can germinate and form seeds within 4 weeks. But the record for shortness of life cycle is probably held by an African herb that is said to take only 8 to 10 days between sprouting and seed production. A brief life cycle is related not only to the restricted duration of the season in which conditions are suitable for growth, but also to the short period during which insects are available for pollination.

Dispersal of seeds is a problem that desert plants have solved in a number of ways. Many species of drought-evading plants produce seeds equipped with dispersal units, which help to distribute them so that the offspring can have a better chance to reach a site suitable for germination. In order to achieve just the opposite effect, the stems and leaves of others are closely curled toward one another when dry, but open wide apart when moistened. By this means, the seeds

Above: in preparation for the dry season, honey ants of arid regions stock up by storing liquid food in the distended crops of selected workers, which hang upside down from the roof of their subterranean nest to serve as living honey pots.

Right: African harvester ants carry grass seeds down into the nest, where they are stored as food for the dry season.

26

are scattered only when they are wet and relatively heavy, during the moist season. This tends to prevent long-distance dispersal—a healthy precaution, because the parent plant is presumably growing in a favorable locality.

Some annual grasses have a particularly interesting method of keeping their progeny alive. Large numbers of their sharp-pointed seeds become entwined into dense balls, which the wind blows over the desert surface. As each ball comes in contact with the soil, individual units are anchored and detached, one after another, until the ball has disintegrated. Subsequent changes in the humidity of the air cause each seed to twist like a drill, forcing it deeper into the soil, where it remains until rain falls. Individual seeds may also become attached to the hairs of animals—goats' legs are sometimes completely covered with them—and are thereby dispersed. Many other desert plants have well-developed barbs and bristles—the spikelets of bur grasses, for example—to aid their dispersal by animals. But much seems to be left to chance. The fruits of some desert plants are simply blown about until they either are trapped in a rock or hollow, where they may eventually disintegrate, or become buried in wind-blown sand. When rain falls, the seeds that have landed in favorable surroundings are able to germinate.

Desert vegetation is not entirely ephemeral, like the plants with brief life cycles discussed so far. There are many plants that habitually grow where evaporation stress is high and water supply low, and that do not need to evade extreme desert conditions. Such plants, all of which show characteristic adaptations to their environment, are termed *xerophytes* (from the Greek words meaning "dry" and "plant"). Among them are trees, perennial grasses, and species that develop bulbs, corms, or tubers. Some xerophytes are characterized by the ability to survive long periods of drought and dehydration of the tissues without suffering injury. They are extremely resistant to wilting, and a few species can lose up to 25 per cent of their water content before they begin to wilt. The creosote bush, one of the commonest species of the North American deserts, provides a notable example of drought tolerance. In an extreme drought, the mature leaves of its buds dry out and turn brown; yet the buds retain the power to continue growth when favorable conditions return once more to the area and water is available.

Top: this huge mound was built by termites of central Australia as a shelter from desert heat and aridity. In nests above and below ground, worker termites in desert areas prepare for the dry season by piling up stores of such foods as the dried petals and grass being collected in the picture shown above.

Above: the weird cissus plant of Angola has the swollen stem and reduced foliage of a typical desert shrub. Left: the giant barrel cactus of Lower California prepares for drought by storing great quantities of water in its stem, whose pleats open and shut like an accordion as moist and dry periods alternate.

Above left: the rounded shape of stone plants, common in Africa's dry regions, reduces the surface area exposed to drying winds. Above right: the welwitschia plant of Southwest Africa has two curling leaves split longitudinally into broad straps, on which fog and dew condenses, providing moisture for shallow roots. Individual welwitschia plants may survive for many hundreds of years.

This close-up of a cactus in Lower California shows the impressive armament of prickly spines that help keep the plant alive by discouraging herbivorous animals from nibbling at it.

Most plants of arid regions, however, have evolved mechanisms not so much of drought tolerance as of resistance to drought. They fight the battle against water loss in a number of ways, often combining different protective devices within a single plant. One means of retaining moisture is to have leaf surfaces coated with fatty substances and resins; these make it harder for water vapor to escape. Other structural adaptations to drought include the presence of dense, hairy coverings (which again keep moisture from escaping) or of pores sunk deep into the leaf tissue so that the dry wind cannot blow directly into them. Smaller and fewer leaves also help resistance to water loss. And—perhaps most important of all devices—a number of desert plants have developed internal tissues for storing water over long periods of time and for giving increased mechanical support to the bloated, water-filled organism after a heavy rainfall. Such plants (among them the cacti) are known, for obvious reasons, as *succulents*. The fluted stems of the saguaro cactus become so juice-filled that they expand and contract like an accordion as the seasons alternate.

Many desert trees shed their leaves at the onset of the dry season—a very good protective device, because it is through the pores of leaves that most water escapes. Some species of acacia, however, usually retain some leaves, and one kind of acacia actually *produces* leaves at the beginning of the dry season! Presumably it grows where subterranean water is available, and it perhaps benefits from producing foliage at a time when there are not many insects around to feed on it. On the other hand, some desert plants remain always leafless or have only very tiny leaves. In such cases, the stems are green (in other words, furnished with chlorophyll) and used for photosynthesis, the process by which organic compounds are produced from carbon dioxide and water by means of energy absorbed from sunlight.

The leaves of desert grasses are often folded or rolled into tubes, with the lower surface thickened and pores concentrated on the upper surface. In this way, with the edges of their leaves curling up and touching each other, the grasses greatly reduce their loss of moisture. Clearly, for much desert vegetation the surest way to survive is to expose the least possible amount of leaf surface to the air. Although, as I have said, such plants as the succulent cacti and euphorbias must depend for their extreme drought resistance upon well-developed water-storing tissues, they also have very small leaf surfaces; and so they have a remarkably low surface-to-volume ratio, for they are always thick and fleshy. It has been said that even a small cactus would transpire (i.e. lose moisture) 300 times faster if it were cut up into thin leaves!

Another characteristic feature of most desert shrubs is that they possess painfully sharp thorns and spikes. The probable function of these is to afford protection against browsing and grazing animals. In the Australian deserts, where there is more choice of vegetation and less grazing pressure than in other deserts of the world, the acacias are less thorny. Desert plants have also developed other defenses against hungry animals. Many contain poisonous or irritant latex. Others secrete resins or tannins in the bark or leaves; the pods of some contain strong purgatives; the creosote bush of North America has an unpleasant, pungent smell. All such devices tend to make the plants unpalatable to animals.

But in spite of such examples the interdependence of plant and animal life is obvious in the desert as elsewhere. For instance, extreme drought is the major menace for all desert life, and in exceptionally dry weather vegetation often does a special service for other creatures. Some plants can survive on moisture from the air; and at night, with the drop in temperature, dew condenses on their leaves and stems and runs down into the soil around their roots. The welwitschia of the Namib Desert in southwestern Africa is such a plant. It bears two curling leaves, split longitudinally into strips, on which dew condenses, providing water for the shallow roots. The ability of vegetation such as the welwitschia to absorb moisture from the night air, even when dew does not form, can make vitally needed water available for snails, insects, and other small animals of the desert.

Finally, I must add a word about a common feature of most deserts—certainly their most attractive feature to plants as well as to all animals, including man. I am referring, of course, to their oases, where water is plentiful, the soil is fertile, and green vegetation thrives. The English word "oasis" comes from the Coptic words *oueh* (to dwell) and *saa* (to drink), and the implication is clear: because oases have water, they are good places to live. In the typical oases of the Libyan Desert, as in many Tunisian and Algerian ones, the water comes from underground sources. Other oases draw their water from rivers entering the desert from nearby mountains; those on the Karakum Desert fringe of Central Asia are examples of this type, as are those of Sinkiang in China and some to be found along the foothills of the Andes in western Argentina. But oases are not merely isolated areas scattered in or around deserts; they can also be green ribbons of fertile land fringing rivers. The short, swift rivers that flow through the Peruvian desert to the Pacific Ocean are lined with such oases, and ribbonlike oases occur all along the banks of the Rio Grande, Colorado, Indus, Tigris, and Euphrates. The Nile valley is, as most people know, the largest oasis of this kind in the world. And, lastly, some oases occur high on mountain plateaus—the so-called *altitudinal* oases, such as Tamanrasset and Tibesti in the central Sahara and Windhoek in South West Africa—where rain is trapped from the upper air.

For obvious reasons, most oases have been exploited by man, and therefore cannot be seen in their natural state. A few, however, like many of those in the great American desert, do still exist in a relatively natural condition. In such oases one can find a number of species of small plants growing in or near the water, and shrubs and trees—such as rabbit-brush, scrub willows, cottonwood, mesquite, and California fan palms —may also occur. In the foothill canyons of the Sonora Desert, for example, where stream flow is either permanent or semipermanent (and periodically torrential), there is a river-bank woodland consisting of cottonwood, willow, ash, sycamore, and walnut trees. This deciduous, broad-leaved forest is bordered by a flood plain dominated by a mesquite-acacia community that is in turn surrounded by desert and grassland.

We have now seen something of what might be called "the amoeba's world"—life within the different kinds of desert soil, from the most nearly barren to the fertile humus of an oasis. Now let us rise to the surface and begin our consideration of the many kinds of animal that manage to live in the desert despite its extreme temperatures, its cruel winds, and its lack of a steady, dependable rainfall.

Oases occur wherever there is fresh water, which often comes from rain that falls on nearby mountains. Here we see one such oasis situated in the foothills of the Aïr Mountains, Niger.

In Time of Rain

Changes of the environment in hot, arid regions result from one or other of two factors that may or may not coincide: precipitation of rain, with a consequent outburst of plant growth; and periods of cooler weather even if rain does not fall. These changes are reflected in the stages of development and numbers of the fauna, so that populations of adults reach their peak at the time of the rains. For example, adult darkling beetles begin to appear in small numbers in Egypt during late October, when the rains and cooler weather usually begin. Their population gradually increases, reaching a peak in March. By the end of May the beetles have disappeared. During the hot season, their life cycle is continued by the larval and pupal stages.

In the case of life cycles like this, which are extremely common among desert insects and arachnids (spiders, scorpions, and related creatures), aestivation (summer dormancy) may or may not occur in the developmental stages. Either way, when rain comes, it brings with it an abundance of plant and animal life. Flowers are visited by butterflies, moths, bees, wasps, hover flies, bee flies, and other such insects. The droppings of camels and goats are rolled away by dung beetles, and grass seeds are harvested by greedy ants. Termites extend their subterranean galleries to the soil surface and make nuptial flights, while such predators as scorpions, camel spiders, spiders, ant lions, bugs, wasps, robber flies, and predatory beetles gorge themselves on an abundance of food. With the rains, too, come swarms of desert locusts, which breed in the damp sand. The ephemeral vegetation is devoured by hordes of caterpillars and crickets, and the air buzzes with a rare abundance of flies, wasps, and bees. Migratory birds appear and build their nests, and most of the resident reptiles, birds, and mammals produce their young while the harshness of the desert is briefly alleviated.

Thus, the appearance of the desert is completely transformed by rain when—whether seasonally or, as so often, unpredictably—it starts to fall. And just as soil amoebas and other protozoans are forced to compress much of their life span into a period of a few humid days, so must great numbers of desert-dwelling animals

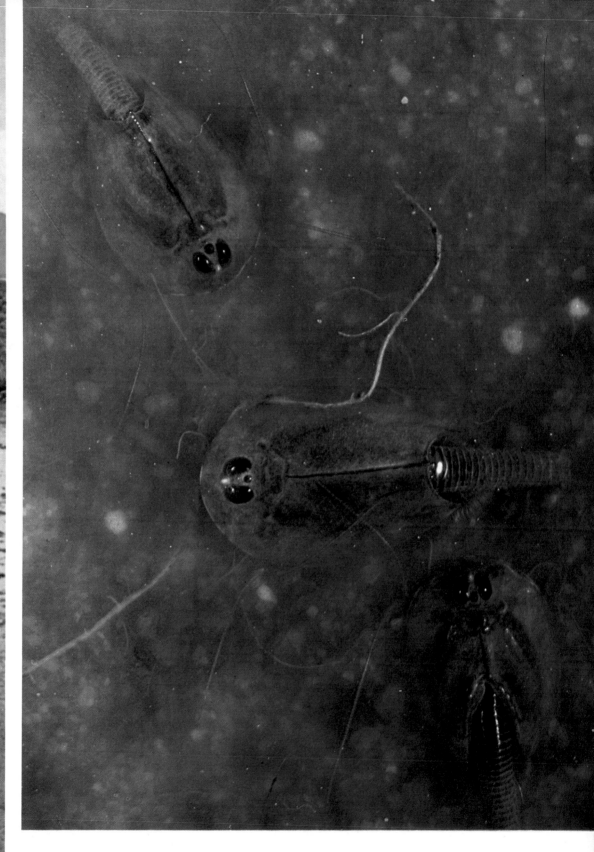

Sudden squalls in desert regions often leave standing water, as in Nevada's Great Basin Desert (left). Residual pools are inhabited by primitive filter-feeding crustaceans, including one-inch-long tadpole shrimps (above), which complete their life cycle within about 10 days and lay drought-resistant eggs before the pool goes dry.

Right: among the primitive crustaceans of temporary desert pools are the fairy shrimps (up to one inch long), which swim upside down with graceful movements of the legs. Like tadpole shrimps, they feed on particles in the water by filtering them through hairs on their limbs and passing them to the mouth.

Below: tiny brine shrimps half the size of fairy shrimps (shown here in the palm of a hand) live in vast numbers in Great Salt Lake, Utah. They are tinged with red and usually occur in such dense swarms that they may color the water. Some of the swarms are composed entirely of females, which can reproduce quite satisfactorily by the development of unfertilized eggs.

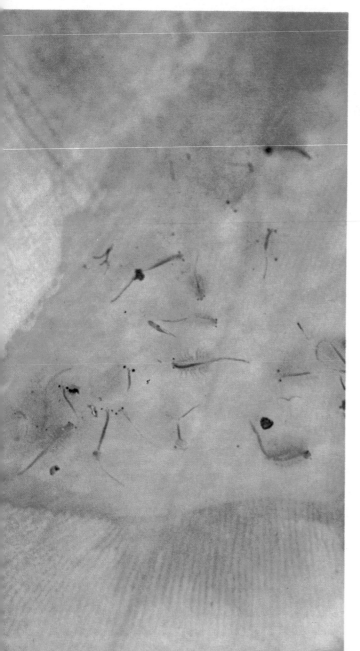

other than those already named. Let us consider the inhabitants of desert pools.

Perhaps the most spectacular of these are the curious crustaceans known as *apus* (the tadpole shrimps) and such others as fairy shrimps, brine shrimps, and water fleas. These creatures have a very ancient lineage; indeed, fossils of tadpole shrimps have been found in Triassic deposits some 180 million years old. Although it may seem extraordinary that these living fossils should have survived in such an uncompromising habitat as the desert, the fact is that therein lies the secret of their success. For tadpole shrimps and their close relatives thrive in temporary pools and pass the dry season in dormancy as drought-resistant eggs. This dormant state, known as *diapause*, is characterized by a temporary halt in growth and reproduction, reduced metabolism, and enhanced resistance to heat, drought, and other climatic factors. In their

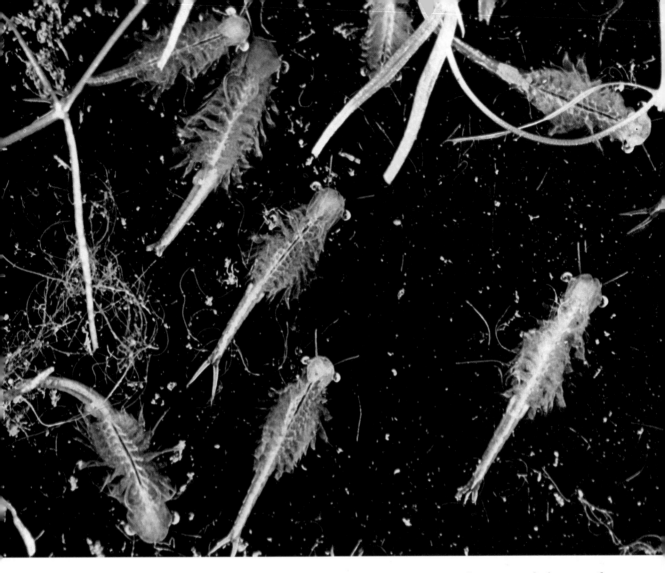

active state, however, these aquatic crustaceans are sensitive to heat and drought; they soon die if removed from water.

The life of a desert crustacean is a veritable race against time, for it must hatch, grow up, mature, and finally lay eggs before its pool dries up. An apus can grow from a microscopic egg to a mature tadpole shrimp, one inch long, in the brief span of 10 days. Few other animals have become adapted to such a short aquatic existence followed by many months of inactivity, and so these crustaceans are largely spared both competition and predation. They themselves feed on amphibian eggs, insects, and smaller crustaceans. The tadpole shrimps also eat bottom sediments, but their fellow-crustaceans in the pools are purely filter-feeders—which means that they have nets of fine hairs on their limbs, and strain water through these nets so as to filter out small particles of food, such as unicellular algae, and convey them to their mouths.

In permanent waters there would be fishes and other creatures to snap up the desert crustaceans before they had time to reproduce. But in temporary desert pools, although some of them may be devoured by spoonbills, flamingos, and a few other birds, they have relatively few enemies. This may account for the long evolutionary stagnation of the group. Because they have largely escaped the rigors of natural selection, the driving force has been removed from their evolutionary development. The only selective factor of importance in their lives is the ability both to survive as resistant eggs in dry weather and to develop and reproduce swiftly after rain has fallen.

What happens to tadpole shrimps and the other desert crustaceans when there is not enough rain for the desert pools to remain wet for as long as 10 days? In such an event, some young shrimps

Above: into the shadows of a rain-washed desert spot in northwestern Africa a distinctively-marked pantherine toad emerges to search for the juicy insects on which it feeds.

Above: the American spadefoot toad breeds only during the rains, and seldom leaves its damp burrow otherwise, except in the cool of the evening. Its "spade" is a broad sharp-edged tubercle on the inner side of the foot, which it uses for digging. Below: its graceful tadpoles swimming in a desert pool.

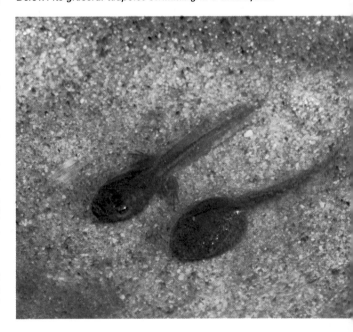

and water fleas will certainly die before reaching maturity and laying their eggs. Luckily, though, not all the dormant eggs hatch when they are wetted the first time. Some will hatch only after two, three, or even more immersions. Sooner or later, there will be enough rain for a desert pool to persist for more than 10 days. When this happens, many of the very resistant eggs will hatch, and many more will be produced.

If the eggs were merely dormant, they would all hatch as soon as moistened. But, as I have said, they are in diapause, and this is a physiological condition, under hormonal control, that can be broken only by a definite shock or a series of shocks. In this respect, the apus eggs are in striking contrast to the larvae of certain desert midges of northern Nigeria, which inhabit small pools formed in shallow hollows on unshaded rocks. These hollows may dry up several times during the rainy season. Each time this happens, the larvae also dry up, but they remain dormant only until it rains again, when, after as little as half an hour, they resume feeding.

These midge larvae will remain viable for many years in the dry state; and while in this state they can survive remarkable extremes of temperature. Their tissues, and even the individual cells of their bodies, are dry. It is possible to cut one in

Left: fresh water seeping from the base of the Namib Desert dunes at Sandwich Harbor attracts such aquatic birds as the flamingo, which has a superbly adapted beak that can filter tiny crustaceans, insects, and other morsels from the water.

37

half, leave it for a few years, and then watch the two halves wriggle if you place them in water. They will not wriggle for long, though, because, having been "killed" long ago, they will quickly die!

Mosquito larvae, water beetles, water boatmen, dragonfly larvae, and various kinds of water bugs may also inhabit temporary rainpools on the fringes of desert regions, wherever these lie within their range of flight. (Oases often act as centers from which such animals become dispersed. This is why mosquitos and malaria pose a constant threat to human populations in the Nile valley and other desert regions where there is permanent water.) And the pools are also the breeding places of desert frogs and toads. The active existence of amphibians in hot, dry climates is extremely limited, not only because their moist skins permit rapid evaporation of water from the body, but also because amphibians are unable to produce urine that is more concentrated than their body fluids. Nevertheless, frogs and toads *are* found in some deserts, and not merely in oases. Those that survive have, naturally, made both behavioral and physiological adaptations to the environment.

For instance, the spotted toad, which is common in the deserts of the southwestern United States and northern Mexico, reputedly stores as much as 30 per cent of its gross body weight as water in the urinary bladder, and this reservoir can be absorbed under conditions of dehydration. The American spadefoot toad, so called because of a spadelike tubercle on the hind foot (which it uses for digging in sand), buries itself deeply in the damp sand when the rainpool in which it has bred dries up, and only reappears when there is heavy rain; thus it escapes extreme heat and desiccation. And the sand-colored tree toad of the California Desert spends most of its time on rock surfaces near sources of water, keeping its body temperature down by evaporation of water from the skin.

One effect of rain that, though less direct than the formation of temporary pools, is nevertheless of extreme importance is that it brings on the urge to breed. Among many desert inhabitants, even when they are physiologically ready, reproduction often needs to be triggered by the immediate stimulus of rainfall or by the appearance of green vegetation that follows the coming of wet weather. Locusts, for example, seem to mature in response to aromatic chemicals

produced seasonally by certain shrubs at the time of the annual rains. These compounds are responsible for the characteristic exotic scents of frankincense and myrrh.

The importance of rain, with a resulting limited season of plant growth, is also clearly seen in its influence on the hereditary adaptation of the rutting and birth of various species of gazelle. There is a close correlation between the birth of these animals and the normal time of rainfall. Calving usually begins about one month after the onset of the rainy season, when plenty of grazing is available. Similarly, the camel, in contrast to most domestic animals, has a pronounced rutting season at the time of rainfall, and its pregnancy lasts for 12 months, thus allowing the young to be born during the annual rainy season. The fertility of jerboas, voles, and other rodents is greatly reduced or even interrupted during dry

Left: insect-pollinated flowers bloom profusely after rainfall near Alice Springs in central Australia. Arid soil all over the world bursts into life when it rains; seeds germinate and green leaves push through the sand, as shown above, in Tunisia.

weather, and at such times the population level of these creatures drops considerably. Their staple food consists of grain and roots, but they also nibble at green plants when these are available. Their sterility in times of drought is believed to be caused by the absence of some essential factor that occurs only in green vegetation.

It can be said that nowhere in the world is rainfall such a tremendous and significant event as in the arid desert. In temperate regions, the cold of winter puts an end to the long growing season; many animals hibernate in a state of diapause, deciduous shrubs and trees drop their leaves, and annual herbs die away. But in deserts, it is drought, not cold, that puts an end to growth. Instead of winter and summer, drought and rain regulate the seasonal rhythms of plants and animals. During the brief rainy season, or

whenever it rains in deserts that lack seasonal rain and have it only spasmodically, there is a period of active growth. This is the time when cacti store water, annual herbs complete their brief life cycles, and perennial plants blossom and set seed. Many insects that survive throughout the dry season in a resting stage now become active. Food is abundant, bees pollinate the desert blossoms, and wasps scour the desert for suitable prey.

Some animals migrate into the desert at the time of rain, either because food is available then, or in order to breed. Dragonflies move down the Nile at this time of year and lay their eggs in temporary rainpools. Fruit bats fly up from East Africa a few weeks after the rains have ceased, because this is when wild figs and other fruits ripen for them to eat. But they have to be quick. Fertile periods are very brief in the desert.

The Scorpion's World

The desert dries up remarkably fast after rain stops falling. Flowering plants bloom, shed their seeds, wither, and die. Grasses turn yellow, so that the landscape takes on a monotonous sandy color. In conditions like this, the uninitiated might be excused for thinking the desert to be lifeless. Most of the insects that assumed temporary abundance on the short-lived vegetation are gone. Gone, too, seem to be the huge camel spiders (Solifugae) that preyed on them. Underneath rocks and down holes in the ground you may find scorpions and insect larvae; but except for ants and darkling beetles (Tenebrionidae), adults insects have become very scarce. In fact, however, there is plenty of life around, even on the driest day. The reason we do not see it is that most desert creatures lie low during the day and become active only in the cool of night.

Of all animals, the scorpion is perhaps most associated in our minds with the desert, even though some species are found in the wet tropics and others in subtropical regions. Nocturnal in habit, desert-dwelling scorpions spend their days in sheltered retreats. In North Africa and southern Europe, they are usually found under rocks and stones, in shallow scrapes that they dig with their claws. In the southern part of the Sahara, however, and the deserts of North and Central America, where climatic conditions are more extreme, they live in deep burrows at the roots of trees and shrubs, and along the banks of rivers and dry watercourses. They avoid oases because of the excessive moisture, but they are numerous around the edges of such fertile areas, where they benefit from an abundance of insect prey.

They are strictly carnivorous, but do not usually stalk their prey, preferring to wait for the insects that wander into their lairs. When hungry, however, they emerge at night and walk about with claws extended, ready to grip the prey, which may then be subdued with a sting—but only if necessary, for these much-maligned

A scorpion stinging a grasshopper. Scorpions use their poison sparingly, injecting only enough to kill. The prey is shredded by alternate movements of the jaws. It may take hours for the scorpion to suck all the juices and soft tissues into its tiny mouth.

creatures are not needlessly wasteful. There are two types of scorpion poison. One type is local in effect and comparatively harmless to man; the other is neurotoxic, like some kinds of snake venom, and also destroys red blood corpuscles. The venom of some scorpions may be as dangerous as that of the cobra, but the quantity injected is usually much smaller.

Like many other venomous animals, some species of scorpion are capable of *stridulating*— that is, of making harsh warning sounds when disturbed. There is no evidence that they themselves can hear the sounds. In fact, the existence of stridulating organs implies an auditory sense not in the producers but in the enemies that might otherwise destroy them.

Even more than scorpions, the solifuges (familiarly known as camel spiders) are typical animals of the desert. Sometimes also called "jerrymanders," "false spiders," and "wind scorpions," the long-legged species are familiar to all who have traveled in arid regions. A large specimen, whose formidable appearance is enhanced by its unusual hairiness and bulk, can, with its limbs, span a width of five or six inches. These creatures avoid fertile oases and seem to prefer neglected places where the soil is broken and bare. Sometimes they can be seen running so fast that they resemble balls of yellow thistledown blowing over the desert (thus justifying the nickname of "wind scorpion"). Often, when going at full speed, they will stop abruptly and begin hunting about like a dog checked in mid-course by the scent of game.

Most solifuges are nocturnal and hide away in deep burrows or under stones during the daytime.

Above: the vinegaroon, a large species of stingless whip scorpion found in the US Southwest and Mexico, where it lives in deep, damp burrows, for it is not well adapted to aridity. When disturbed, it exudes a vinegar-like acid.

Left: these scorpions have fought, and the one on the right has been defeated. Behind its back legs can be seen the pectines— comblike sense organs that can detect vibrations of the ground caused by the approach of large potential enemies.

This tiny inhabitant of a coastal sand dune is a "false" scorpion, an arachnid related to scorpions but lacking a sting. The picture is highly magnified; note the size of the sand grains.

They are exclusively predatory and carnivorous and have enormous appetites: they will devour almost any insect, spider, scorpion, or other camel spider, as well as small lizards, birds, or mice, and will continue feeding until their abdomens are so distended that they can scarcely move. In addition to this wide range of diet, they have considerable powers of water conservation and can tolerate extremes of both drought and temperature, so that they are superbly adapted to desert life.

Other relatives of the scorpion are less common in the desert, except possibly for the vinegaroons, which can be found in some numbers in the deserts of the American Southwest. Their strange name was originally given them by settlers from the French West Indies, because of the vinegarlike defensive secretion that they

Above: a long-legged solifuge (or camel spider) caught in the act of devouring an ant. Camel spiders are formidable predators, and feed on a wide variety of insects, spiders, scorpions, and other camel spiders. They are extremely voracious and will keep on eating until their abdomens are so distended that they can scarcely move.

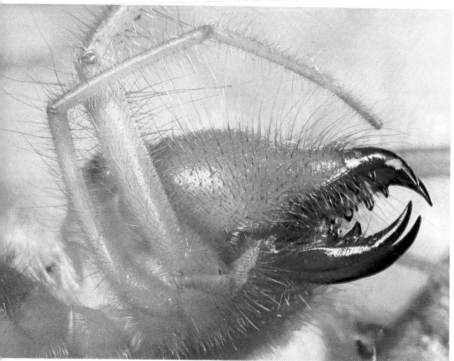

Left: in keeping with the solifuge's appetite are its massive jaws, which—as shown in this much-magnified photograph—are probably the largest in proportion to body size of the entire animal kingdom. The camel spider usually holds its prey crossways and munches it until it has been reduced to a soft pulp and absorbed in a semifluid condition. A solifuge is not venomous, but its bite can be painful to a human being.

exude when disturbed. They are not really well adapted to dry conditions, however, and their survival in the desert depends upon deep burrowing, sucking up water from a damp substrate, and obtaining moisture from the bodies of their prey.

Of the remaining orders of arachnids, only spiders and mites are important inhabitants of the desert. Desert spiders are usually white or pale in color, without the markings found among those that live in humid climates. Some species can change color quite quickly so as to match their background closely enough to be almost invisible to enemies. A few of them have brushes of hair on the underside of their limbs, to facilitate movements on sand. At least one of the larger hunting spiders in the Namib Desert digs a tube in the sand to live in. It pushes loose sand up the slope of the tube with its mouth-parts and cements the "walls" with a crisscross of webbing. Other species live on the trunks of acacias and other trees. True spiders are numerous in oases, where they can climb up trees and other plants both to avoid water and to find plenty of insects to feed on.

Several desert species of jumping spiders are especially notable in that they mimic the insects on which they feed, and thus themselves escape the attention of hungry predators. In one Sudanese species the male is an ant mimic, whereas the larger female mimics wingless mutillid wasps. The resemblance is so exact that it is difficult to recognize the spiders as spiders. In the ant mimic, the appearance of a narrow waist is created by a strip of dark color on a white background. Furthermore, the spider walks in the jerky manner of ants and holds up its front legs so that they look like insect antennae. In general, jumping spiders are small, with broad heads and short, stout legs, but with extremely large eyes; keen sight permits them to stalk prey from afar.

In contrast, wolf spiders hunt in the open and overcome their prey by sheer strength. As you would expect, they have longer bodies and limbs but smaller eyes than the jumpers. Other types construct funnel-shaped cobwebs, each consisting of a triangular sheet with its apex rolled into a tube, in which the spider awaits its prey instead of hunting for it. Those that spin the familiar circular web (known as an "orb" web) are also relatively plentiful in the desert. One such common inhabitant of sand dunes in the Mediterranean region is very large and has a remarkably irregular shape. This, with its sandy color, makes

Here a fly that has alighted on a flowering welwitschia plant alongside a crab spider's silk nest has met its doom. Crab spiders lurk in desert plants where they cannot easily be seen, wait patiently for the arrival of nectar-thirsty insects, and then pounce.

Jamaican trapdoor spiders inhabit sandy tropical regions, where they dig burrows with the aid of comblike spines on the margins of their jaws. The burrow out of which this spider is peeping is lined with silk over a coating of earth and saliva.

Above: a dikbens cricket of Southwest Africa. Crickets and bush crickets are an important element of the desert fauna. They appear in abundance on the vegetation that springs up after rain, and are a major food for many animals.

Right: giant velvet earthmites like these appear on the desert sand each year after the rains; after mating, they return to their burrows for another year. The adults feed on termites, but the larval stages are parasitic on grasshoppers and locusts.

it extremely inconspicuous in its desert habitat.

All the arachnids that we have been considering so far are predatory carnivores that feed on insects and other arachnids. There is another group—known as the Acarina—that includes mites and ticks, and this is unusual in that most of its members are parasitic and only a few are predatory. Some of the acarine arachnids get fluid nourishment from plants or decaying organic matter; others attach themselves to the bodies of insects or mammals and live as parasites while they are larvae, but become free-living and predatory when adult; still others are permanently parasitic.

An example of the second type is provided by the giant velvet mites that often appear in the deserts of Africa and America a week or two after rain and probably feed on termites and other insects. The larvae are parasitic on grasshoppers. A high rate of water loss—or *transpiration*, as evaporation from plants and animals is termed—indicates that they are not well adapted to drought, and for this reason the adults dig burrows where the sand is damp. Their scarlet

color has a warning function and is associated with *repugnatorial glands*— glands that produce an unpleasant secretion that makes them unappetizing to such potential enemies as scorpions and camel spiders. In dry weather they disappear underground.

Much better adapted to life in arid places are many species of ticks. When not attached to their hosts, these animals have remarkable powers of water conservation, and some can live for 10 years or more without food or drink. The ticks that live on goats and camels are extremely common throughout the Great Palaearctic Desert. Some of the larger kinds have a notably vicious bite and can cause serious loss of blood to the host.

In contrast to the arachnids, desert insects are mostly vegetarian, and only a few of the many kinds are predatory. It should be emphasized that there *are* many kinds. A high proportion of the known orders of terrestrial insects are found in desert areas. Among them, crickets, grasshoppers, and locusts are important. The desert locust exists in the Great Palaearctic Desert as a result

A swarm of desert locusts like the one shown above may contain 10,000 million insects, travel 2000 miles in a season, and consume its own weight of food in a day. A potential pest over 11 million square miles of Africa and Asia, they threaten the livelihood of one eighth of the world's population. The immature "hoppers" (left) are conspicuously black and yellow in color. If crowded together during this early stage, they form migratory swarms; if not, they remain solitary. African migratory locusts (right) are less of a menace to agriculture than desert locusts; but rapidly breeding swarms may spread out in Africa over an area of 7 million square miles.

of its migratory habits. Solitary locusts are normally found among sand dunes on coastal plains, in scrub belts along wadis, in oases, and in similar habitats that represent ecological islands in the arid deserts. But the migratory locusts appear in great numbers when population densities build up. Long-distance movements of swarms take place high in the air, where wind speeds are often greater than the speed of flight of the insects. Consequently, it does not much matter in what direction they are actually heading; inevitably they get carried into areas of low barometric pressure, where rain is most likely to fall.

Here they feed on the ephemeral grasses that spring up after the rain, and later they deposit their eggs. The female prefers to lay her eggs in sand that is dry on the surface but damp underneath, and the eggs do not develop unless kept moist. There is no doubt that the instability of the environment and, in particular, the unreliability of rainfall make the lives of desert locusts very precarious. But their mobility, linked as it is with weather dynamics, helps them to overcome their physiological handicaps. Then, too, there are so many of them! Locust swarms often comprise 10,000 million insects, travel up to 2000 miles in a season, and consume their own weight of food in a day. As you might expect, they soon cause almost complete defoliation in the arid regions they attack.

Grasshoppers and crickets, though common throughout the deserts of the world, are much less of a menace to the vegetation than the sudden swarms of locusts. Grasshoppers show little adaptation to the environment, apart from desert coloration, but some crickets (such as the sand treaders of North America) have combs of long hairs on their lower hind legs, which help them to get about in the sand. They lie buried during the day and emerge at night to feed on the sparse plant life.

Many species of Hemiptera (bugs) also live on that sparse vegetation. The most conspicuous members of this group are no doubt the cicadas, but perhaps more interesting are the coccid bugs. The manna that, according to the Bible, sustained the Israelites during their wanderings in the wilderness of Sinai might well have been the secretion of one kind of coccid. Another kind, which lives in arid parts of South America, encysts itself in a waxy coating, in which condition it can resist prolonged drying up for very long periods, even as much as 17 years.

Termites are also vegetarian, but they have the unusual ability to digest cellulose, which is the fundamental supporting material of trees and other woody plants. They can do this because of a "fermentation chamber" in the hind gut, which is populated by a rich and varied fauna of protozoans that contain the enzymes required for breaking down cellulose. Dead desert shrubs are usually eaten by dry-wood termites, and other kinds of termite commonly live among the roots of such woody plants as agaves, ocotillo, and cholla and other cacti. In more arid deserts, only subterranean species of termites occur (though they do come to the surface after rain). They live in nests composed of dried grass, sticks, and other fragments of vegetation, which they cover loosely with a coating of dry sand particles glued together with saliva or bits of excrement. In this way the workers, which are sensitive to air currents, are protected from the dry air outside their tunnels, for there is room enough for them to walk between the plant debris of the inner nest and the outer covering.

Most of the ants of arid regions also live in subterranean nests, although a few nest in the wood of dead trees or under the bark. They are generally omnivorous. Paradoxical as it may appear, their primary adaptations to life in the desert are less directly related to the dryness of the air than to the nature of the terrain. Most of the ants in the Sahara Desert, for example, live in comparatively moist localities, and only a few are found in really arid soils. Even the most drought-resistant species bring water to their nests from the salty, damp sand of water-bearing strata. Similarly, the harvester ants of California are susceptible to extremes of heat and cold, and so they live in deep nests and forage only during a brief period each day when the temperature is favorable.

In fact, it becomes increasingly apparent to the observer of insect life in the desert that, although a great variety of insects can be found there, only a few can be said to have truly adapted to desert conditions. Bees, for instance, require nectar and pollen, and so their activities must be restricted to the rainy season. This is equally true of moths and butterflies, which rely on pupal diapause to carry them through the dry periods—but this can hardly be considered a desert adaptation, because pupal diapause also carries them through

Butterflies, which need flowering plants (because they feed mainly on nectar), live only on the fringes of deserts and must often (as shown below) suck moisture from drying mud. The caterpillars feed on growing plants during the wet season and pass the dry season in a state of diapause—as inactive pupae, from which adults emerge when the rains come and flowers are once again in bloom.

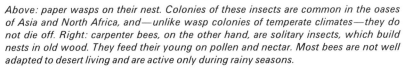

Above: paper wasps on their nest. Colonies of these insects are common in the oases of Asia and North Africa, and—unlike wasp colonies of temperate climates—they do not die off. Right: carpenter bees, on the other hand, are solitary insects, which build nests in old wood. They feed their young on pollen and nectar. Most bees are not well adapted to desert living and are active only during rainy seasons.

the winters in temperate regions. A behavioral adaptation of small blue butterflies and some others is the power of continued flight within the shelter of a small bush, even when the wind is blowing too strongly for them to fly outside. Hairy caterpillars, rolled up into a ball, are sometimes blown about by the wind; and the larvae of some American desert species inhabit long tubes of sand attached to plant stems. Small moths are numerous in the American deserts. The pupal life of many of them is spent underground, but a few—called "bagworms"— are conspicuous because of peculiar pupal cases that they hang onto plants. Bagworm pupae festoon acacia trees in desert and semiarid regions of Africa.

Without doubt, however, the darkling beetles of the family Tenebrionidae are of all insects the best-adapted to desert life. These insects are able to live on dry food without any water. Most of them are twilight-active or nocturnal creatures; but a few are day-active except in extremely hot weather, when they burrow in the sand. In general they lack wings, and the *elytra* (the pair

of protective forewings characteristic of beetles) are fused together. The airspace below the elytra helps to insulate the body, and is even more important in reducing the amount of water lost through evaporation, because the respiratory tubes open into it. All the tenebrionids are omnivorous; they feed on vegetable matter, carrion, and dung.

Some other beetle families also show remarkable structural adaptations to desert life. Take, for example, the dung beetles—a family that includes the well-known Egyptian scarab beetle, which acts as a scavenger by breaking up and burying the droppings of camels, goats, and other animals. The female detaches a portion of dung and forms it into a pellet, which she compacts by rolling it with her hind legs. She then excavates a subterranean chamber, where she remains with her ball of dung until she has eaten it all. In the autumn, she digs an even larger chamber and collects a large quantity of dung for the benefit of the young.

Among other families particularly well adapted to desert life are the burying beetles, blister

51

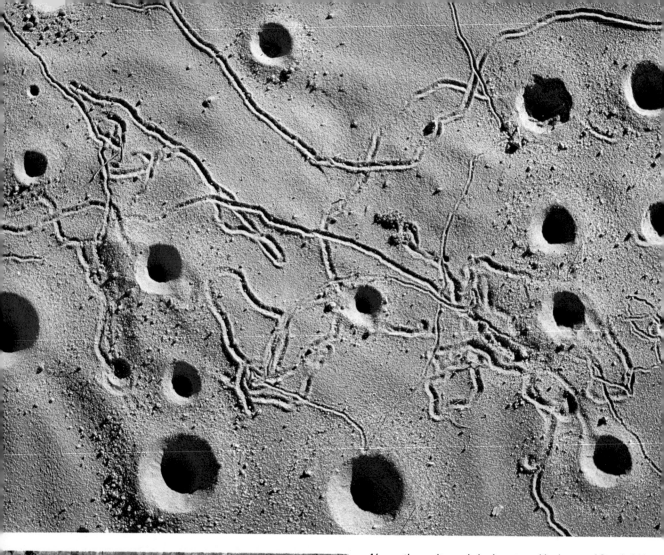

Above: these pits made in desert sand by larvae of South African ant lions—which are insects, despite their name—are connected by trails, showing where the larvae move at night. Left: an ant-lion larva burrows into its hole. The soft, vulnerable abdomen is soon concealed, and only the jaws of the inch-long larva appear above the sand (below) ready to grab a passing ant.

beetles, ground beetles, and tiger beetles, to name only a few. But some dung beetles are especially noteworthy in that they show more advanced social behavior than the rest: male and female work together in excavating a big earthen chamber, within which they deposit up to seven ellipsoidal balls of dung, in each of which an egg is laid; and the parents remain with their offspring until they mature, their presence acting as a deterrent to predators and parasites.

Many American dung beetles have become secondarily adapted to eating vegetation and fallen leaves. But there are also beetles that are exclusively herbivores—for instance, the blister beetle, which gets its name from the fact that an oily fluid that it secretes from the joints of the limbs raises painful blisters on human skin. Adult blister beetles have conspicuous warning coloration: vivid black and green, or brown (or blue) and red.

In contrast to the varied assortment of arid-region insects that are primarily vegetarian, there are only a small number of carnivores. One of these is a gigantic wingless ground beetle; like the blister beetles, these nocturnal predators have a striking coloration (black and white), which warns of their horrible flavor and thus protects them from larger predators, such as small mammals and birds. Also carnivorous are the ant-lion larvae, which have been called "demons of the dust." You can see their cone-shaped pits clearly in fine sand. At the bottom of each pit lies buried an ant-lion larva, waiting in ambush for passing ants and other insects that may slip into the trap. The prey is assisted in the slide down to its doom by particles of sand flicked with surprising force and accuracy by the larva lurking below. In very hot weather, these larvae orient themselves within their pits so that their bodies are in the coolest spots.

Among other predatory desert insects are, of course, those belonging to the order Diptera (comprising such familiar pests as houseflies, mosquitos, and gnats). Bloodsucking horseflies attack camels, horses, and donkeys, and botflies are even more unpleasant. One of the botflies develops in the nose of a camel, which eventually sneezes the mature larva out onto the sand, where it pupates. Mosquitos, sandflies, and other bloodsuckers are particularly prevalent in oases, along with the common housefly. The dipterans need nearby sources of water in order to survive, and so do the predatory tiger beetles, which are common mainly on the banks of rivers, near temporary rainpools, and on the seashore. Tiger-beetle larvae inhabit tubes in the sand, from which they watch for passing prey. One American species cements the sand grains with saliva, and the burrow serves as a pitfall to trap insects.

Not all carnivorous insects are predatory. Some—including certain ants and, as I have already pointed out, darkling beetles—are scavengers, feeding on plant material as well as on dead insects and arachnids. Desert animals tend to have less restricted diets than those of their relatives in more humid regions. This is because the scarcity of food in arid regions denies them the luxury of specialization, and so they have to make do with whatever they can get. Of course, plant matter must form the basis of animal food chains in the desert as elsewhere, but the type and extent of the vegetation depends upon the amount of rainfall and is therefore more or less seasonal in its availability. Under desert conditions, a considerable part of the vegetation survives periods of drought in a state of inactive diapause, which only rain ends. Seasonal rainfall, therefore, results in a yearly period of abundance; irregular rains result in food at longer intervals, or none at all. Thus, the advantage of diapause to vegetarian animals is obvious: it enables them to endure long periods of food shortages as well as heat and drought. But even when not in diapause, desert animals are often astonishingly resistant to prolonged starvation. A darkling beetle that I once collected in southern Tunisia went on living in my laboratory for over five years without eating.

In the most extreme deserts, where precipitation is negligible, the fauna must depend for food upon dried vegetable matter blown from elsewhere by the wind. Part of this is eaten or destroyed immediately. The remainder becomes buried and, in the absence of bacteria, does not decompose; instead, it comes to the surface, often years later, when it feeds the larvae of beetles and also supports bristletails, which are abundant sand-dwellers commonly found under rocks, camel dung, and so on. In turn, the larvae and bristletails are eaten by scorpions and other carnivorous animals. Therefore, the basis of the food chain in regions where no plants grow is windblown seeds and vegetable fragments!

Ecologists have often drawn attention to the fact that an unusually high proportion of desert animals—apart from a variety of insect vegetarians—are carnivorous. It is the vegetarians, of course, that support the predators and scavengers. Each predator must kill many herbivores during the course of its life, and each herbivore must eat many times its own weight of plant material. In any one food chain there are usually between three and five major links. For instance, dried grass may be eaten by beetle larvae, themselves devoured by camel spiders, which, in turn, feed lizards or birds. As we ascend the food chain, the size of each predator increases until, at the top, the animal is not preyed on at all. As the predators become progressively larger in food chains, their numbers decrease. Thus there is a pyramid of numbers, with very many small animals at the base supporting a few large ones at the apex. The Chinese proverb that one hill cannot shelter two tigers expresses this concept.

It is therefore surprising to find so many predatory forms in the food web of the desert, with so few prey species, as compared with humid environments. Obviously, the proportion of herbivorous *individuals,* if not of species, is large.

The problem of food in the dry desert is only one of many, however. As we have seen, the desert provides a particularly inhospitable environment for life; and although the biological problems that confront animals in hot, dry regions are essentially the same as those in other land areas, the difficulties present themselves in a more acute form. Water conservation is, naturally, the first of these. And the problem of preventing water loss by transpiration through the body surface is far more acute for the arachnids and insects that it is for bigger animals. The reason is that larger forms have a smaller surface area in proportion to their mass. If a flea and a man transpired at the same rate, for instance, the man would need to sweat 4500 times faster than the flea in order for both of them to lose 10 per cent of their body water in the same period of time. Some oasis-dwelling arthropods, such as woodlice and centipedes, are unusually large, and this may well be an adaptation to the generally arid habitat: although they tend to lose water rapidly by evaporation, their size reduces the surface-to-volume ratio, and so diminishes the loss.

One obvious way for an animal to tackle the problem of water loss is to develop an impervious covering. Spiders, scorpions, mites, and most insects do just this. They avoid becoming dried up by secreting on their cuticles a thin layer of

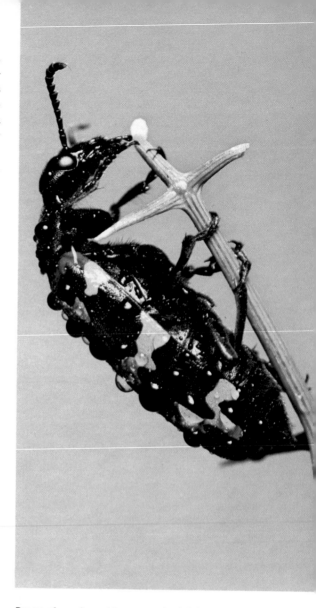

Drops of condensed fog cover the brightly marked body of this blister beetle—so-called because it secretes an oily liquid containing cantharidin, which raises painful blisters on the skin.

wax, which is relatively impermeable to water vapor. Such a layer is also impermeable to oxygen and carbon dioxide and so these creatures have evolved a respiratory mechanism that permits gaseous exchange to take place even while water loss is kept down. The *spiracles* (breathing holes) of insects and the so-called "book lungs" of scorpions, spiders, and other arachnids are normally kept closed by special muscles; only when carbon dioxide begins to accumulate in the body are they opened to facilitate respiration. Before molting takes place, the animal secretes a new wax layer beneath the old cuticle, so that the casting-off process is effected with a mini-

Scarab beetles rolling a ball of dung across the desert sand of South Africa. These insects are scavengers; they break up, carry away, and bury the droppings of cattle, camels, goats, and other animals both for their own use and as nourishment to be stored for their developing larvae. Although only a little over an inch long, the scarab beetle can make a ball of dung as big as a man's fist.

mum loss of water. Such structural adaptations, though by no means uniquely designed for life in the desert, are important there. So too are the excretory products evolved by insects and arachnids—uric acid and guanine, respectively—which, because they are extremely insoluble, allow nitrogenous waste matter to be eliminated from the body in a dry state, with no water lost.

A method of avoiding desiccation in desert areas that is rather less complex than those just described is, quite simply, to find the occasional damp places and stay there. Such animals as worms, woodlice, centipedes, millipedes, and springtails remain for most, if not all, of the time in a damp environment under stones and fallen leaves, in cracks and burrows in the soil, or in crevices under the bark of trees. Therefore they usually penetrate only into the desert fringes and oases, where tolerable conditions are available. In the oases and wadis where the woodlice live, they dig communal burrows deep in the damp sand. Their body covering, however, does tend to be somewhat less porous than that of woodlice from more humid areas, and the desert species have long legs that permit them to walk with their bodies raised well off the hot, dry ground. One species of woodlouse, found in Arizona, almost equals some of the dry-desert insects in its ability to restrict water loss through evaporation. Millipedes are much less well adapted to the desert environment, but centipedes are found in quite arid places. They survive by crawling deep into crevices, and they emerge only at night and when it rains.

But it is their physiological adaptations to dry conditions that permit most desert-dwelling invertebrates to survive. Some of them are even able to absorb moisture through the cuticle, and they can do so even when the atmosphere is unsaturated. This capacity, which is characteristic of certain ticks, fleas, and roaches, is probably far more widespread than naturalists now realize. Another common adaptation of both herbivorous and carnivorous desert insects is the ability to live on moisture obtained with food. For example, by conserving the high moisture content of plants or by absorbing the moisture present even in desiccated vegetation, their bodies may contain water greatly in excess of what their diet seems to provide.

Many desert animals also show structural adaptations for living in sand. For instance, the bristletails, which are extremely numerous in the Namib Desert, take refuge at the base of tussocks of grass, where they can wriggle or almost swim with fishlike movements in the sand. At least one species of hemipteran has the same habit. And several species of darkling beetle have become flattened, with short legs and with the thorax and abdomen expanded into thin, wide plates with

Sex and food are the keys to survival in the desert, as elsewhere. Right: black and white darkling beetles mate on a dune of the Namib Desert. Below: other members of the darkling-beetle family feed on a dead gecko. Darkling beetles are widely distributed throughout the world's deserts. Their larvae eat vegetable matter, but the adults scavenge on dung and the corpses of scorpions, insects, reptiles, and other carrion. Most of the beetles are active only at night, but a few are day-active except in very hot weather, when they burrow in the sand.

sharp edges. Their platelike form allows them to edge their way into the sand with alternate sideways movements. Some of these flattened beetles, which feed on the leeward side of the dunes, orientate themselves horizontally, so that the smallest digging movement of the legs starts a cascade of sand from above; the sand covers them very rapidly and protects them from predators. Many of the invertebrates associated with dunes and ergs in the Sahara have their own types of adaptation. Some are modified to swim through a loose substratum of sand without making a hole; some excavate pits; others mine tunnels in more cohesive sand. And, as has been said, a number of insects and arachnids have brushes of flattened hairs or bristles on the undersides of their legs, and these act like snowshoes to ease their movements through the sand.

Whereas a solitary insect must depend on selecting a favorable *microclimate* (that is, the climate of the limited area within which it lives), social species are able to work together and actually change the climate of their habitat to their advantage. Some tropical termites extend their nests in a north-south direction, so that the smallest possible surface area is exposed to the noonday sun. During dry seasons, they vacate the section of the nest above ground and move down to regions where the humidity is greater. They keep the nursery area moist by secreting saliva or bringing up wet particles of sand from the water table (which may lie nearly 150 feet below the soil surface). And they stabilize temperature in the nest by means of a number of ingenious devices. The outer wall of the mound is very thick and provides good insulation; this

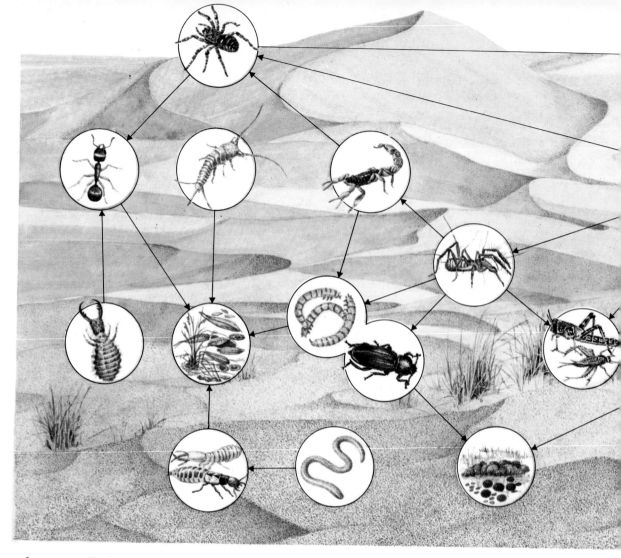

reduces ventilation, but termites are adapted to survive in unusually high concentrations of carbon dioxide. Air circulation in the nest is based on convention currents; the activity of the termites in the central area warms the air and raises the content of carbon dioxide, which causes the air to rise to the upper air spaces; the slight excess pressure thus generated forces the air through radial canals to vertical canals at the sides of the nest. Here the carbon dioxide diffuses out and oxygen comes in, and the cooled air sinks to the cellars of the nest.

Microclimatic conditions are less well controlled in the nests of ants. But bees can cool their hive by spreading water on the combs and fanning air over it with their wings.

The importance of nocturnal habits as a means of evading the daytime heat of the desert can scarcely be overestimated, but there are many other advantages to nocturnal activity. Loss of moisture is reduced because the air is more

nearly saturated. Large enemies are more easily avoided, and food is more readily obtained, in the dark. Communication between members of the same species is facilitated, because odors are more readily conveyed by the night air. All these are good reasons why only a very few animals— including some grasshoppers, beetles, and spiders —are active in the desert during the heat of the day. (Many of these, incidentally, have long legs, which raise their bodies above the hot sand.)

Some creatures are active only during a certain period of the day or night. Others, however, indulge in different kinds of activity at different times. Many aquatic insects, for example, spend the daytime swimming about in rivers and temporary rainpools; during the hours of darkness, they usually fly from one locality to another. Rhythms of activity are to be found in thriving communities, whatever their environment, but such rhythms are especially marked in desert regions, where the changes in physical condi-

58

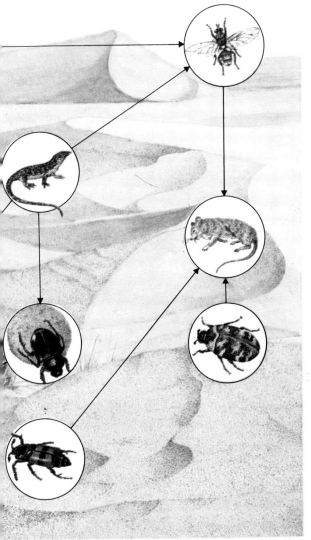

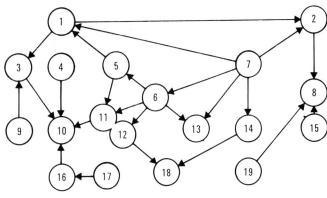

1 Spiders	11 Darkling beetle larvæ
2 Flies	12 Darkling beetle adult
3 Ants	13 Grasshoppers
4 Bristletail	and crickets
5 Scorpion	14 Dung beetle
6 Camel spider	15 Carpet beetle
7 Lizards	16 Termites
8 Corpses	17 Worm snake
9 Ant lion larvæ	18 Mammal dung
10 Seeds and dry vegetable matter	19 Burying beetle

A simple food web showing the interrelationships of some smaller desert animals, principally insects. Seeds and dry vegetable matter provide the primary source of energy, but a secondary supply appears in the form of corpses, both of desert-dwelling animals and of migrating birds. The arrows in the diagram point from predators to prey or from plant-eating animals to their food.

tions between day and night are so sharp.

As I have indicated, scorpions, camel spiders, and most desert insects are nocturnal, and spend the day deep down inside their dark burrows or hiding under rocks. The question therefore arises: How do they know when it is dark enough outside for them to emerge? The answer seems to be that their rhythm of activity is *endogenous*—i.e. it rises from a kind of "biological clock" operating within themselves. Scientists have discovered this by monitoring the activity of such animals in *aktographs*. An aktograph is a box that pivots about its transverse axis, so that any movement of the animal within causes the box to rock slightly, and this is recorded. Even when the aktograph is placed in an incubator at constant temperature and humidity and in darkness, the experimental animal inside can maintain its rhythm of movement and rest, at least for several days.

During the last 20 years or so, an enormous amount of research has been carried out, much of which indicates that "biological clocks" in plants and animals operate on a cellular level. But we can still only guess at how the innumerable cellular "clocks" are coordinated and synchronized; we do not even know whether one or many mechanisms are involved. But in searching for the answer to this and other questions, biologists have made a number of fascinating discoveries. Under constant conditions, the diurnal cycle of cells has a period of *approximately* 24 hours; it may be as short as 22 or as long as 26 hours. For this reason, such endogenous rhythms are called *circadian* (from the Latin *circa diem*, meaning "about a day"). There are also lunar and annual rhythms in many organisms. Moreover, the response to an external stimulus varies critically with the phase of the rhythmic cycle that the organism happens to be in at the time.

Many species of desert beetle adapt to seasonal climatic changes, for instance, by being nocturnal in summer, day-active in winter, and crepuscular (twilight-active) in spring and autumn. In temperate regions, the circadian rhythms of nocturnal animals tend to be delayed as the days lengthen, whereas those of day-active animals are accelerated; the shortening of the period of daylight has a reverse effect. Thus, the time of activity is adjusted to keep pace with changing day-lengths in areas where these change as the year progresses. But this mechanism appears to be either absent or not pronounced among tropical desert creatures, which is not surprising, because there is little seasonal change in day-length near the equator.

The physiology of circadian rhythms can be tested only under constant experimental conditions because, in nature, the rhythm is constantly being synchronized with cyclical changes in the environment. If a scorpion, for instance, begins to come out too early, it will have to wait until night falls before commencing its usual activities, and this will resynchronize its biological clock. On the other hand, if it should delay the return to its lair, it will be driven quickly back when the sun rises. But both such eventualities are unlikely to happen. In general, the circadian rhythm of nocturnal animals tends to be synchronized with sunset, that of day-active

As the setting sun silhouettes the saguaro cactus of Mexico's Sonora Desert, nocturnal animals emerge to mate and feed.

animals with dawn. And associated with rhythms of locomotive activity are rhythms of oxygen consumption and other metabolic processes, for most of the desert animal's physiological processes are coordinated by the biological clock.

The final—and, from a biological point of view, most important—problem for the desert animals is survival not of itself alone but of its species. The object of a scorpion, insofar as it can be said to have one, is to produce more scorpions, and so on. The survival of an individual depends upon living in a suitable environment, avoiding enemies, and obtaining food. The survival of the species depends upon reproduction.

In many marine animals, reproduction consists merely of shedding the sexual products into the sea, where fertilization takes place externally. All that is required is that the animals should be fairly close together, so as to facilitate union of eggs and sperm. On land, however, external fertilization would be impossible. After being emitted by the male, the semen would dry up before achieving its function. This would be especially likely, of course, in the desert. The random spawning characteristic of primitive aquatic animals is extremely wasteful and inefficient. Insemination (internal fertilization) is a much more economical and efficient means of propagating the species. Although worms, snails, and many insects copulate for the purpose of insemination, many other desert creatures reproduce by means of indirect transfer of sperm. This process, though primitive, is far less random than the spawning of marine animals.

The primitive method of fertilization among terrestrial arthropods (arachnids, insects, etc.) is by means of spermatophores. These are small bags or packets secreted by the male and containing semen. Spermatophores almost certainly evolved before the ancestors of the terrestrial arthropods left the sea and came to the land. They were a development that avoided the dilution of sperm that occurs with external fertilization in water. And on land they have proved valuable because they prevent desiccation of the semen. Moreover, they permit extensive rituals of courtship. Courtship, which precedes mating in many animals, has several biological functions. We do not fully understand all these functions among the invertebrates, but it is obvious that courtship synchronizes the sexual activities of the partners and ensures that the partners are of the same species and that the union will be fertile. In pre-datory creatures, it may also temporarily allay the carnivorous instinct and prevent the partners from killing each other. Let us now watch fertilization at work in a pair of scorpions.

Close behind the genital operculum (the lidlike covering of the reproductive organs) of a scorpion lies a pair of sensory appendages known as the *pectines*. The pectines have a dual function; first, they act as tactile organs for determining whether the ground is suitable for mating; and secondly, they sense vibrations and give warning of the approach of danger. It is also possible that they may act as humidity receptors and absorb moisture from a damp surface. This would account for the fact that not only males but also females in all stages of development have pectines. (It is not easy to distinguish the sex of scorpions. The male is usually more slender than the female and has a longer tail, but this is not always the case, and there are no external genitalia on which to base a sure diagnosis.) Courtship takes the form of a special dance or *promenade à deux*. On finding a female, the male grasps her claws in his and walks forward and backward while she follows him. Other behavior patterns include "kissing," in which the mouth parts of the two scorpions are brought together, and "juddering," during which the male jerks his body rapidly while his feet are held still.

Finally, when the male scorpion walks across a rock or some other firm object that his pectines tell him is suitable for mating, he deposits a spermatophore on it. Then he maneuvers the female in such a way that the spermatophore is taken up in her genitalia. The fertilized eggs of the scorpion develop inside the mother, and the young are born alive, enveloped in what is called a *chorionic* membrane; they escape from this envelope by tearing it with their stingers. Until their first molt, the little creatures are plump and weak, and they ride on their mother's back.

As in scorpions, the mating of camel spiders involves the transfer of a spermatophore from the male to the female. Courtship is brief, after which the ball of sperms is inserted directly by the jaws of the male without being deposited on the ground. The eggs are laid, usually at night, in an advanced stage of development and hatch within a day or two. As with the scorpions, the mother guards her young until after their first molt, but they do not climb onto her back.

Copulation represents an evolutionary advance over the primitive method of fertilization practiced by the scorpions, solifugids, and such related creatures as the vinegaroons. Cockroaches, grasshoppers, and a number of other desert arthropods copulate, but they resemble the scorpions in one respect: in the act of copulation, the male ejects not free sperm but a spermatophore into the female. Free-sperm copulation occurs in millipedes, some mites, bugs, flies, beetles, butterflies, moths, bees, wasps, and ants. Interestingly enough, spiders do not transfer semen by means of spermatophores, but neither do they copulate directly. In these creatures (as also in dragonflies), the semen is transferred indirectly. When the male reaches maturity, he weaves a small pad of silk on which he deposits a drop of sperm. He then sucks the sperm up with especially modified appendages (pedipalps) that lie on each side of his head and eventually inserts these into the vagina of the female. Each species has pedipalps shaped to fit the genitalia of females of that species.

Before the transfer of sperm, the male spider courts the female. As I have said, although we know that such courtship has considerable biological significance, we do not entirely understand its function. It may serve to stimulate the female's mating instinct or to protect the male by blocking her hunger drive. In any event, it is obviously of the utmost importance to the male to establish his identity, so that the female does not treat him like an insect victim. This is undoubtedly why the sense most appealed to in courtship is always the one on which the species chiefly relies for the capture of its prey. For instance, jumping spiders—which, you will remember, have keen sight in order to stalk their prey—make use of visual signs in courtship, whereas spiders that spin webs use distinctive tweaks on the threads of the female's snare.

One way or another, then, the smaller desert animals manage to secure the survival of their species—just as they manage to cope as individuals with the various problems of living in the harsh environment of the desert. The intensity of these problems varies according to the size of the animal that experiences them. As we have seen, very tiny forms can survive long periods of drought as spores or eggs in a state of diapause. Diapause is also possible for somewhat larger creatures—those the size of a scorpion or insect. It is not feasible, however, for such mammals as antelopes, donkeys, and camels. Unless an animal is small enough to hide itself in a burrow, it

Above: extending her abdomen to more than twice its normal length, a locust deposits a pod of about 70 eggs 4 inches deep in moist sand. White foam seals the pod against water loss.
Right: a male buthid scorpion (bottom) holds the claws of a female as they carry on a courtship dance. When the male feels firmly grounded—on a stone, for instance—he deposits a bag of semen (spermatophore), to be taken up by the female scorpion.

cannot afford to become torpid, because it would be too vulnerable to enemies and to the demands and fluctuations of the environment.

Similarly, there is a vital relationship between weight or mass and surface area that determines how an animal can solve such problems as water loss and the maintenance of body temperature. There are three ways for animals to survive in a hot desert. They can withstand the heat, but only in diapause or when completely dehydrated; they can evade it by burrowing and nocturnal behavior; or they can actively combat it by some form of sweating. The last possibility is available only to really large mammals such as camels, goats, and gazelles. These are discussed later in the book. First, though, we must look at the reptiles and small mammals, which have their own solutions to the problems of desert life.

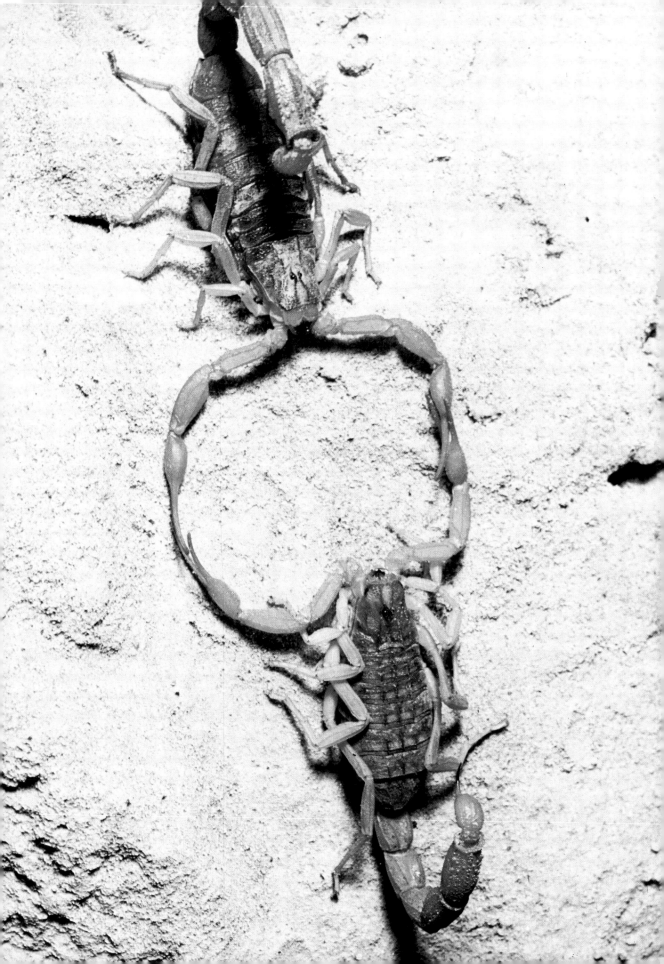

Reptiles and Small Mammals

Scorpions may be maligned, but people seem even more prejudiced against snakes—in fact, they are ready to believe almost anything nasty and inaccurate about them. Two misconceptions are particularly prevalent: that snakes are cold and that they are slimy. Cleopatra committed suicide by letting an asp bite her, and one of the characters in Shakespeare's play *Antony and Cleopatra* speaks of the asp as leaving a trail of slime. This is, of course, nonsense. Snails leave trails of slime. Snakes do not.

The asp with which Cleopatra killed herself must have been either the Egyptian cobra or a horned desert viper, to both of which the name "asp" has been applied. Cobras and vipers are the two most dangerous types of poisonous snake. Let us begin our survey of desert-dwelling reptiles by concentrating on them.

The Egyptian cobra, an admittedly unpopular animal, is by no means confined to Egypt; it is widely distributed throughout the continent of Africa, and can be found as far south as Natal. It seems to prefer dry, sandy places, and its often brownish coloration blends with its dusty surroundings. A quick, irritable creature, it rears up at the slightest disturbance and strikes with loud hisses; but, as we shall see, it could not possibly be either cold to the touch or slimy. It may leave a trail, however, though not a slimy one. All desert snakes leaves trails in dry sand, because of their method of locomotion.

To move forward, the cobra moves its body in a series of horizontal waves, which flow continuously from head to tail. As it does so, its sides press against irregularities in the ground, such as stones or vegetation, and propel it ahead in a seemingly effortless manner. The entire animal seems to flow along, every part of the body following the winding track. In sand, these lateral undulatory movements produce a trail consisting of curved piles against which the body has pressed. The snake would be unable to

A sidewinding desert viper slithers into the shade of a grass tuft. Though snakes need warmth, they are less able than lizards to withstand the intense midday heat of the desert sun. Thus they tend to be either nocturnal or active at dawn and dusk only.

move on a perfectly smooth, frictionless surface. The broad, backward-pointing scales of the snake's underside catch against the ground and keep it from slipping backward.

In some other species these scales can be moved by special muscles, so that the snake can creep forward with its body extended in an almost straight line. This "rectilinear" form of movement is mainly found, however, in such thickset snakes as pythons and vipers, not in the more slender species. The horned viper, like the American sidewinder rattlesnake, propels itself forward by looping its body sideways in a flowing S-shaped curve. Thus, the trail that it leaves in the sand is a ladderlike succession of furrows. Such spiral sidewinding causes the horned viper to move obliquely in the direction toward which its head is pointing.

The muscular contractions employed in sidewinding are like those used in the normal undulatory movement of such snakes as the Egyptian cobra. But each segment of the body remains at rest on the ground while the other segments are pushing ahead. A series of such segments forms a fixed track, or "tread." Successive regions of the body are then added to the front of the "tread," whose hinder end is being lifted. This adaptation is closely related to life in the desert, for it not only halves the area of the body in contact with the hot surface, but also prevents the snake from sinking into soft sand. And it has an additional function in that it enables the prey to be approached in a devious manner so that it is not alarmed until too late.

Horned vipers and sidewinders are also alike in being bleached, sand-colored creatures with an upright spine over each eye. They can bury themselves rapidly in the soft sand, which forms an insulating layer over their bodies when the sun is extremely hot. Their poison fangs are similar, too, in that they are normally folded back in their mouths, concealed in fleshy tissue, and erected only in the act of biting. In cobras and other so-called *elapid* snakes (many of which, such as the mambas, do not ordinarily live in desert regions), the fangs are permanently erect, though covered by folds of flesh. Nonpoisonous snakes and the usually mildly poisonous back-fanged ones have smaller teeth, and their bite leaves a double row of tooth marks. In most cases, a snake strikes rapidly and disappears before it can be identified. The characteristic punctures made by the fangs, however, often enable diagnosis to be made. Where human beings are concerned, this may be important in deciding what kind of treatment should be given. Even in the desert, only one snake in three is venomous; only if two (and no more than two) bleeding fang marks are present is the bite that of a dangerously poisonous species.

It should hardly surprise anyone to learn that desert-dwelling snakes are exclusively carnivorous. Because they feed mostly on small mammals, birds, and other reptiles, they represent a link in the food chain on a higher level than that of the arachnid and insect predators discussed in the last chapter. When eating, all snakes seize their prey with their teeth and swallow it whole. The venomous fangs of back-fanged snakes are grooved, but those of vipers and cobras are not merely grooved but tubular; the venom that kills the viper's or cobra's victim flows through the tubes and out of holes near the tips of the fangs, which are situated at the front end of the upper jawbone.

Of all the reptile predators in the desert, the various snakes known as vipers are perhaps the most efficient. The term "viper," incidentally, is used rather loosely; but for our purposes here it should be understood that so-called "true" vipers are confined to the Old World, whereas rattlesnakes and a number of related types called "pit" vipers are concentrated mainly in the New World, with a few in Asia. In contrast to the sinuous cobras, whose necks broaden into hoods when they are excited, vipers are stout-bodied snakes with wedge-shaped heads. The name "pit viper" is derived from the sensory depressions between the eyes and the nostrils; elaborate supplies of sensory nerves and blood vessels within these depressions cause them to act as directional heat receptors that make it possible for the viper to strike at warm prey, even in complete darkness, at distances of 18 inches or more. The victim rarely dies immediately, however. Viperine venom, though powerful, acts less rapidly than cobra venom. So the snake may follow its prey for some distance before it drops.

Rattlesnakes trail their victims by means of a specialized sense organ called "Jacobson's organ" (for the 19th-century Danish physician who first described it). This comprises a pair of internal cavities at each side of the snout, with ducts leading to the roof of the mouth. Odorous particles that the snake picks up from the air or ground on its forked tongue are transferred to

The similarity between desert environments, and the high intensity of natural selection common to all of them, has resulted in a considerable degree of similarity between unrelated animals that inhabit deserts in different parts of the world. The North American sidewinding rattlesnake (above) bears a very close resemblance to the horned viper of the Great Palaearctic Desert, pictured below.

As a sidewinding viper moves across the loose sand of the desert, it loops its body sideways in a constantly flowing S-curve. Thus it leaves behind a ladderlike succession of furrows in the sand.

these openings, and the snake can then follow the scent. Jacobson's organ is also employed in mating, for it enables the two sexes to find one another (after which there may be a ritual courtship involving a remarkable complex of stereotyped dance figures). Indeed, much snake behavior is conditioned by instinctive response to odors, whether through the Jacobson's organ or through a normal sense of smell, which many snake families have in addition to the specialized organ. Thus, when a rattlesnake is exposed to the smell of a king snake, which feeds on other snakes, it reacts to the enemy by adopting a defensive, head-down posture. If the rattlesnake's tongue is removed, however, this response does not occur, even though the king snake is in full view. Obviously, rattlesnakes are dependent for the sense of smell on the Jacobson's organs.

A diamondback rattlesnake of the American desert can kill a 200-pound man in an hour. But, as I have said, cobra venom may act even faster. It is questionable which of the two venoms is the more lethal, for the physiological effects tend to be quite different. Viper venom is likely to cause collapse and heart failure; cobra venom is predominantly neurotoxic and induces paralysis. Viperine poison usually includes an ingredient that causes clotting of the blood, whereas elapine venom more often contains an anticoagulant and, at the same time, causes hemolysis (breakdown of the red blood corpuscles).

Reptile teeth are replaced throughout the lives of the animals, and each fang has a series of successors behind it, ready to take its place in time. The snake's ability to swallow large objects is related to the structure of the lower jaw, which is only loosely attached to the skull and can easily be disarticulated. Moreover, the two sides of the lower jaw are united in front only by elastic ligaments, and so they can be moved separately as the prey is forced down the throat. Ingestion is aided by a copious flow of lubricating liquid from the salivary glands. And, finally, not only can the skin of the neck and body be stretched to accommodate very big chunks of food, but the windpipe can be protruded from the throat, so that breathing is not obstructed while the prey is being swallowed.

The rattle of a rattlesnake is composed of a number of interlocking horny pieces of cast skin, which, when rapidly vibrated, produce an angry buzz. The function of this, like the hiss of an adder, is to warn potential enemies to avoid its

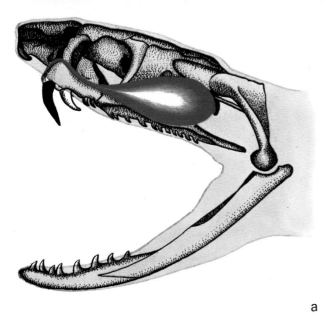

a

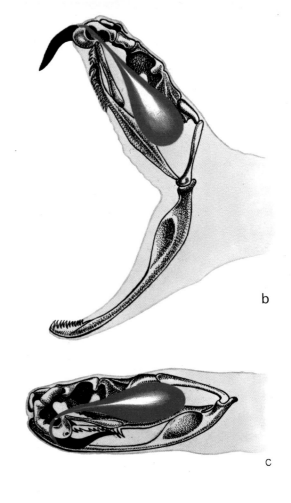

b

c

The venom of a poisonous snake is carried in a sac (here colored red), with a tube leading to the hollow fangs (black). The two large poison fangs in the top jaw of a cobra (a) are permanently erect, whereas in vipers they are erected only in the act of biting (b). Normally, viper poison fangs are folded back, concealed in fleshy tissue (c). In nonpoisonous snakes and the usually mildly poisonous back-fanged snakes, there are no large fangs, and bites leave double rows of tooth marks. The presence of two bleeding fang marks is a clear indication that the victim has been attacked by one of the dangerously poisonous snakes.

dangerous possessor. No doubt it often allows the snake to save its venom for more profitable use than self-defense. There is a kind of natural economy that governs most snakes' use of their weapons; they do not often waste their poison. For instance, during their mating displays rival rattlesnakes wrestle and try to push each other over, but they neither rattle nor bare their fangs in such disputes. Cobras do not immediately strike at potential enemies. Instead, they dilate and expand their necks, thus displaying characteristic markings that are clearly warning signs. The venomous saw-scaled viper, widely distributed throughout the arid regions of Asia and Africa, shows typical cryptic desert coloration. This doubtless helps to conceal the snake. When disturbed, however, it inflates its body, throws it into a tight figure 8, and rubs the oblique lateral scales against each other. The resultant vibration of these saw-toothed scales makes a noise like violently boiling water.

Many harmless snakes protect themselves from their enemies by mimicking the hiss and threatening gestures of venomous species. The most im-

portant nonvenomous snakes found in deserts are the worm snakes and the harmless (harmless to people, that is) members of the family Colubridae, which also includes the mildly poisonous back-fanged snakes. The nonpoisonous snakes have no special method of killing their prey, and so they either crush it or eat it alive; it ultimately dies of suffocation or from the action of digestive juices. The worm snakes, which are found in deserts in tropical regions only, lead secretive lives under logs and stones, or burrow into the ground. Their eyes are rudimentary and their dentition is reduced, and they feed on termites and other small insects.

Snakes, a conspicuous and important element of the desert fauna, are well adapted for life in arid regions. Their skin has a thick, horny outer layer, with few skin glands, so that water loss is minimal. They eliminate urinary wastes as a pulpy or semi-solid mass, which contains a high proportion of uric acid with little water in it. And their diet, which consists exclusively of animal matter, is very rich in moisture. The evaporation of water from their bodies is also

Left: the Egyptian cobra, or asp, reaches a length of over six feet. Its name is misleading, because it is found from Egypt to Morocco and Natal. The hood, which is formed by a lateral spreading of elongated anterior ribs, serves as a threatening display to deter enemies.

Below: by disarticulating their jaws, snakes are able to engulf surprisingly large prey. A four-foot rattler can gulp down a full-grown cottontail rabbit. Here a red diamondback rattlesnake, a rather large species with a limited distribution in California, swallows a rat.

Above: the western diamondback rattlesnake is widely distributed in desert regions of Mexico and the US Southwest. The picture shows both the forked tongue, used for sensing nearby prey, and the rattle, which serves to warn off potential aggressors.

70

greatly reduced by either a daily or a seasonal state of quiescence, when they conserve their energy in a relatively cool and humid burrow.

Other reptiles, however, are even better adapted for life in the desert, where they are much more common than snakes. For instance, many kinds of lizard can in general tolerate much higher temperatures than can the snakes. A desert rattlesnake cannot survive in heat that exceeds about 107°F, whereas lizards inhabiting the same area can withstand a temperature as much as 10 or 11 degrees higher. As we shall see later, the great problem of desert living for mammals is not the extreme heat but the dryness, because the temperature of a mammal's body is regulated by physiological means. With the reptiles, on the other hand, body temperature varies somewhat according to the external temperature. They require warmth, because their metabolism increases with higher temperatures. But there is a point at which the metabolic processes begin to suffer damage and disorganization. This is the point at which heat can become lethal. I shall be saying more about the question of body temperatures later in this chapter.

Many lizards have a pair of glands opening into the nasal cavity. Through these they void excess salts taken up with their food. And such salt glands are, of course, a highly useful adaptation to desert living, especially for insect-eating

lizards, which build up accumulations of potassium salts because insects contain these in large quantities. Nor is it only the carnivorous species that have salt glands. Some of the vegetarian species, such as the chuckwalla, also have them. The chuckwalla is one of the largest and most bizarre of the lizards of the North American deserts. It may reach a length of 18 inches and a width of 4 inches. Its tolerance of heat is not high, however, and so it lives in rocky areas where it can get shelter from the sun. When threatened, it darts into a deep crevice in the rock, where it inflates its body so greatly that it cannot be extracted.

A great number of lizard families are widely distributed throughout the world's deserts. The agamids occur only in the Old World. They are generally terrestrial in habit and flattened in shape, and mostly feed upon insects and spiders. In an ecological context, therefore, they and the other insectivorous lizards are more comparable with scorpions and camel spiders than with most snakes. Like the New World's chuckwalla, some Old World species, in particular the scaly-tailed lizards, are entirely herbivorous. In the scaly-tails the short, thick tail is covered with whorls of large scales, the body is much flattened, and the head is smooth and covered with very small scales. Then, too, there are the lacertid lizards, which are a familiar sight throughout the deserts of Asia and Africa, as are the iguanid lizards in those of America. Perhaps the most imposing of desert lizards are the African monitors—speedy and rapacious creatures up to five feet long, which will eat any animals they can overcome.

Most iguanid species are insectivorous, but a few appear to be largely herbivorous. Among the latter are the horned toads, whose flattened bodies are covered with spiky scales, and the desert iguanas, abundant in valleys and plains where shelter is provided by creosote bushes with rodent holes and burrows under them. Adaptations of iguanid lizards include scales fringing the edges of certain toes, thus widening them; these widened toes serve as sandshoes on the surface of the sand, and assist movements beneath the surface. The lizard's nasal valves restrict the entry of sand into the nasal passages, which are specialized by being convoluted and having absorbent surfaces that reduce loss of moisture through the nostrils. Their wedge-shaped heads help them to "swim" through the sand, as do the enlarged lateral scales on their

Above: the Texas horned lizard, seen crawling on a cactus, avoids the midday heat by burying itself in the desert sand. When attacked, it can squirt blood from its eyes as a defensive measure. Left: the American desert iguana is able to withstand a remarkably high body temperature, but must nevertheless seek any available shade at midday.

legs and tail. These scales tend to press the animal down into the sand when it moves its limbs. Similar adaptations occur in desert-inhabiting members of many lizard families.

The lizards of sand dunes and ergs are also well adapted to the environment, whether they are "sand-runners" on the surface or "sand-swimmers" underneath. The runners have all their toes fringed with elongated scales, which evidently widen the surface that presses on loose sand and thus distribute the weight, on the principle of a snowshoe or sandshoe. A modification that serves the same function is found in the ducklike webbed feet of a nocturnal gecko that lives on the sand of the Kalahari Desert. In this animal there is a complete webbing between the fingers and toes for support on loose sand. These various dilations of the toes are probably also of use in burrowing.

"Sand-swimmers" include the skinks, as well as other lizards and snakes that show several profound modifications for rapid burrowing in loose sand. The nose is pointed or shovel-like, and some species can dive head first into loose sand as though it were water. In addition, the nostrils tend to be directed upward instead of for-

ward, and this slant protects them from being clogged with sand. (In most snakes and lizards, incidentally, the nostrils are either shielded by complicated valves or reduced to pinhole size.) And in some sand-dwellers, including skinks and geckos, the eyes have a remarkable feature: a window in the lower eyelid. In some species this takes the form of a circular, transparent disk occupying the whole eyelid, which is permanently closed, thus providing protection from the sand. The ear opening is also either small and protected by fringes of scales or even non-existent. Desert lizards—and snakes, too—often have widened bodies for burrowing by lateral and vertical movements instead of plowing straight forward into the sand.

Geckos are widespread throughout the tropics, and a number of species are adapted to desert life. The heads of these lizards are broad, their bodies flattened, and their toes usually equipped with pads that adhere by means of friction; these enable the animals to run up smooth, vertical surfaces. In some desert species, the feet are completely webbed for support on loose sand. Unlike the majority of reptiles, which are not nocturnal creatures, most geckos are active only at dusk and during the night—a behavioral adaptation of special value in hot, dry climates. Geckos are also able to withstand considerable desiccation and starvation. Some can lose over half their body weight without ill effect, and then recover when food is again available.

Lizards that live in sandy deserts usually move with extreme rapidity. When not running, they stand alert, with head high and the front of the body raised on the forelimbs so as to keep clear of the hot sand. In swift motion, the tail is held well above the ground as a kind of counterpoise. Such adaptations are found in a number of unrelated families in different parts of the world. Similarly, several quite distinct species of desert lizard have adopted a snakelike form of locomotion. Their bodies are covered with smooth scales, which cause little friction, and their legs are either of a reduced size or even lost, so that movement through the sand is accomplished entirely by wriggling the body. One small species, which inhabits the sand dunes of California and Arizona, can move very fast in this way, but spends much of its time lying in wait for its prey, with only the fore part of its head exposed.

Although every reptile loses a certain amount of water—perhaps 10 times the amount formed by metabolism—by evaporation through the skin, it is doubtful if this contributes much to cooling the body. A reptile can keep cool in lethal heat only by hiding from it in one way or another (unlike the larger mammals, whose body surfaces are cooled by their own transpiration). Small reptiles have a higher rate of water loss per unit body weight than larger ones, the difference probably being related to the relatively larger surface area in small animals. At high temperatures, an increase in respiration rate or panting takes place, but even this does not cool the body to an appreciable extent, although it may serve to dissipate metabolic heat. Even so, evaporative water loss may be as high in some reptiles as it is in small mammals; at high temperatures, therefore, the production of metabolic water becomes inadequate for the maintenance of water balance. On the other hand, carnivorous reptiles get a considerable amount of water from their food, and this helps to redress the balance.

The ability of a species to resist desiccation is clearly correlated with the habitat it normally selects. The permeability of reptile skin is variable and depends upon external conditions. It is comparatively permeable when saturated with water, but is almost completely impermeable

Many desert reptiles can change color so as to be inconspicuous against their background. The body and tail of this American chuckwalla (right) are adapted to different background colors. Another form of protection from predators is the sharp spines on the tail of the North African scaly-tailed lizard shown below.

Above: the skin of the Australian moloch, or "thorny devil," soaks up moisture, which travels to the mouth by capillary action—a convenient adaptation for making the most of limited water.

Left: walking across soft sand can be a problem. The web-footed gecko of the Namib solves it by having built-in sandshoes—webbed feet that act like snow-shoes to ease the lizard's nocturnal excursions.

This Australian shingle-back is a large lizard—sometimes reaching two feet long—in contrast to the two reptiles pictured at the top of the page, which are not more than a few inches in length. The shingle-back has rough scales and a short, stumpy tail, and eats both plant and insect food. It is one of the largest members of a very widely distributed family of lizards called the skinks.

in dry air. An apparent exception to this general truth about permeability may be found in the curious spiny lizard that inhabits the sandy districts of western and southern Australia, where it feeds on ants. Its rough skin is hygroscopic—very sensitive to moisture—and sucks up water like blotting paper. This water travels to the mouth by capillary action and is swallowed.

Although it is commonly assumed that lizards can withstand extraordinarily high temperatures (probably on account of their habit of basking in the sun), this is not so. Most species do indeed seem to prefer temperatures at the higher end of the normal activity range; but, as I have already indicated, they are stricken with paralysis and soon die when the temperature goes much higher than 113°F. In the Sudan, neither day-active skinks nor nocturnal geckos can survive a 24-hour period of over 104°F heat. The geckos can withstand a very high degree of desiccation, however—perhaps in compensation for their comparative lack of mobility. But all lizards, in spite of their deserved reputation for liking warmth, do all they can to avoid the sun at its peak.

Like lizards, desert tortoises escape the worst heat by burrowing deeply in the ground. The tortoise scrapes the earth loose with its forefeet, then turns around and pushes the loose earth away with its carapace, or shell. Often it takes advantage of initial excavations by other animals, such as ground squirrels. American desert tortoises do not normally drink, because they get enough moisture from the succulent plants on which they feed, but they will search for water when necessary. They can exist without water through the entire dry season. The female lays her eggs in early summer, and the eggs hatch in three or four months. It takes about five years after hatching for a young American tortoise to develop a really hard shell, and it does not reach maturity until it is 15 or 20 years old.

The Old World equivalent of the American desert tortoise is the spurred tortoise, which occurs throughout the Mediterranean region and Asia Minor, its range extending eastward as far as Iran. Like their American relatives, these tortoises generally feed on juicy plants, but in the absence of succulent vegetation they will eat the astringent green fruits of the dwarf palm. They spend the morning and evening hours basking in the sun, but seek shade when the temperature begins to approach lethal limits. At all seasons they are diurnal in their habits. The pairing season begins in May and lasts until September. During courtship the male makes a piping or grunting sound and bangs his shell against that of the female. The eggs are laid several weeks later and buried in the ground; they hatch the following summer, at the time of the annual rains. The eggs of the African desert tortoise are less predictable. Within a single batch, some may hatch in April or May before the rains begin, others as late as July and August. This is doubtless an adaptation to the irregularity of the Sahara Desert rainfall. It helps to ensure that at least some of the baby tortoises will appear when food is available.

Evaporative water loss from tortoises increases greatly when the air temperature exceeds 105°F; the temperature of the body is maintained at this level by the evaporation of urine, which is discharged over the back legs, and of copious saliva, which wets the head, neck, and front legs. This is analogous to the emergency salivation that, as we shall see, enables small desert rodents to withstand high environmental temperatures for short periods. The tortoises also have very large bladders, whose function used to puzzle naturalists. We now know the answer: urine is stored there, both as a defense against enemies (it is discharged when the tortoise is disturbed) and for use in emergency cooling when the animals are unable to find a cool, shady hiding place.

Within the same size range as many reptiles are such small mammals as jerboas and kangaroo rats. The physiological problems posed for mammals by the desert environment, however, are not the same as those faced by reptiles, because they are warmblooded, whereas the reptiles are not. (We shall be discussing the interesting question of blood temperatures later on.) Thus, their main problems in arid regions are concerned with the shortage of water rather than with the stresses of temperature. Rodents are the most numerous of small desert mammals; they inhabit different deserts of the world but have many qualities in common, even though some of them are only distantly related. They all tend to be about the size of a small common rat (except for the spring hares of southern Africa, which are bigger) and have short forelegs for burrowing, long hind legs for jumping, and a long tail for balance with a tuft of hair at the tip.

North American kangaroo rats and other small rodents can survive indefinitely on dry food without drinking a drop of water. Indeed, some can

Typical Readings Inside and Outside a Jerboa Burrow		
	Relative Humidity (%)	Temperature (°F)
Day—Noon		
Surface	5	94
Burrow	40	80.5
Night—Midnight		
Surface	45	71.5
Soil (at same depth as burrow)	60	72.5

The Sahara jerboa achieves a kind of air-conditioned comfort by digging a burrow deep in the sand, where —as indicated in the adjacent chart—the temperature remains at a relatively constant average of about 76°F, no matter how high the thermometer rises on the surface. Jerboas eat very little and leave their burrows for food-hunting excursions only at night. Note the position of the tropical crescent moon: it hangs in the sky like a balance pan.

The American desert tortoise can get all the water it needs from a diet of plants. Its bladder stores large quantities of smelly urine: this is not merely waste matter, but is discharged to deter predators, is deposited around eggs as a protection against drying out, and may be used for cooling the legs in extreme heat. The American desert tortoise can also burrow into the ground to avoid the scorching sun.

even gain weight on an exclusive diet of dry grain! Because they must have water in order to live, how do they manage? The answer is a very complex one. No physiological water storage is drawn upon, nor is there any increase in the concentration of the blood while the kangaroo rat is living on a dry diet. This means that the animal does not conserve water by retaining waste products, but the urine is almost twice as concentrated with respect to salts as is the urine excreted by the white rat. Kangaroo rats are even able to utilize seawater for drinking, because they can excrete such large amounts of salt and yet maintain normal water balance. They can also eliminate an excess load of urea—about 23 per cent, which is nearly four times as much as in man.

It is also true that desert rodents lose very little water by evaporation through the lungs. The air breathed out by most mammals is full of water vapor at a temperature close to that of the body. But desert rodents manage to cool the air that they breathe out, and cool air contains far less vapor per unit volume than warm air

A Namib golden mole devouring a beetle larva. Such moles are plump and cylindrical, with short broad front limbs adapted for burrowing and for "swimming" through the sand. Also helpful adaptations for life in sand are the small eyes and ears.

The kangaroo rat of America (above), like the Sahara jerboa (right), can survive in desert regions on a diet of dry seeds by emerging from its comparatively cool, moist burrow only at night. Both also produce very concentrated urine and do not sweat. The two species are superficially very similar and inhabit similar desert environments.

does. They achieve this desirable economy by means of what biologists call a "countercurrent heat exchanger" within the nasal passage, which warms the air that is breathed in, then cools warm air from the lungs as it is exhaled and, in so doing, condenses the moisture. Thus the water vapor is retained in the rodent's body instead of being lost at the tip of the nose. By means of this and other adaptations, the burrow-dwelling animal can cope with the arid desert, because it can retain most of the water already in its body and need not constantly replenish its store by drinking or by eating moist foods. How, then, does the rodent maintain its basic supply of body water? The answer is obvious: by reducing the amount of water lost in respiration and excretion so that it does not exceed the amount of moisture taken in with food and the amount of water produced by metabolism.

Kangaroo rats, for example, are nocturnal and do not emerge from their holes during the day. Measurements of temperature and humidity

recorded in their burrows show that the moisture content within the burrow is likely to be two to five times higher than that of the desert atmosphere outside. Consequently, with the considerably reduced rate of evaporation of water from the lungs brought about by the nasal-passage adaptation just described, so little water is lost in respiration that the amount lost is exceeded by metabolic water production; and so there is actually an ultimate gain in water for the rodent. As long as it breathes the moist air in its burrow during the day, it needs no other water.

Desert rodents do not sweat. Indeed, it seems likely that the general absence of sweat glands in most small mammals results from the necessity to conserve water that is imposed by their small size, which means a very high surface-to-volume ratio. In order to maintain a constant normal body temperature when the external air temperature is around 104°F, a kangaroo rat would have to lose 20 per cent of its body weight per hour by evaporation. But there is a regulatory process with-

in the rodent, which is held in reserve for emergencies. If the body temperature approaches the lethal level of about 107.5°F, copious salivation occurs automatically, and the saliva wets the fur of the chin and throat. The cooling effect of this has kept experimental desert animals alive for up to half an hour at temperatures fatal to other small rodents. But of course there is a strict time limit on this emergency salivation mechanism, because small animals gain heat rapidly and their bodies contain a very limited amount of water. Clearly, the desert rodent's supply of water can be used for heat regulation only in the greatest emergency, and any loss by evaporation normally takes place only through the lungs.

The adaptations of jerboas to their desert environment are similar to those of the American kangaroo rats and other small mammals. Underground living and the nocturnal habit are partial solutions that jerboas have found to the three main problems of the desert—scarcity of water, rarity of food, and solar radiation. Like the kangaroo rat, the jerboa can live for a long time on a dry diet by eating little and excreting little. The urine is concentrated and the feces are dry.

A number of desert rodents—the ground squirrels, for instance—aestivate: that is, they become torpid during the summer and early autumn. Deep in their comparatively cool burrows, their body temperatures drop to that of the surrounding air, their respiration rate is much reduced, and other physiological processes likewise slow down. This mechanism tides these animals over periods of food shortage, when it would not benefit them to wander outside their burrows, especially with environmental conditions as extreme as they are at that time of year.

Rodents are primarily herbivores. Little is known about the adaptations of desert carnivores, but they no doubt obtain considerable quantities of water from the body fluids of their prey, and so they have few problems of water shortage. Among the small carnivores are foxes, jackals, hyenas, coyotes, cats, badgers, skunks, ferrets, some carnivorous marsupials, and the Australian dingo. Most of these live in or near oases or on the desert fringes. Only the foxes inhabit extremely arid regions, where they must often be entirely deprived of drinking water.

The delightful fennec fox of the Sahara has a number of adaptive characteristics that parallel those of the American kit foxes (which are more common in America's semiarid plains than in her dry deserts). The fennec is much smaller than its relatives from temperate climates; it has well-developed sense organs and large eyes and ears; and by spending the day in a deep burrow it avoids extremes of heat. Like many other desert species, it is a pale sandy color. It enjoys a much more varied diet than other foxes, too, for it feeds on insects, lizards, rodents, dates, other fruits, and virtually anything else it can get. Its liking for sweet things lends an element of truth to the fable of the fox and the grapes. The fennec's young are born in the burrows at the time of the spring rains; when they reach adulthood, they never weigh more than a couple of pounds. If they get overheated, they pant like dogs, and their strikingly large ears probably serve to radiate heat. To conserve water, they excrete a highly concentrated urine.

A number of kinds of rodents and other small mammals such as the fennec are able to live in the desert by subsisting on moist food. The sand rat of North Africa, for example, lives and nests in places where the vegetation consists of succulent plants. These are usually extremely salty, but sand rats are able to eat them in great quantities because the animals secrete urine that may have as much as four times the concentration of sea-water. The American pack rats and ground squirrels, which feed on juicy cholla fruits, also excrete a concentrated urine, although they do not have the sand rat's ability to eliminate vast quantities of salt. Also American are the grasshopper mice, so named on account of their insect diet, which provides them with all their water requirements. And, to mention only one other in this category, the crest-tailed marsupial mouse (or mulgara), which inhabits the most arid parts of Australia, lives mainly on insects, supplemented by lizards and small rodents, and thus satisfies all its water needs.

We have seen that almost all small mammals of desert areas excavate tunnels and burrows in which to spend the hot hours of the day. Although this is equally true of most species of desert hares

and rabbits, the American jack rabbit remains a notable exception; it lives above ground and has no underground retreat. Yet it inhabits areas where no free water is available, and depends upon the moisture obtained from its green food. It is not entirely clear how these jack rabbits can survive in the desert, but the suggestion has been made that their very large ears, which contain a network of blood vessels, may serve (like those of the fennec fox, already mentioned) to radiate heat to the sky while the animals are resting in the shade. Large ears are a characteristic of many desert animals. The Sahara hare, for instance, has ears much large than those of its relatives of temperate climates.

Most of the reptile and mammal inhabitants of deserts have adaptive coloration; that is, they are pale in color, resembling their background. In many desert mammals the undersurface is white, and this coloration often extends over the flanks.

Similar animals tend to evolve in similar habitats. For example, the American kit fox (above) and the Sahara fennec fox (below), small nocturnal carnivores with a wide range of diet, look remarkably alike. They both have large ears, which may radiate heat; and they get moisture from the body fluids of their prey.

The backs of the animals may be fawn-colored, brown, cream, or gray, generally depending on where they live, for there is often a very close similarity between a given species' color and the soil of the particular type of desert in which it lives. For instance, the rodents that inhabit dark isolated lava beds of New Mexico have a very different coloration from that of the closely related species to be found in nearby light soils and white gypsum sands.

The most striking support for the hypothesis that such adaptations are correlated with the environment is afforded by the extraordinarily close resemblance between unrelated animals that occupy similar ecological niches in different areas of the world. Just as there is a structural similarity between the kangaroo rats of America and the jerboas of the Old World deserts, so do the jack rabbits of North America, the hares of the Great Palaearctic Desert, and the marsupial quokka of Australia resemble one another. The prairie dogs of the New World deserts are similar to the ground squirrels of the Sahara; the American kit fox is superficially very much like the Sahara fennec; there are marked parallels between the iguanid desert lizards of America and the Palaearctic lacertids, as well as between the horned lizards of Arizona and the spiny-tailed lizards of the Sahara; and the desert rattlesnake of Arizona, California, and northern Mexico, apart from its rattle, is almost indistinguishable from the horned viper of the Great Palaearctic Desert. If structural similarities are adaptive, it seems that color is likewise an adaptive factor.

In our survey of the fauna of the world's deserts, we have so far discussed the adaptations of microscopic animals and the inhabitants of temporary rainpools, of arthropods, which represent a higher stage in the food web, and of reptiles and small mammals, which are higher still. Just to sum up, it should be remembered that reptiles are mostly predatory, feeding on arthropods or small mammals, and that the small mammals are mainly—though by no means exclusively—herbivorous. Because of their elongated shape, lizards and snakes have a higher surface-to-volume ratio than mammals. Consequently, the metabolic expense of maintaining a constant body temperature by physiological means, as mammals do, would be prohibitive, and so the reptiles must depend almost entirely on behavioral thermoregulation to keep their bodies from either freezing or burning up. Even if they

Above: the night-active blacktail jackrabbit does not burrow but passes the day resting in shade or a shallow depression. This is unusual for a desert animal that drinks no water. Heat is probably radiated from the body by way of the large ears, which contain many blood vessels and are usually held erect.

had evolved an insulating covering of hairs o feathers, they would still be at a thermal dis advantage as compared with mammals.

From this it follows that most reptiles must be predominantly day-active, so that they can warm their bodies from solar radiation. In hot weather however, they need to retreat to the shelter of a cool microclimate during the middle of the day when the heat of the open desert becomes in tolerable. In contrast, small mammals are able to afford the energy to maintain a constant warm body temperature through the production of metabolic heat. But, as I have pointed out, they cannot spare too much water for evaporative cooling, and so it is inevitable that they should be strictly nocturnal during hot weather.

Each group benefits ecologically from the setting of its "biological clock." Lizards are most active diurnally because it is during the day that grasshoppers, flies, and other succulent day-active insects are available. Seed-eating mammals, on the other hand, can gather their food under cover of darkness. You might assume, then, that snakes that feed on small mammals must be at a disadvantage, because reptiles are generally day-active whereas mammals are not. However, such snakes are not strictly diurnal like most other reptiles; some of them are nocturnal, others are active at dusk and dawn. As we have seen, desert snakes have a much lower tolerance of high temperatures than have lizards. They also have a thermal optimum much below that of lizards and better adjusted to the desert surface at night. Nevertheless, they require as much

Right: as with the jackrabbit, no water is required by the African desert hedgehog; it obtains both food and water from its insect prey. The cactus in the background is a prickly pear—a desert plant originally a native of the New World, but which has been introduced by man into the arid regions of other continents.

82

warmth as they can get. That is why rattlesnakes are found lying on warm road surfaces at night in the American Southwest, where they are frequently crushed by cars.

It used to be thought that reptiles were cold-blooded—that is, not actually cold, but simply unable to regulate their body temperatures—and that warm-blooded mammals could maintain a fairly constant body temperature in spite of fluctuations in the temperature of the environment. The words "cold" and "warm" are so inappropriate in this context that biologists eventually discarded them and adopted the terms *poikilothermic* and *homeothermic* instead. Reptiles were called *poikilothermic* (meaning that their body temperature varies according to that of the surroundings) and mammals were called *homeothermic* (meaning that they maintain a relatively constant temperature). But, as we have seen, poikilothermic reptiles and arthropods often have body temperatures as high as, or even higher than, those of homeotherms living in the same environment; and—chiefly as a result of their behavior—their temperature really varies far less than does that of the environment. So a more truly descriptive pair of terms was needed.

For this reason, most scientists now speak of the two groups as *ectothermal* (from the Greek words for "outer" and "heat") and *endothermal* ("inner heat"). Ectotherms (the reptiles) get most of their body heat from the surroundings, by basking in the sun or pressing their bodies against a warm surface, whereas endotherms get theirs from metabolic sources. Even these terms are not entirely suitable, and some authorities prefer to speak of poikilothermic animals as "adjusters," because they adapt themselves to a somewhat variable body temperature, and homeotherms as "regulators," because they regulate their body temperature by physiological means. The distinction between the two groups is not sharp, and no terminology can be absolutely satisfactory. Even among reptiles, metabolic heat production reaches significant proportions in such large creatures as pythons and boas. Indian pythons have long been known to incubate their eggs. When the environmental temperature falls below about 91.5°F, the body muscles of a brooding python undergo spasmodic contractions, which bring about an increase in metabolism and body temperature. In contrast, as we have seen, lizards and other small reptiles depend upon external sources for warmth.

Because the reptiles have relatively impermeable outer skins and therefore do not transpire rapidly, they are not restricted to nocturnal activity, as are most small desert animals (other than insects). This is an advantage—but, of course, they would be killed if they became too hot. Therefore they must spend quite a lot of time adjusting their temperature by moving into the sun or the shade, by orienting the axis of the body to the angle of the sun or to the direction of the prevailing wind, by increasing or decreasing contact with the soil, by perching on branches, or by burrowing. Heat regulation by basking or the avoidance of excessive heat, supplemented by more subtle types of behavior, is associated with rhythmic activity. The reptiles' inner time clocks send them out of their retreats at dusk or dawn, independently of cyclical environmental changes in temperature or light intensity. But for this, these ectothermal creatures would be unable to make full use of their burrows without losing valuable time at the start of their normal periods of activity.

By means of their circadian rhythms, the reptiles mirror internally—or even preadapt to—diurnal changes in the external environment. At the same time, the daily rhythm is itself constantly modified both by an internal seasonal rhythm and by environmental changes in day length, ambient temperature, and so on. For example, day-active desert lizards often have two daily peaks of activity during the summer, when the weather is very hot at noon; these peaks occur at dawn and dusk. In spring and autumn the animals have a single peak around midday; and during the winter they hibernate. Their preferred body temperatures also reflect seasonal changes. Thus, the physiology of circadian rhythms in the desert is closely interrelated with temperature regulation and the avoidance of climatic extremes.

The habits of desert animals are controlled by the physical environment—first through its influence on the vegetation that forms the basis of every desert food chain, and then more directly in all the many ways that we have been examining. The interrelationships between larger animals and the desert environments in which they live are even more complex than those we have studied so far. The animals are too big to escape from the rigors of the desert by burrowing. Instead, they must adapt themselves physiologically to the aridity and the extreme daytime heat.

Larger Mammals

As has been pointed out, larger desert animals such as camels, asses, and antelopes are in a completely different situation from that of the creatures so far discussed, because they are too big to hide from the heat by burrowing. Instead, the big creatures must employ physiological adaptations to reduce water loss and to avoid thermal stress as much as possible during the daytime. Still, they have an advantage in that their bulk reduces their surface-to-volume ratio. This means that they do not need to use so much energy for metabolic heating in cold weather and at night. Moreover, their insulating hair not only keeps them warm at night but shields them from the heat of the sun.

The camel is one of the best adapted of the larger desert animals. There are two species of camel: the single-humped Arabian camel (or dromedary) and the two-humped Bactrian camel. The dromedary is widespread throughout the Middle East, India, and North Africa, whereas the Bactrian camel lives only in the deserts of central Asia, where the winters are very cold. It has a longer, darker winter coat and shorter legs than the dromedary, and it seldom measures more than seven feet from the ground to the top of the humps—about the height of the shoulders in the taller and more slender dromedary. The dromedary has been almost entirely domesticated, but there are wild Bactrian camels; and the small humps and feet and short brown hair of those that inhabit the Gobi Desert indicate that they are genuinely wild and not merely feral (that is, descendants of domesticated animals that have escaped in previous centuries).

Dromedaries had been domesticated on the borders of Arabia by 1800 B.C. (a fact confirmed by the finding of Middle Bronze Age remains of camels at ancient urban sites in Israel). Later, they were introduced into North Africa, the Nile valley, and northwestern India. In the 19th century, 20 of them were imported into Australia as carriers for a cross-country expedition, and

Bactrian camels grazing in the Gobi Desert, Mongolia. This sturdy animal, whose thick fur is an adaptation to Central Asia's cold winters, has been domesticated by man as a pack animal.

their descendants still live there in a feral state; dromedaries were also used in the United States, after the Mexican War, on mail and express routes across the newly acquired arid regions, but the only camels now in America are in zoos. As for the Bactrian camels, we know very little about their history. They were probably widely distributed as wild animals in central and north-western Asia in prehistoric times, and they were domesticated in Persia by the sixth century B.C.

Camels are still of great importance in desert countries as beasts of burden. In the course of evolution, they lost all but two of the toes on each foot, and subsequently increased the surface area of the feet by developing fleshy pads that do not

Above: adaptations of the single-humped dromedary to life in the desert sands include long, protective eyelashes and muscular nostrils that can be closed tightly to exclude dust and sand.

Right: dromedaries being used as pack animals in Egypt. As early as 1800 BC these camels had already been domesticated on the borders of Arabia. The normal walking speed of a fast dromedary is about 3.5 miles an hour, the maximum around 10 miles an hour.

sink into the sand. Their eyes and noses, too, are well adapted to life in sandy places, for the eyes are protected by long, thick lashes and the nostrils can be closed at will to prevent the entrance of sand. A pack dromedary can carry up to 600 pounds, a Bactrian camel up to 1000, for 30 miles a day. When moving fast, they raise both legs on the same side of the body and advance them simultaneously while supporting their weight by the legs of the opposite side. In this way they can maintain a speed of six miles an hour for a few hours at a time, although their normal walking speed is only about three miles an hour. Racing camels can go almost twice as fast as the pack animals; but to keep a racing camel at its fastest pace, the long trot, the rider must cultivate a rankling sore on its neck and prick the sore continuously.

Camels are herbivorous cud-chewers, but they differ from such true ruminants as oxen and giraffes in that the adults retain two incisor teeth in the upper jaw and lack an *omasum* (the third section of the true ruminant's stomach). The smooth-walled *rumen* (the anterior section) has *diverticula* (small sacs) leading from it. These used to be called "water sacs" because of an erroneous notion that water was stored in them. Actually, these glandular sacs serve as accessory salivary glands and produce a watery fluid that has the same salt content as the rest of the body.

It looks like green-pea soup, but far less appetizing. Yet there are many tales of people who have saved their lives by killing camels to drink the rumen-sac fluid; and these may be true, for any fluid is attractive to a parched traveler.

People also used to believe that the camel stores water in its hump, or that the fat of which the hump is composed is itself essentially a water store. Neither of these ideas is correct. The camel's hump is in fact a food store—a splendid desert adaptation, because by concentrating the nutriment in one large depot and not distributing it as a layer of fat beneath the skin, the hump allows the rest of the body to act as a radiator for cooling purposes.

The main problem for a camel, of course, is how to keep cool without undue loss of water, and this is solved by a number of adaptations. The rate of urine flow is low, and little water is lost with the feces. Instead of eliminating all the urea produced in metabolism, the camel, like other ruminants, can use it for microbial synthesis of protein. In this way, the amount of water excreted is reduced, and the body makes greater use of the food. Furthermore, the coarse hair on a camel's back acts as a barrier to solar radiation and slows the conduction of heat from the environment. At the same time, the camel avoids undue water loss by having a temperature that varies over a range greater than that of other mammals; it does not need to begin sweating until its body temperature has risen to 105.3°F. Thus heat is stored in the body during the day and lost at night, when the environmental temperature is lower. Moreover, when the camel's temperature rises, the difference between it and that of the air is reduced, so that less sweat is required to prevent a further increase.

A camel can also tolerate a much greater loss of body water than most other mammals. Without ill effects, it can lose up to 30 per cent of its body weight, as compared with only about 12 per cent in man. And it has an unusual capacity for drinking, with an ability to assimilate 25 gallons or more in a very short space of time—an amount that would cause other mammals to die from water intoxication. This ability is related to the

physiology of the blood, whose red corpuscles are remarkably resistant to dilution and can swell to twice their initial volume without rupturing.

When most mammals are subjected to high temperatures in dry air, desiccation proceeds steadily while the body temperature remains constant. If water is lost through evaporative cooling and is not replaced, the blood gradually becomes more viscous until, eventually, it cannot circulate quickly enough to carry metabolic heat away to the skin. At this point, as we have already seen, the body temperature suddenly rises and "explosive heat death" results. In camels, this is avoided by a physiological mechanism to ensure that water is lost from the tissues only, and the blood volume remains fairly constant. Thus, it is not the camel's ability to do without drinking water that makes it so well adapted to its environment, but its ability to economize the water it does drink and to tolerate wide variations in body temperature and water content. In winter, when the air temperature is comparatively low and camels do not need water for heat regulation, they become independent of drinking water for several months. In summer, the length of time between drinks depends on the environmental temperature and the amount of work that the animal must do. The camels used for policing the desert in the northern Sudan require water every third day in order to keep fit during the summer.

In contrast to most other domesticated animals, which mate in the autumn and produce their young in the following spring, the dromedary has a pronounced rutting season at the time of the rains, and its pregnancy is prolonged for nearly a year. The Bactrian camel has an even longer gestation period of from 370 to 440 days. The young of both species are born singly, are suckled for three or four months, and are not fully grown until they reach 16 or 17 years of age. Yet they live only about 25 years. Droves of wild Bactrian camels in the Gobi Desert usually consist of one or two males and from three to five females. They sleep at night in open spaces and graze during the day on grasses, brushwood, and shrubs. They migrate to the northern part of the range in spring and return southward in the autumn. The males of both species are quarrelsome during the rutting season, when they fight and bite savagely unless separated. Otherwise, they are the most phlegmatic of animals—stupid, obstinate, and without much spirit.

A day-old dromedary in the Danakil Desert of Ethiopia. Young camels can follow their mothers by the end of the first day. Camels' rutting season coincides with the rains, and gestation takes a year; so the young are born when food is again plentiful.

Day
1 Vulture (flying)
2 Flies (flying)
3 Wasp (flying)
4 Lark (flying)
5 Peregrine falcon (flying)
6 Oryx (in the open)
7 Ostrich (in the open)
8 Gazelle (in shade)
9 Hare (in shade)
10 Owl (in rock cracks/caves)
11 Bats (in rock cracks/caves)
12 Nightjar (in rock cracks/caves)
13 Camel spiders (in hole)
14 Jerboas (in hole)
15 Wolf spider (in the open)
16 Swallowtail butterfly (flying)
17 Termites (in underground nest)
18 Dung beetles (in the open)
19 Scorpions (in hole)
20 Horned viper (buried)
21 Fennec fox (in hole)
22 Ants (in the open)
23 Darkling beetles (under stones)
24 Crickets (under rocks)
25 Moths (resting)

Night
Vulture (roosting)
Flies (resting)
Wasp (resting)
Lark (roosting)
Peregrine falcon (roosting)
Oryx (sheltering)
Ostrich (sheltering)
Gazelle (in the open)
Hare (in the open)
Owl (flying)
Bats (flying)
Nightjar (flying)
Camel spiders (in the open)
Jerboas (in the open)
Wolf spider (under stone)
Swallowtail butterfly (resting)
Termites (active in tunnels)
Dung beetles (under stones)
Scorpions (in the open)
Horned viper (in the open)
Fennec fox (in the open)
Ants (in nest)
Darkling beetles (in the open)
Crickets (swarming)
Moths (flying)

Where the desert creatures are, by day (left) and at night (right). While nocturnal forms sleep, day-active animals come out into the open, although they may occasionally need to take shelter from the heat. Most birds soar in the sky, where the air is comparatively cool. When evening falls, the diurnal forms retire to their shelters, and only night-active animals are at work. Owls and bats take to their wings; gazelles browse on acacias; the fennec fox, scorpion, camel spider, and other predators emerge to hunt for food in the African deserts.

Above: a male pronghorn herding his harem. The male (at the extreme right of the picture) is larger and has more prominent horns than the females (here shown with very small horns).

Left: the oryx antelope, photographed here in the Awash valley of Ethiopia, is found in both deserts and plains. Its horns are long and—unlike those of most antelopes—almost straight. They are splendid defensive weapons.

Above: the addax can tolerate more extreme desert conditions than any other species of antelope. Its horns are long, ringed, and wound in an open spiral. The record length is 43 inches.

Apart from the camels, the larger mammals of the Old World deserts are mainly antelopes and wild asses. In the arid regions of North America their ecological niche is occupied chiefly by the pronghorn (which used to be very common on the prairies but was drastically reduced in numbers by hunting over the past 200 years and is only now on the increase again) and the mule deer. The larger equivalents in the Australian deserts are marsupial kangaroos and wallabies, whose young are born at an early stage of embryonic development and carried by the mother in a *marsupium* (pouch) until they are big enough to fend for themselves.

Because of their size, none of these animals can escape the rigors of the desert climate by burrowing; instead, they have many of the physiological adaptations of the camel—though to a lesser degree—and have fairly low water requirements. They are all much more fleet-footed than the camels, however, and their mobility enables them to travel long distances to get water if they need it. Among the most mobile and widely distributed of the large mammals are the many types of

Springboks and zebras at a water-filled natural basin in South Africa. Adapted to arid conditions by nomadic habits, such graceful mammals existed in vast numbers on the dry, treeless plains of southern Africa up to the middle of last century. Easily shot during migrations in search of food, however, they are now becoming rare. Springboks are renowned for their 10-foot leaps into the air.

Above: antelopes are not always as gentle as they look. Here two male gemsboks of South Africa are locking horns in combat. The horns of both sexes of gemsbok—a species of oryx antelope—are long and straight, reaching lengths of up to four feet, which matches the typical shoulder height of these sturdy animals.

Right: saiga antelopes like the male shown here live in herds on the steppes and sandy deserts of eastern Russia and Siberia.

desert antelope. These are found throughout the deserts of Africa and the Middle East, and the different kinds show considerable variations in coloration and size.

Oryx antelopes, for instance, live in the deserts and plains of Africa south of the Sahara, and in Arabia and Iraq. The white oryx is one of the smallest of the many species, but it has unusually large horns. Mostly a dirty white color, with chestnut markings on the head and legs, it stands only about 35 to 40 inches high, but its scimitarlike horns may exceed 45 inches in length. Among other oryx species are the small Arabian, with its tail tuft and blackish-brown markings, and the gemsbok of the deserts of southwest Africa, which prefers less arid country than do most of its near relations. The gemsbok's shoulder height is about four feet, and, like the related beisa of East Africa and Ethiopia, its coloration is more striking than that of the white species. The beisa is mainly fawn-colored with black head markings; the gemsbok, reddish-gray with a white head marked with black, a white belly, black thighs and tufted tail, and

The wild ass of the plains and desert regions of northeast Africa, photographed here in Somalia, can manage without much water and is thoroughly at home in arid surroundings. It can tolerate a considerable degree of dehydration without damage to its body tissues and can make up its water loss very quickly.

black stripes along its back and flanks.

The oryx, whose numbers have been greatly reduced in recent years, are formidable creatures when attacked. Charging with head down, thrusting their swordlike horns to either side with a scything movement, they emit a curious vocal challenge through their nostrils. Most of the other antelopes are much more gentle creatures —even the odd-looking saiga antelope, which roams the arid plains of western Asia. Though small—about three feet high at the shoulder— the saiga can indeed look rather menacing, with its greatly elongated and swollen nose, which contains a network of bones and mucous membranes that may serve either to warm inhaled air or to filter out dust. But it is much more timid than the oryx.

All antelopes are swift and can cover long distances; they have these traits in common with most other mammals of steppe and desert, where concealment from foes is hard to achieve and sources of water are infrequent. Swiftest of all are the gazelles, the smallest, most lustrous-eyed, and most graceful members of the extensive antelope family. Perhaps most common of them are the dorcas gazelles, which are widely distributed throughout the Sahara Desert region. The dorcas has a shoulder height of no more than 24 inches. Its back and sides are colored a sandy reddish brown and its belly white, with an indistinct dark stripe separating the two colors. In many of their habitats—for example, in Morocco, Palestine, and other desert regions of the Mediterranean basin—dorcas gazelles do not require water, because they get all the moisture they need from succulent roots and plant material; but in the Sudan they lose weight steadily when deprived of drinking water, and they are unable to withstand a loss of more than 14 to 17 per cent of their normal weight. During the dry summers, in fact, they cannot survive for more than five days without drinking. Thus their survival depends upon the speed and endurance that permit them to travel great distances to water. Gazelles can run for some time at a steady speed of 50 miles an hour. They migrate from the western Sudan to the Nile during the dry season, and they tend to be rather solitary creatures in dry weather, whereas they often run in herds of 24 or more when it rains.

Probably the most gregarious of the larger desert mammals is the species of wild ass known as the *onager*, of which several different subspecies can be found all the way from the steppes of central Asia to northwestern India, Baluchistan, Iran, and Syria. Onagers—the "wild asses" of the Bible—are white with a large yellowish area on each flank and a black dorsal stripe, black mane, and black tail. They travel in herds, each herd led by an old stallion. Another type of wild ass, the reddish-brown kiang, is a much more solitary creature, which inhabits the high desert plateaus of Tibet, Ladak, and Sikkim. And there are a number of other species and subspecies ranging throughout the arid regions of Asia and Africa. It seems probable that none of the wild asses of today is a pure descendant of the original, true wild ass; there has undoubtedly been much inter-breeding with domestic asses.

The desert asses are surefooted, long-eared animals, and they resemble the camel in one respect: they can tolerate a water loss of up to 30 per cent of their body weight. Their drinking capacity is also impressive; within a few minutes they can ingest more than a quarter of their body weight. They apparently lose water more rapidly than camels, however—partly because the fluc-tuations in their body temperature are smaller, partly because their fur coats are thinner and provide less effective insulation, and partly be-cause their behavioral adaptations for reducing heat-gain from the environment are less extreme than those of the camels.

Neither antelopes nor asses normally sweat. Among the rare desert mammals that do lose water by sweating are the Australian marsupials. The kangaroos that range widely throughout the inland desert regions of the continent exist on the water content of their vegetarian diet supple-mented by infrequent drinking. In hot weather they cool their bodies by sweating, accompanied by copious salivation and licking of the feet, tail, and belly. And this is equally true of the quokka, a medium-sized marsupial (about as big as a rabbit) that inhabits the offshore islands and coastal regions of southwest Australia, where no fresh water is available. The quokka gets its moisture from the vegetation it eats and from an occasional drink of seawater. It obviously gets all the moisture it needs, for it sweats freely—and this is an uneconomical method of

The quokka (above), a stocky Australian marsupial, lives in dry scrub as well as in swamps. Whereas the red kangaroo (right) is day-active, the quokka rests by day and seeks food at night. Unlike most desert mammals, marsupials such as quokkas and kangaroos cool off by sweating in addition to panting. Yet they drink little, obtaining moisture mostly from their vegetarian diet.

Probably because of the scarcity of vegetation in which to hide, large predators have been exterminated by man in most desert regions. One that continues to flourish is the caracal lynx; though shown here in wooded country, it is widely distributed throughout the barren deserts and savannas of Africa, western Asia, and India. It is a fast-moving predator of antelopes, hares, and birds.

cooling the body if water is at all hard to find.

The camel's method is certainly more economical. Let us pause here for a moment to consider why. A comparison of the camel's performance with that of two kinds of mammal with which we are more familiar—man and dog—provides an interesting illustration of the different ways in which various species react to high temperatures. Both man and dog begin to transpire as the body temperature starts to rise above normal. A human being sweats and cools himself by evaporation from the skin; a dog pants and evaporates from its respiratory surfaces. But, as we have seen, the camel simply allows its body

temperature to rise so that heat is stored during the day and lost at night. This puts the camel at a great advantage over both human beings and dogs in a hot, dry climate.

In man, sweating increases as the heat load gets larger, until the amount of sweat reaches 2.6 pints an hour. This high rate of water loss can persist, in spite of desiccation, until dehydration reaches an advanced stage. When supplied with unlimited quantities of drinking water, man's capacity for physical work in the desert is great —far greater than that of the dog, which can cool its body only by panting. But a limitless water supply is not easy to find in the desert. And there

Above: pumas, or mountain lions, once abounded in the New World's plains and forests from Patagonia to Canada; but except for a few that still manage to exist in America's deserts, these animals are now confined to very remote areas. Those shown here in mountain snow are feeding on an elk that they have killed.

are other complications that sweating men must face, such as loss of salt. Dogs transpire only through the lungs, and do not lose any salt in the process. Human sweat, on the other hand, is saline, and the salt lost through sweating in hot climates needs to be replaced. The human desert-dweller who does not take more than a normal amount of salt in his food may soon feel sick and listless, unable to exert himself.

Moreover, because the dog does not sweat, its skin becomes much hotter than that of a transpiring man. It can reach 113°F, at which point heat may even be lost by conduction to the air, whereas heat flow in human beings is in the reverse direction. In this situation, by not sweating through the skin and by having a high skin temperature, the dog is better able to withstand a temporary shortage of drinking water. Indeed, it would be true to say that where water economy is concerned, greater efficiency is achieved by cooling the lungs through panting than by cooling the skin through perspiring. Only comparatively large mammals can afford to cool their bodies in so wasteful a manner. Why, then, did sweating evolve in man? The answer may be that our ancestors lost their covering of hair and developed their extraordinarily effective—but uneconomical—sweating mechanism when they left the rain forest and became hunting animals of the savanna; here there would have been a selective pressure to reduce overheating during the chase.

As we have seen, the camel can and does sweat, but not very much, and only after its body temperature rises above 105.3°F. Its sweat, moreover.

is much more effective than, for example, the sweat of a horse, because the camel's sweat evaporates on the skin under its coarse hair, where it provides maximum cooling, whereas a horse's sweat evaporates outside the animal's coat. Actually, horses are likely to sweat only when driven by man or chased by predators; sweating is for the most part an emergency procedure for them rather than a normal one. And, apart from the marsupials, this is equally true of antelopes, wild asses, and other desert herbivores.

To sum up, one might say that desert mammals conform to expectation. Small ones *avoid* extreme conditions by burrowing and other methods, and large ones *resist* them in all the ways we have been discussing. Perhaps the most salient feature of the mammalian fauna of deserts is the wide array of adaptive patterns that they exhibit. This diversity can be correlated with the many different ecological niches that mammals occupy.

We have limited our discussion so far to the varieties and habits of herbivorous mammals. What about the carnivores? The largest common desert carnivores today are hyenas, foxes, coyotes, dingoes, and so on—animals far too small to prey on the bigger herbivorous mammals. Yet natural food chains are normally headed by a large carnivore, and you may well wonder why substantial numbers of large carnivores do not roam the deserts of the world. The explanation is that they once did, but man has either removed most of them from the fringes of the desert or has made the desert unsuitable for them by altering the environment. Certainly, natural desert areas are not a particularly unfavorable habitat for large carnivores if there is enough shade for them to lie in during the day. They have a low surface-to-volume ratio, and the blood of their prey provides them with an adequate intake of fluid. A fair number of pumas still manage to exist in the American deserts, and lions are distributed throughout the Kalahari. There would be plenty of other big carnivores in those deserts and elsewhere if it were not for the intervention of human beings.

For instance, the marsupial thylacine (also known as the Tasmanian tiger or wolf) is a carnivore that used to wreak much havoc among the sheep and fowl of Tasmania's colonists. In 1888, a government bounty was introduced; from then to 1914, at least 2268 animals are known to have been killed, and the total figure was probably much higher. It seems probable that thylacines were exterminated much earlier in Australia, as a result of competition with dingoes introduced by the aborigines. At any rate, these animals, which may reach a length of more than five feet (of which one third is tail), are now almost extinct in Tasmania as well. Similarly, lions used to be common in the Sahara. The ancient Egyptians worshipped them, tamed them, and trained them for the chase. Cheetahs, leopards, wild cats, hyenas, and wild dogs were also plentiful within Egypt's frontiers and throughout the arid regions of Asia and the Middle East. Lions and cheetahs were common in Algeria until the time of the French occupation of that country. By the middle of the 19th century, however, their numbers had greatly diminished. In fact, cheetahs are now probably extinct in North Africa except, possibly, for a few in the Tripolitanian Desert of northwestern Libya.

In the absence of large desert predators, one might logically expect an increase in the numbers of wild herbivores, limited only by a shortage of food resulting from overgrazing. But this does not occur, because man has proved to be a far more efficient predator than any wild carnivore. In place of lions and leopards, he has introduced domesticated cattle, goats, and sheep, which are far more harmful, because less mobile, than any wild game. For instance, in contrast to gazelles, which nibble at grasses and the leaves of thorn bushes "on the run," as it were, goats stay put. If the lower leaves give out, they climb the trees to reach the upper branches; and they eat shrubs and smaller plants to the ground, so that the vegetation does not recover.

We have already begun to construct a food web of the interrelations between the flora and fauna of the desert. The higher links of the main chain can now be added to it. Small herbivores are eaten by small carnivores; large herbivores were formerly eaten by large predators such as lions, pumas, leopards, cheetahs, and marsupial wolves, but today they are killed mainly by man. Man has harvested plants by using domestic animals since pastoralism first began. In arid regions, however, the domestic herds need larger areas in which to graze than in more fertile parts of the world. Thus desert man has gradually squeezed out other forms of desert life. And in so doing he has compounded his own survival problems by enlarging the world's arid regions. We shall have more to say about this subject in the final chapter of the book.

Goats grazing on an argan tree in Morocco. Overgrazing by goats has been perhaps the most important factor among the many that have helped to create most of the Sahara Desert during the last 7000 years or so. Certainly the enormous extension that has taken place during the last 100 years is due to such misuse of the land. Goats destroy vegetation by eating plants to the ground.

Bird and Bat

The conquest of the air opened up a new dimension in the lives of the animals that achieved it. Such large desert birds as vultures, eagles, and lammergeiers (those enormous Eurasian "bearded vultures," with a wingspread of up to 10 feet) are able to soar in the cool air far above the scorching heat of the desert sand. This more than compensates for the loss of forelimbs—or, rather, their conversion into wings—that makes it impossible for most birds to escape the heat of the day by burrowing. The large birds' ability to fly probably explains why their form and appearance show very little specialization for desert life. Apart from being generally paler in color, most desert species—even the small birds—are hard to distinguish from their relatives in humid climates. The most numerous are insect-eating species, followed by seed-eaters; least numerous are the carnivores (those that eat animals higher in the food chain than insects). Many of the carnivorous birds feed chiefly upon reptiles. The golden eagles and lanner falcons of the Sahara, for example, live to a large extent upon spiny-tailed lizards. The Sonora white-rumped shrike impales its lizard prey on sharp thorns. And the American roadrunner, a relative of the cuckoos, regularly feeds on snakes.

Although many species have been sighted in desert regions, their distribution is usually closely related to the presence of surface water for drinking. They are most numerous, naturally, in and around the vegetation and pools of oases, which are the winter haunts of such migratory birds as swallows, swifts, and pintail ducks; and doves and pigeons drink the water and feed on grain and dates all year long. But where no such hospitable region is within their range of flight, birds are very scarce, in contrast to the relative abundance of reptiles and small mammals. Water loss by evaporation is the most serious physiological factor that limits their distribution in arid regions. Even though the birds that cannot keep cool by high flying rest in the shade

Carrion-eaters thrive in time of drought. Here white-backed vultures crowd around the carcass of a cow killed by drought in the Kalahari Desert. At such times, hunger engenders aggressive behavior, even among those animals not noted for a fiery nature.

as much as possible during the hottest part of the day, they are exposed to much more radiant energy than are burrowing rodents. Owls and nightjars are an exception, however; in the daytime they hide in rock clefts and fissures.

Early in the morning, most desert birds feed actively. Later in the day, the smaller species shelter in trees and bushes with their wings hanging and their beaks open, and large ones circle in the sky. But the largest of the desert birds—the largest of all living birds, in fact—can neither fly nor find easy shelter from the heat. An adult ostrich may be seven or eight feet tall and weigh up to 300 pounds, but its wings are short and ineffectual. So the ostrich depends for its mobility

Above: American turkey vultures (also called turkey buzzards) perching on a cardon cactus in Lower California, Mexico. Turkey vultures, which are related to the condors, feed mainly on carrion and offal, but sometimes eat eggs and young birds.

on ground speed. In a single stride it can span 25 feet, and it can run at a speed of 50 miles an hour. More important than the ostrich's speed, however, are its physiological adaptations to desert life, for the ostrich is more specialized in this respect than most other birds.

Another name for the ostrich used to be "camel bird," and some observers say that from afar it does seem to them to look like a camel, with its humping walk. At any rate, it *is* like a camel in some significant respects. It can go without water for days on end, can tolerate considerable desiccation, and can rapidly make good the loss of weight suffered during dehydration. At higher temperatures, the ostrich's rate of respiration

Above: the lammergeier, or bearded vulture, inhabits arid and mountainous regions of southern Europe, Asia, and Africa. With a wingspan of from 8 to 10 feet, it is even more gigantic than such large American species as the condor and turkey vulture. Like other vultures, it may supplement its carrion diet from time to time with small living animals.

Left: a roadrunner, or chaparral cock, of Arizona feeds on a lizard. These birds prey on various animals and are even able to kill—and devour—rattlesnakes. As their name suggests, they are also noted for their ability to run at great speeds.

An Egyptian vulture cracks an ostrich egg with a stone. This procedure, not recorded until quite recent times, is one of the few examples of the use of tools by animals other than anthropoid apes. (Another is the Galápagos woodpecker finch's use of a cactus spine to probe for insects in crevices.)

They are very gregarious; not only do they group together with their own kind, but they commonly join forces with such game animals as antelope, zebra, topi, and wildebeest. This sort of association benefits all concerned, for the tall bird has exceedingly keen eyes, which can spot potential predators, whereas its mammalian companions are able to detect hidden enemies with their powers of scent. Furthermore, as the mammals move along, they flush out the insects and reptiles that the big birds like to eat. The ostriches also—perhaps chiefly—feed on fruit, grass, leaves, and seeds whenever these are available.

The ostrich, then, is a case apart. Just as the camel is the best adapted of all large mammals for life in the desert, so the ostrich is the best adapted of the non-high-flying birds. The water problem is an ever-present one for many small birds, which can survive only by eating plenty of succulent food or by drinking. This is why most desert species are insectivorous; they and the few carnivorous species get the water they need from their juicy prey. It is the seed-eaters that must depend for survival on adequate supplies of surface water. Their problem is complicated by the fact that birds lose water by evaporation much more rapidly than do mammals of comparable size. This is quite possibly due to the fact that a bird's body temperature is normally higher than that of most mammals. Consequently, the air that it breathes out is warmer and has a higher moisture content.

The fact that birds in general have a higher body temperature than mammals gives them one big advantage in the hot desert; it allows them to rely to a greater extent upon the dissipation of heat by conduction and radiation. The temperature of most species varies from 104 to 107.5°F, and the lethal temperature is very high indeed— about 116.5°F. But this is true of all birds, not of the desert species only. For example, the capacity of the American mourning dove to endure high body temperature (hyperthermia) and extensive dehydration, combined with its ability to fly long distances, allows it to meet the demands of a desert existence even though it is not primarily a desert bird.

Most of the water that small birds lose by evaporation is lost in panting, not through skin transpiration. They have no sweat glands; when their body temperature rises, panting increases evaporative cooling through the respiratory tract. Some species, such as the American desert

quickens considerably, thus increasing respiratory cooling. Its head, neck and legs are nearly naked, but its body has an insulating layer of thick feathers (the ostrich plumes that stylish ladies used to wear in their hair); and when the bird fluffs its feathers, it can increase the thickness of insulation by nearly three inches. When dehydrated, it reduces its daily food intake, and its body temperature tends to rise; there is a resultant increase in the amount of heat lost from the naked parts of the body. Finally, although it must either drink water from time to time or eat very succulent food, it has nasal salt-excreting glands that enable it to live off brackish—or even salty—water.

A native of Africa and the Middle East, the ostrich is not exclusively a desert bird, for colonies of ostriches are found over Africa generally wherever the country is open and dry.

Above: an ostrich family with chicks, in the Kalahari Desert. Ostriches live not only in sandy wastes and deserts, but also in savanna with low bushes and thorn trees. Although they usually congregate in parties of only 5 or 6, troops of 40 to 50 ostriches will occasionally assemble in one place.

Right: three female ostriches in full dance, with their wings twisted backward. Adults of both sexes indulge in displays of remarkable agility, to the accompaniment of wing-flapping, twisting, and swerving at great speed. Such behavior is in keeping with their gregarious habit of traveling in groups.

The mourning dove, one of the common birds of southwestern US deserts, is especially numerous within a few miles range of open water, for it needs to drink at least once every day or two; an excellent flier, it can reach the needed water rapidly. Adults (both male and female) supply the nestlings with a milky secretion from their crops, as is the case in other doves and pigeons.

Chakers drinking at an open puddle in Death Valley, California. Unlike mammals, which can evade the desert blast by sheltering in burrows, and thus become relatively independent of water, most desert birds must fly long distances to find open water where they can drink.

poorwill—which is like the whippoorwill but smaller, and with a song truncated (as is its name) to only two syllables—also keep cool by rapidly flapping the loose skin on the ventral surface of the throat. Both cooling processes, which can take place simultaneously if necessary, entail loss of water. And most terrestrial birds cannot compensate for the loss, as the ostrich can, by drinking salt water, for they have a low tolerance for saline fluids. There are, of course, a few exceptions to this generalization. Among desert birds, one example is Pallas's sand grouse, which feeds on salty, succulent plants in arid regions of central Asia. But the great majority of desert birds share a need for fresh water with their nondesert relatives.

A very serious drawback to desert life for birds has to do with reproduction, and thus with the very survival of a given species. Birds' eggs, particularly those of the smaller species, are highly vulnerable to overheating by exposure to direct sunlight. Only the largest, those of the ostrich, can withstand prolonged exposure to the desert sun. Different species must therefore adopt a variety of devices for sheltering the eggs.

Larks nest as much as possible under shrubs and bushes, wheatears in holes or small caves. Certain species in Arizona and California lay their eggs in holes that woodpeckers hollow out in the saguaro cactus. By means of such holes, woodpeckers manage to colonize several of the world's desert areas where no other large plants grow; and when they eventually move on to other homes, the deserted holes provide shady retreats for many different species, including elf owls, screech owls, sparrow hawks, and flycatchers. Of these, only the elf owl is found exclusively in deserts where the giant saguaro grows, but the others all use woodpecker holes as nesting sites wherever they can find them.

Of the birds that breed in the open without protection, most species sit on the nest from the time the first egg is laid, so that the eggs are never exposed to daytime heat or nocturnal cold. Pratincoles and terns in hot regions are reputed to stand over their eggs, thus shading them from the sun. When the eggs hatch in desert places, the parents must also find ways to quench the thirst of their babies. The sand grouse that inhabit the Great Palaearctic and Kalahari deserts and that nest far away from rivers and lakes have adopted an extraordinary method of watering the young. The male rubs his breast on the ground before drinking, so that his feathers are awry and easily saturated as he bends to the water. He then flies back to the nest, where the little birds pass the wet feathers through their beaks and keep changing places until their father's feathers are dry and the supply of water is exhausted. Until they can fly, the young sand grouse take water in no other way.

Although the timing of the reproductive cycle in birds depends primarily upon day-length, breeding among the desert species is frequently coordinated with either rainfall or the visual stimulus provided by green vegetation. Many desert birds do not reproduce at all in dry years. Others appear to be undaunted by both aridity and heat. The double-banded courser of South Africa, for instance, breeds continuously regardless of weather or season; and the sooty falcon of North Africa can also breed in harsh conditions.

To complete our brief survey of the problems posed for birds by desert living, let us examine one last question: How do they cope with the dry season and the consequent loss of food as insect life disappears and what little vegetation there is in the desert dies down? One obvious answer, of course, is that many species migrate to preferable regions at such times; as we know, that is something that birds can do more easily than most other creatures. But some species do not bother to go away; and it seems likely that more birds than we now realize can become temporarily torpid and assume a state not unlike the hibernation of other animals. Centuries ago, it was believed that such birds as swifts and swallows did this. As late as the 18th century, the great English lexicographer Dr Samuel Johnson wrote that swallows "certainly sleep all winter." He even thought he knew how it was done: "A number of them conglobulate together by flying round and round and then, all in a heap, throw themselves under water and lie in the bed of a river." Most modern naturalists, however, looked upon all notions of torpidity in birds as myths.

Above: when desert woodpeckers abandon their holes, elf owls often move in. The elf owl, which is little bigger than a sparrow, lives exclusively in deserts where the saguaro cactus grows.

Left: this Gila woodpecker perched on a dead saguaro cactus is one of many species of woodpecker at home in arid regions.

They did so, that is, until 1946, when a torpid desert poorwill was discovered in California. Subsequently, it was found that hummingbirds regularly reduce the consumption of their energy reserves by allowing the temperature of their bodies to drop during the night, if not for longer periods. And there is now plenty of proof that periodic torpidity in response to low temperature exists among not only hummingbirds but also nighthawks and swifts. The American poorwill is a nocturnal bird that spends much of its time on the ground, occasionally rising in a fluttering way to snap up small nocturnal moths

Birds, like other animals, have various ways of coping with aridity and heat. Sand grouse (above) fly daily to the nearest watering places. Water is carried to the young in the male's breast feathers. Shade for the eggs is as much of a necessity to birds as is water to drink. Below: a Temminck's courser in the Kalahari Desert shields its eggs from the sun to keep them cool.

and other insects. And so winter hibernation doubtless enables it to survive in the desert during times when such food is scarce or absent.

One other type of desert adaptation is quite common among birds: cryptic coloration (which means coloration that blends in with the background). Among familiar examples are the desert poorwills and nightjars, whose soft-tinted plumage makes them extremely hard to see when they perch on the sand or hide themselves in rock crevices. One of the crested larks of the Sahara is represented by a dark race in northern parts of Algeria that are not desert; in the semideserts that fringe the Atlas Mountains southward, the dark larks give way to a paler race; and in the northern Sahara itself we find a still paler race. The color of this last group is so wonderfully adapted to the soil that a crested lark is easily overlooked if it does not happen to be on the wing or singing. And in the reddish, stony desert that stretches between Laghouhrat and Ghardaia in Algeria, there is a reddish form of the same bird, whose distribution corresponds fairly closely with the limits of the red area. Simi-

lar examples could be singled out from many other species of bird, as of mammals. Moonlight and starlight are so bright in the clear desert air that adaptive coloration has important survival value even for nocturnal animals.

It may seem paradoxical, but in addition to cryptic coloration, a brilliant black—which does just the opposite of concealing—is also common among not only desert birds but other desert-dwellers. The occurrence of blackness in widely separated groups of animals is worth remarking on. Examples include ravens, wheatears, beetles, bees, flies, and so on. Because black is conspicuous, it can be considered as a warning coloration—a "you'd-better-not-touch-me" sign to potential enemies—in distasteful or poisonous animals. Its prevalence among desert animals may result from a fascinating adaptation known as Müllerian mimicry (so named after a 19th-century German zoologist), in which two or more noxious species all have a special attribute—in this case, the color black—that causes them to resemble one another. Predators learn to avoid creatures with the *aposematic* (warning) attri-

One means of protection from hungry enemies is by cryptic coloration—that is, a coloring that blends with the background. The South African nightjar (above) is active during twilight or night hours, and is difficult to detect in its shelter when the sun shines. The color of the crested lark (below) closely matches that of the soil and differs according to its desert habitat.

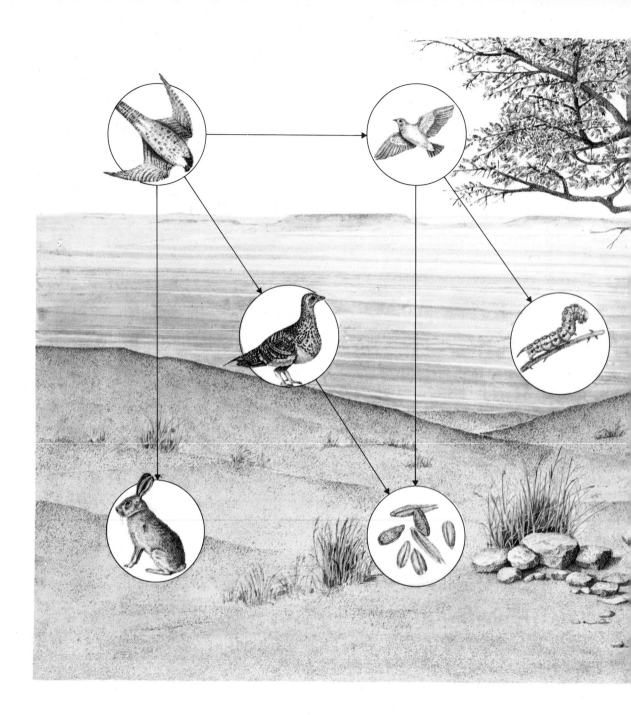

bute, and the numerical losses of all the species that look alike are thus reduced. A second type of mimicry, called "Batesian mimicry" after the English naturalist H. W. Bates, who spent the years 1849–60 collecting butterflies in the forests of Brazil, is even more helpful to some species. In Batesian mimicry, a relatively harmless and unprotected species, such as a bee fly, resembles a potentially dangerous species such as a bee and, on account of its realistic disguise,

is therefore carefully avoided by predators

The struggle for existence is especially severe in desert regions, as we have seen. Poisonous species tend to be more dangerous than their relatives from less arid environments, speedy animals faster, senses more acute. In a similar way, natural selection has had an unusually strong effect on coloration. Cryptically colored species are exceptionally inconspicuous, and Müllerian and Batesian mimicry are extremely

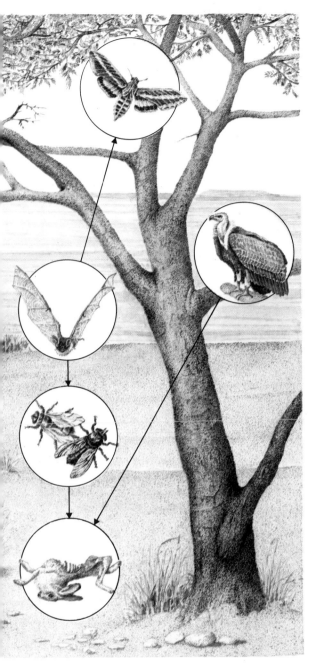

A Simple Food Web for Desert Birds

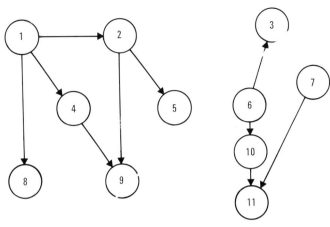

1 Lanner falcon	7 Vulture
2 Skylark	8 Hare
3 Moths	9 Grass
4 Sand grouse	seeds
5 Caterpillars	10 Flies
6 Bats	11 Corpses

Vegetation, which is at the base of all food chains, is the primary source of energy for birds as for other living creatures. In extreme deserts, vegetable matter may consist of nothing more than dry seeds and plant material blown from elsewhere. A secondary source of nutrition consists of the local fauna both alive and dead, as well as of the corpses of migrant birds. The dead bodies support flies and other insects in addition to carrion-eating mammals and birds. Corpses soon become mummified in deserts as they do not keep moisture for long.

common. That is why we seldom find colors without marked adaptive significance, even among the birds.

When day-active birds retire to rest, their place is taken by nocturnal bats. Bats are the only mammals to have evolved flapping flight; and they are the only aerial mammals of the desert, because such gliding forms as flying squirrels and flying lemurs occur only in forests. (Bats also glide from time to time, but they do not seem to be able to use upward air currents or to practice soaring flight, as many birds do. In any case, upward thermal currents are much less common at night than during the day, when the surface of the ground is heated by solar radiation.) Like birds, bats are unable to burrow because their forelimbs have become delicate wings. Insectivorous species exist only where adequate food is available, and the kinds known as "flying foxes" are fruit-eating and so tend to be restricted in desert regions to river valleys and oases. Consequently, although bats are very common throughout the Nile valley, where they can roost in caves and ruins during the day, they do not penetrate far into the Sahara Desert.

A comparable situation is found in other desert

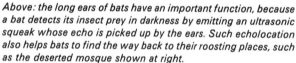

Above: the long ears of bats have an important function, because a bat detects its insect prey in darkness by emitting an ultrasonic squeak whose echo is picked up by the ears. Such echolocation also helps bats to find the way back to their roosting places, such as the deserted mosque shown at right.

regions of the world. We find bats around the fringes and in oases, but not in great numbers where there is little but hot sand and sky. But nocturnal habits are a useful adjunct to life in the desert. If there are roosting places and water holes within flying range, small bats can be found in almost all desert places; they appear at sunset, just after kites and other day-active birds have gone to roost. However, the existence of bats is not possible unless there are crevices large enough to shelter them, for they must have cool places in which to hide from sunlight.

Many riverine species visit water regularly at the beginning of their evening flight, but we do not know whether this is a general rule. What we do know is that water is even more essential for insect-eating bats than for most mammals. No other desert mammal seems to be as exclusively insectivorous as the bats, probably because the number of insects tends to fluctuate greatly according to the season, and so no earthbound desert mammal can survive throughout the year on insects alone. The fluctuations may well be less marked among the aerial insects on which bats feed than among terrestrial species; and because of their nocturnal habits and the ability to hibernate, bats can avoid not only the daytime heat of the desert but perhaps also the season

when insect food is not abundant.

A diet of insects is inordinately rich in protein, however, and requires much more water for the excretion of nitrogenous waste than does a carbohydrate diet. Insectivorous birds get all the moisture they need from their juicy diet; but bats do not, because mammals cannot excrete insoluble uric acid (as the birds do) but must excrete urea in solution. Dusk at a desert water hole is therefore characterized by clouds of bats, which may have flown from quite distant roosting places, swooping down to drink as they glide low over the water surface.

Bats show no special modification in relation to the desert environment. They appear fairly high in the food chain and are eaten by owls, kites (when the bats come out of their shelters too early in the evening), foxes and snakes. Their numbers, though, are probably regulated more directly by occasional food shortages and disease than by predation. Although not especially adapted to desert life, they are clearly an important element in the ecology, for a bat eats up to half its own weight of insects in the course of a single night. Furthermore, the species that feed on fruit and nectar, such as the American long-nosed bats, may well play an important part in the pollination of cacti and other desert plants.

Desert Man

The year 1973 witnessed the culmination of a long drought in the savanna regions fringing the southern border of the Sahara Desert. These depend for their very life on monsoon rains that usually come when the intertropical front moves north during the summer, but that had failed to fall adequately for seven successive summers. In July 1973, when my wife and I traveled by rail and road from Abidjan on the Ivory Coast northward to Mopti on the Niger River, rain had at last begun to fall and the countryside was green again. But the sheep and cattle of the nomads who inhabit this region had died in thousands, and their owners were facing starvation.

Failure of the monsoons is a natural hazard of the fragile, unstable ecosystem on the desert's fringe. It results in disaster when the land has been overexploited. Each such disaster adds to the relentless advance of desert conditions, which have frequently been brought about by human misuse of the environment. And although arid regions are readily degraded into desert, it is far more difficult to reclaim them and bring back their natural climax vegetation.

The world's desert places are so vast, so awe-inspiring, and so desolate that it is hard to realize that they are not as old as time and that a very large proportion of them are man-made. Yet the evidence is irrefutable. Not long ago, I met a botanist from the western part of India who told me that he had been born in a village surrounded by a forest. He had recently gone back to see his old home and had found, to his horror, that it was now situated in a desert. The spread of the great Thar Desert of western India has been accelerating in recent years as a result of the felling of trees for firewood and of the trampling and overgrazing of the land by domestic stock. Only 2000 years ago, the entire region was jungle!

Until very recently, too, the fauna and flora in the central part of the Nile valley were compara-

A typical scene in a mountainous region of the central Sahara Desert: a party of nomads pausing to water their livestock— camels, donkeys, sheep, and goats—at a communal well. Acacia trees provide them with scant shade in the searing heat.

Dunes and desert grasses in the central Namib. Natural causes are responsible for this ancient desert, for it adjoins a sea whose cold Benguela Current flowing from the Antarctic brings only fog and mist, not rain. It is man's misuse of the environment, however, that has increased the area of established deserts and created equally barren conditions in many other parts of the world.

tively rich. Elephants and lions were plentiful there, and so were cheetahs. As we saw in an earlier chapter, none of these animals can flourish in a true desert environment. But many of the animals that are normally associated with desert places—such as antelopes, mouflons, and ostriches—have been exterminated over large areas; even gazelles are becoming scarce. It is difficult to imagine large animals surviving today in the barren land that was able to support them until the 19th century. In the diary of his journey up the Nile during the years 1821 and 1822, a French traveler, Linant de Bellefonds, com-

mented on the wooded nature of the countryside of the northern Sudan; he heard a lion roaring at Ed Debba, near Old Dongola. Today, away from the river, that region of the Sahara is almost complete desert, with practically no vegetation. Similarly, lions abounded around Shendi, 120 miles north of Khartoum, in 1835, and game was abundant at Kassala as late as 1883. None of these Sudanese areas could now support that kind of life.

In Kenya tradition has it that the area around Lake Rudolf, now semidesert, was once lush and fertile. Within living memory, much of Somalia that is now overgrazed and eroded was forested, with permanent springs and a rich fauna of elephants, lions, and other game. One could go on for a long time enumerating such man-made desert areas in tropical Africa. Through shifting cultivation, forest has been transformed into savanna. The savanna has been maintained by regular burning, which affects the composition of the vegetation, favoring some kinds and eliminating others. Through overcultivation without the use of fertilizers, woodland savanna eventually becomes agriculturally unproductive. It is then used by herdsmen whose cattle, sheep, and goats can create desert conditions even where the rainfall is sufficiently high to support forest trees. Increasing sterility in some areas causes further overgrazing in others that remain relatively fertile. Soils, climates, vegetation, and fauna interact with one another to produce an unstable biological environment that tends with misuse to deteriorate steadily. In the fragile regions bordering existing deserts, such trends are greatly accelerated.

Nor has man's destruction of the environment been confined to the Old World. At the beginning of the present century, the area of Chihuahua Desert east of Las Cruces in southern New Mexico was covered with long grass, grazed by

Much of the African savanna and of the Sahara itself would probably be fertile and forested but for the past centuries of shifting cultivation and intense overgrazing by domesticated animals. In the process, many of the wild animals have been exterminated. This view of the Blue Nile River in Ethiopia shows riverine forest that has so far escaped being destroyed and reduced to desert.

Above: Bushmen hunting an eland, a large African antelope, in the Kalahari. Bushmen neither cultivate the soil nor maintain herds of domesticated animals; they live by hunting and food gathering. Magnificent archers, they can hit moving antelopes with poisoned arrows at 150 yards. They then follow the wounded prey for hours or days until it succumbs.

Left: the hunt has ended satisfactorily for the Bushmen. They discard the meat around the site of penetration of the poisoned arrow before cutting the flesh into strips and drying it in the sun to form biltong (a South African name for strips of dried meat). The Bushmen use the skins for constructing temporary shelters (or skerms) in which they spend the cold nights typical of desert areas.

cattle. Too many people, however, made their fortunes too quickly. The productivity of the land was destroyed, and it is now just a waste of creosote bushes, which are too unpalatable for even the hungriest grazing animal.

Human beings are remarkable creatures, however. Having created desert places, they have also learned how to live in them. Human occupation of the desert relies on one or more of three possible ways of life. The simplest is that of nomadic hunters and food gatherers, such as the Bushmen of the Kalahari and Namib and the Bindibu of central Australia. Such peoples are living at a level no more advanced than that of the Stone Age. They plant no crops, have no permanent homes, and keep no domesticated animals except dogs.

Bushmen are excellent hunters and can hit a moving antelope with a poisoned arrow from a distance of 150 yards. The women and children dig the earth with grubbing sticks for their staple diet of edible bulbs, roots, and *tsama* melons, which are prized as a source of moisture. Naturally, they need to be extremely economical with water, which they store in gourds and empty ostrich eggshells. They avoid activity while the sun is high. In very hot weather, they even urinate into pits dug in the ground and lie in them throughout the day, keeping as cool as possible so as not to waste body moisture by sweating. They wear little clothing, but their pigmented skins shield them from ultraviolet light. At night they rest in temporary shelters made from animal skins laid across the branches of thorn trees. And they have one remarkable physiological adaptation for desert living—the anatomical peculiarity of *steatopygia* enables them, in times of plenty, to store fat in their protuberant buttocks, which shrink during periods of drought. Extremely shy but cheerful and good-natured, the Bushmen have a well-developed sense of art and beauty, as shown by their wonderful rock and cave paintings.

Like the African Bushmen, the Australian Bindibu are extremely skilled at tracking game. Their only shelter is a flimsy windbreak made of sticks or clumps of grass; at night, fires and sleeping dogs provide the sole sources of warmth for their naked bodies. Australia has no counterpart of the water-storing *tsama* melon, and these aborigines are forced to camp near water holes and to try to follow the course of the rare desert rains. The womenfolk trudge long distances

Above: a Bushman woman in Botswana drinking water from an ostrich shell. Like all desert-dwellers, Bushmen have to be extremely economical with water, which they also store in gourds.

Below: like the men, Bushman women must also help to gather food for the tribe: it is their job to scour the desert, grubbing with sticks for edible roots. Here we see a Bushman woman roasting the fruit of her toil in the glowing embers of a fire.

daily in search of food and firewood while the men are hunting. Yet, again like the Bushmen, the Bindibu are intelligent and courteous in spite of the harshness of their desert existence.

A second possible way of life in the desert is that of the herdsman. Many desert peoples depend for food upon their flocks and herds—and thus only indirectly upon the sparse vegetation. An exception is the nomadic herdsman of the western Gran Chaco in South America. He and his family do eat some tubers and roots, mainly for the water content, during the long dry season.

Apart from the vegetation in wadis and drainage basins, extreme deserts have little wood for burning or, indeed, for any other purposes. Thus, the primitive shelter of those who dwell in some parts of the Sahara, for instance, usually consists of skins or cloth, and their fuel is often dried camel dung. Desert rainfall is so variable, in both time and place, that they can often take advantage of it only by wandering with their cattle, goats, and sheep over large areas. That is why, as a result of natural selection, even the domesticated breeds of animals tend to be speedy, with long limbs and slender bodies, like many of the wild desert mammals. And, just as camels store fat in their humps, so the desert sheep store reserves in their fat tails. Their nomadic habits enable the human beings and their herds to live permanently in regions where effective rain falls at any one place only once in every two or three years.

An extreme example is the Teda people of the Libyan Desert, who until recently wandered in small groups, with a few sheep or goats, across hundreds of miles of almost lifeless country, where effective rain falls on an average of only once in 30 to 50 years (except on a few isolated patches of high ground, where the rain can come as often as once every 4 to 10 years)! Like the Tuareg of the Hoggar and Ajir mountains in Algeria, the Teda used to roam over an enormous area, but the present range of their nomadic groups does not extend much beyond the limits of the Tibesti massif close to the south-central border of Libya. Similarly, the Tuareg used to range from Touggourt in northern Algeria eastward deep into Libya, westward to Timbuktu in

Rock paintings made by Bushmen in the Botswana hill country. The richness of this art form has excited considerable interest among students of art and anthropology and many different styles have been described in various parts of southern Africa.

125

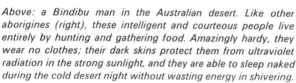

Above: a Bindibu man in the Australian desert. Like other aborigines (right), these intelligent and courteous people live entirely by hunting and gathering food. Amazingly hardy, they wear no clothes; their dark skins protect them from ultraviolet radiation in the strong sunlight, and they are able to sleep naked during the cold desert night without wasting energy in shivering.

Mali, and far south into Nigeria. During the last few centuries, however, Arab and European pressure has forced them to limit their wanderings considerably. A tall, proud race, the Hamitic Tuaregs undertake no menial work, keeping black serfs to do it for them. One night a year or two ago, when we were camping near Agadez in northern Niger, some heavily veiled Tuareg men came and greeted our party, speaking Arabic so that we could understand them. An hour after they had left, they came back with a welcome

gift of cow's milk. Courtesy seems to be an almost universal trait of the nomadic desert peoples.

Nomadic tribes are found all over the Sahara. Some tribes are so small that they have little social organization beyond the framework of isolated family bands of wandering hunters who sleep in the open, dress in skins or rags, and are desperately poor. Others, numbering up to several hundred thousand persons each, are subdivided into clans with elaborate social, political, and economic systems. The nomads cause deteriora-

tion of desert vegetation in direct proportion to the size of their herds. There is no evidence at all that food-gathering hunters such as the Bushmen and Bindibu have ever had an adverse effect on the desert environment; like wild desert animals, they are too mobile and there are too few of them to do any harm to the ecosystem. And even the herdsmen are unlikely to be guilty of overgrazing if they are true nomads, because their few camels and small flocks seldom remain in one area for very long. Serious damage, how-

ever, is caused by the semisedentary people who live in villages near bodies of water for at least part of the year, and who become nomadic only during and after the rains. They tend to have the largest herds and to be responsible for the greatest amount of overgrazing and soil erosion.

It has been argued that such desert people would do less harm and achieve greater productivity if they replaced their sheep and goats entirely by camels, which are more mobile and require water less frequently, and which can

Above: a Mozabite shepherd near Biskra, Algeria. He and his people are not nomads but tend their flocks of sheep and goats in and around the small towns that have grown up at large oases. The Mozabites—a Moslem sect—are Berber-speaking and are notoriously fond of dog meat.

Above: Bedouin nomads with their sheep and goats in the northern Sahara. These Arab people do not have a self-contained economy but are dependent on the presence of flourishing oases in the general area within which they wander. Until recently, such pastoral nomadic tribesmen had a very long history of warfare, raiding, robbery, and blood feuds.

Left: Tuareg nomads in Niger. At the heart of the modern Tuareg economy are their herds of camels and flocks of sheep and goats, all of which extend desert areas by treading, grazing, and browsing on plants. In times past, the blue-robed Tuareg warriors were much feared in the Sahara, where they used to waylay and pillage merchant caravans over a very wide area.

therefore exploit larger areas of vegetation without overgrazing any one area. The big drawback is that camels are a less attractive source of food than are sheep and goats. Camel milk is nutritious, but the meat is not popular (though the liver is considered a delicacy by the people of Arab countries). It is unlikely that the sedentary or semisedentary herders of most desert regions would agree to participate in any serious effort to force a change in the general diet.

Let us turn now to an examination of the third way in which human beings can obtain a livelihood in the desert: by dwelling in oases. This is

the way of life that most of the inhabitants of the world's arid regions have chosen. As I pointed out in an earlier chapter, only a few oases still exist in their natural condition, and these are largely in the New World, chiefly because the pressure of population has not been as great there as in the Old. The oases of Asia and Africa have been greatly changed through the centuries, with every drop of water being utilized by man. Although the original flora probably consisted mainly of tamarisk, oleander, and other shrubs, these have long since been replaced by such things as date palms, fruit trees, and vegetables,

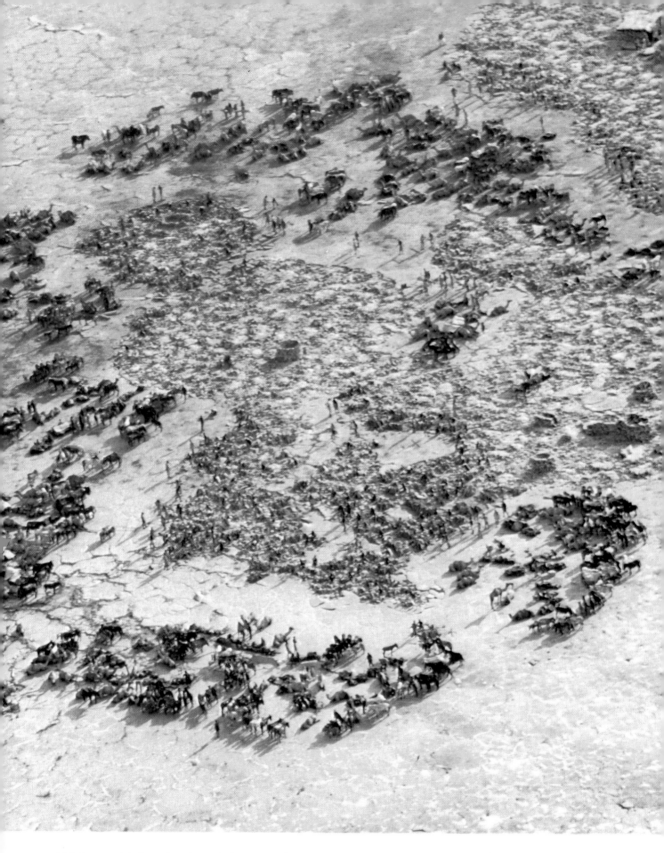

This is an aerial view of a salt works in the Danakil Desert, Ethiopia, where saline waters are concentrated by evaporation. Salt is essential for desert people, because the body eliminates so much in sweat. Though the body adjusts to heat and the salt content of sweat diminishes with acclimatization, some increase of intake is necessary when the rate of sweating is high.

together with agriculturally introduced weeds.

The vegetation and pools of oases are the winter haunts of migratory birds such as perching birds, swallows, swifts, and pintail ducks, and doves and pigeons feed on cultivated grain and dates throughout the year. But because all fresh water is controlled by the human inhabitants, wild animals must either be capable of doing without water (the jerboas and gerbils, for instance) or must sneak in and drink at night (as do the gazelles, foxes, jackals, and hyenas). Smaller creatures abound, of course—grasshoppers, locusts, crickets, spiders, termites, bees, wasps, ants, butterflies, moths, and flies of various kinds, including mosquitos and other blood-sucking pests of man and domestic animals. Dragonflies and other aquatic insects may also be locally plentiful.

I have suggested that it is difficult to reclaim arid regions and make them bloom again once they have been degraded into desert by misuse of the land. Yet in virtually all the deserts of the world, oases are today being extended; and new ones are being created by the exploitation of underground water supplies. In areas where the annual rainfall exceeds six inches, sand dunes can support permanent vegetation if the dune surfaces can be stabilized. This is sometimes done by spraying the dunes with a mixture of oil and synthetic rubber before planting seedlings of acacia or eucalyptus. When the trees have become established, their roots draw upon the moisture that has been stored, from one wet season to the next, below the surface. By extending oases in this way, planners can to some extent reverse the desert expansion caused by overexploitation and mismanagement. The importance of oases, therefore, lies not only in their own productivity but in the fact that they are bridgeheads from which to fight the slow, hard battle of desert reclamation. Naturally this requires large sums of money; more such projects would be a worthwhile investment for the revenues that many of the developing countries are now enjoying from their rich stores of oil and minerals. But overexploitation of underground water could lead to the wells running dry.

In the long run, the world's deserts may prove to have an economic value for humanity quite apart from the productivity of their oases. For example, the sunbaked sands might be exploited as sources of solar energy, which could provide power for industry—and an industrial com-

Above: unloading blocks of salt at Gao, Niger.

Below: salt slabs from mines at Timbuktu in Mali.

munity uses far less water per head of population than does an agricultural one. (Indeed, it seems paradoxical that the industrial heart of the world should be centered in temperate regions where soils are fertile and there is abundant rain. If it were possible to remake the world, we should surely zone the temperate regions for agriculture and the deserts for industry!) On a practical short-term basis, however, the most obvious method of increasing the productivity of arid lands immediately is by the formation of oases through irrigation. This is not possible everywhere, of course; much of the underground water of the Sahara, for instance, is saline and not suitable for either crops or domestic animals. But where fresh water is available and soils are favorable, large parts of the desert can be transformed into green and productive oases.

For the people who live in oases, their isolation has both advantages and disadvantages. The outstanding advantage is that conditions in the surrounding desert are inimical to life and act as a barrier to the introduction into the oasis of agricultural pests and human diseases. Unfortunately, however, where they *are* introduced—usually as a result of human activity—both pests and diseases tend to flourish. To be sure, there are ways of fighting such scourges. Malaria was endemic in the large oases of the Algerian Desert until half a century ago, when gambusia fish were imported from Texas and put into all the permanent waters of the country. These fish, which are efficient predators of mosquito larvae, eradicated the insects from several oases—a splendid example of successful biological control. Nevertheless, there is always a danger of reintroduction, both of mosquitos and of the disease. This has already occurred in more than one place.

Desert irrigation schemes are almost certain to become focal centers for bilharziasis, malaria, and other diseases transmitted by insects and other invertebrates. For example, at the time of the rains from July through September, there is an annual outbreak of malaria among the peoples who inhabit the semiarid belt of savanna and desert land that lies across Africa south of the Sahara. And the crops produced in irrigated desert soil appear to be particularly vulnerable to attacks by locusts and other insects, probably

Overgrazing by sheep and goats near Quarzazate, Morocco. This is how deserts are made; plants are killed, and young seedlings are eaten, so that the vegetation is unable to regenerate. Moreover, the tracks made by the animals as they search relentlessly for fresh plants to graze act as avenues along which water erosion begins, and more plants die when their roots are exposed.

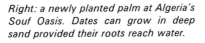
Above: date palms, which are a valuable food source for desert-dwellers, being engulfed by sand at the oasis of Taghit in Algeria. Naturally, efforts are often made to save such trees, but with only limited success. Attempts to replace them are fraught with difficulty.

Right: a newly planted palm at Algeria's Souf Oasis. Dates can grow in deep sand provided their roots reach water.

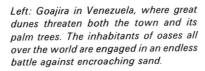
Left: Goajira in Venezuela, where great dunes threaten both the town and its palm trees. The inhabitants of oases all over the world are engaged in an endless battle against encroaching sand.

because in such areas these pests enjoy conditions suitable for year-round breeding.

Although much could still be done to reclaim the semiarid and desert lands of Africa and Asia, it is well to be realistic. Much of the money and technical aid supplied to developing countries by national and international agencies is misapplied or wasted. In order to offer intelligent help to the people of the desert, we must understand and sympathize with their traditions, religious attitudes, problems, and ways of life. Because of a lack of understanding, grandiose schemes often go awry, whereas small improvements may be immediately and immensely effective. In recent years, for example, there has been a gradual replacement by pulleys of the acacia branches that rest across the tops of many Sudanese wells. Such branches serve as a support for the leather rope that runs across them and down into the well; and pulleys reduce wear on the ropes as well as easing the work of the donkeys that draw up the water in goatskin bags.

More ambitious development plans must be accompanied by education. The best projects rely less on money than on the latent abilities and resources of the people they are intended to help.

Above: terraced hills and walled villages in the Afghanistan mountains southwest of Kabul mean relative wealth for the inhabitants. Rainfall engendered by mountains causes high-altitude oases.

Right: poor people must make the best use of what they have. Here a plow is drawn by a mixed team consisting of a camel and a donkey at Safi in Morocco.

Right: desert reclamation depends upon the presence of adequate supplies of fresh water for agricultural purposes. In this photograph of a scene in Libya, water brought up from a depth of 130 feet is being sprayed, together with fertilizer, over crops. Under such happy conditions, from 10 to 12 crops of alfalfa or up to four crops of wheat can be produced every year, but the water is being used faster than it can be replaced.

Below: a donkey draws water in a goatskin bucket from a well at M'Zab in Algeria. Most people who live in the Sahara Desert are still denied the advantages of mechanical irrigation. There is a sharp contrast between the scene at right and this one.

Certainly it will take many years before most desert peoples can learn to understand and act upon modern scientific concepts. For a long time, science will have to coexist with superstition; otherwise its impact will be limited to a tiny minority of highly educated inhabitants of the desert. Knowledge of deeply rooted religious and cultural beliefs is a prerequisite to helping the vast majority, whether nomads or sedentary farmers and shepherds, to adapt themselves to the modern world.

But we should be wrong if we were to dream wistfully of conquering the desert wherever it exists and turning the whole earth into fruitful land. As world population increases and we be-

come more and more crowded, we must soon realize that open space itself is a valuable natural resource. Our desert ecosystems may then be treasured as are the national parks of forest and savanna lands today. For the type of ecosystem that we have been examining in this book is one of great biological interest.

We began with an investigation of the amoeba's world in the sand grains, and of the rain fauna of desert pools. Then we saw how small animals manage to avoid the heat and to survive the desert drought without drinking—something quite impossible for larger forms such as the ostrich and camel. We glanced at the lives of birds and bats in their aerial surroundings. And finally we have been considering the entire desert scene, chiefly from the standpoint of its human inhabitants. This man's-eye view of the desert should make us humble, for it helps to show not only that man is as much a part of nature as any other animal, but also that he can be extremely destructive of the ecosystem. Unless we occasionally find ways to adapt ourselves to our natural surroundings instead of aggressively altering them to our fancied requirements, the prospects for humanity may well be bleak. We can invest our inheritance of desert spaces wisely and with understanding by neither overexploiting nor underestimating the value of that heritage.

Index

References in *italics* are to illustrations or captions to illustrations.

dung: beetles feeding on, 32, 51, 53, *55*, 90; in food web for insects, *59*
dust devil, 15
dust storms, 15

Eagles, 102
ears: of bats, *116*; of small mammals, 80, *81*, 81–82, *82*
earthmites, *46*
earthworms, 20
ebliss, 15
echolocation, by bats, *116*
ectothermal and endothermal animals, 83
eggs: of birds, vulnerability to overheating, 109; of crustaceans, resistance to drought, 34, 35, 37; of tortoises, 75
eland, hunted by Bushmen, *122*
environment, effect on habits of animals, 83
ephemeral plants, 26
ergs (sand-dune areas), 25
erosion: by overgrazing, 100, *101*, *133*; by rain, 10; by wind-borne sand and dust, 8, 13, 23
Ethiopia: Blue Nile in, *121*; salt works in Danakil Desert in, *130*
euphorbias, 29
Euphrates River, oasis, 30
eyelids of lizards, 72
Eyre, Lake, Australia, salt flats of, 25

Fairy shrimps, 34, *34*
falcons, *90–1*, 102, 110, *114–15*
fangs, of venomous snakes, 66
fat storage, 123, 125
feet and legs, adapted for movement in sand: of camels, 86–7; of insects, 45, 56; of lizards, 71, 72, *74*
feral animals, 84, 86
filter feeders, 35
finch, woodpecker, *106*
flamingos, 35, *36–7*
flash floods, appearance of toads and insects in, 10–11
fleas, absorb moisture through cuticle, 55
flies (Diptera), 32, 53, *90–1*, *114–15*
flowers, insect-pollinated, after rainfall, *39*
flycatchers, 109
food chains and webs, 53–4, *59*, 100; for desert birds, 102, *114–15*
food stores: in buttocks of Bushmen, 123; in hump of camel, 89,

125; in tail of desert sheep, 125; of ants, *26*; of termites, 27
foxes, 81: fennec (Sahara), 80, 81, *81*, *90–1*; flying, 115; kit (America), 80, 81, *81*
frankincense, 38
frogs, 38
fruit bats, 39
fruits, of desert plants, 27

Gambusia fish, eats larvae of malaria-carrying mosquito, 132
gazelles, *90–1*, 96, 120; dorcas, 96; reproductive cycle of, related to rainfall, 38
gecko lizards, 72–3, *74*, 75
gemsboks, 95, *95*
Gila monster of Arizona, *12*
gnats, 53
Goajira, Venezuela, *135*
goats, overgrazing by, 100, *101*, *133*
Gobi Desert, *14*; remoteness of, from sea, 10; wild camels in, *84*
grama grass, 26
Gran Chaco, nomadic herdsmen of, 125
Grand Canyon, Colorado River, *11*
grasses of desert: rolled leaves of, 29; seeds of, 26, 27, *114–15*
grasshoppers, 47, 49, *59*, 62; as prey of scorpion, *40*; larvae of giant velvet mite parasitic on, 46
Great Palaearctic Desert, 8, 47, 81
ground beetle, 53
ground squirrels, 79, 80, 81
grouse, sand, 109, *112*, *114–15*

Haboob winds, 15
hammada (rocky desert), 25, 26
hares, 80, 81, *90–1*, *114–15*
harmattan wind, 15
harvester ants, 50
heat death, explosive, 18, 89
heat receptors, in pit vipers, 66
hedgehog, African desert, *82*
Hemiptera (bugs), 49
herbivores, 81
herdsmen, 125
homeothermic animals, 83
honeyants, *26*
horseflies, 53
horses, sweating by, 100
houseflies, 53
humans: as predators, 100; death of, in desert, 17–18; deserts made by, 100, 118, 121, 123; sweating by, 98–9
humidity, 10, 11, 13; beneath

desert soil, 23, 78
hyenas, 100

Iguanid lizards, 71, *72*, 81
Indus River, oasis, 30
insectivores: bats, 116–7; birds, 102, 106; lizards, 71
insects, 8, 32, 47; aquatic, 58; mainly nocturnal, 58; mimicked by spiders, 45; in Sahara, after rain, 11, 39
Iranian desert, *14–15*
irrigation, 132, *138*

Jack rabbit, 80, 81, *82*
Jacobson's organ (scent-detecting), in rattlesnakes, 66, 68
Jamaican trap-door spider, 45
jaws, of scorpions, 44; of snakes, 68
jerboa, 38, *76*, 78, 79, 81, *90–1*

Kalahari Desert, *14–15*; salt pans of, 25
kangaroo rat, 75, 77, 78, *78*, 81
kangaroos, 93, 97, *97*
Karakum Desert, oases in, 30
Kenya, spread of desert in, 120, 121
khamsin wind, 13
Kuiseb River, *8*

Lacertid lizards, 71, 81
lammergeier (bearded vulture), *102*, *105*
larks, *90–1*, 109; crested, 112–13; *113*; sky, *114–15*
lemurs, flying, 115
leopards, 100
Libyan desert: *ergs* of, 25; irrigation of, *138*
lichens, on seaward side of rocks in coastal deserts, 25, *25*
lions, 100, 120
lizards, *59*, 71–5, 81, 82, 83, 102, horned, *72*, 81; scaly-tailed, 71, 73; shingle-back, *74*; spiny, 75; spiny-tailed, 81, 102; *see also individual species*
locomotion: of lizards, 73; of snakes, 64
locusts, 32, 47, *48*, 49, 132; egg-laying by, *62*; reproduction in, 38
lynx, caracal, *98*

Malaria, 38; in oases, 132; in savanna, 132
mammals: large, 83–95; small, 75,

Picture Credits

Key to position of picture on page: (B) bottom, (C) center, (L) left, (R) right, (T) top; hence (BR) bottom right, (CL) center left, etc.

Cover: George Holton/Photo Researchers Inc.
Title page: Des Bartlett/Bruce Coleman Limited
Contents: Wardene Weisser/Ardea

9 U.S. Space Administration
10 Giorgio Gualco/U.P. Bruce Coleman Inc.
11(R) J.A.L. Cooke/Bruce Coleman Inc.
12(L) G.D. Plage/Bruce Coleman Ltd.
12(TR) Kit Flannery/Bruce Coleman Inc.
12(BR) Ray Tercafs/Jacana
13(R) G. Behrens/Ardea
16(TL) D. P. Healey/NHPA
16(CL) Adam Woolfitt/Susan Griggs
16(BL) Grant Heilman
17 Robin Smith/Photographic Library of Australia
18 Ian Berry/Magnum
19-20(T) Dr. Edward S. Ross
21(BL) G. R. Roberts, Nelson, New Zealand
21(R) Roger Wood, London
22 W. Garnett © Time Inc., 1974
23 Dan Freeman/Bruce Coleman Ltd.
24 G. Behrens/Ardea
25 R. Borland/Bruce Coleman Inc.
26(L) M.W. Larson/Bruce Coleman Inc.
26(R) Anthony Bannister/NHPA
27(T) Peter Knowles/Photographic Library of Australia
27(B) Jane Burton/Bruce Coleman Ltd.
28(TL) Dr. Edward S. Ross
28(BL) Anthony Bannister/NHPA
28(R)-29 Dr. Edward S. Ross
31 Jon Gardey/Robert Harding Associates
32 Richard Weymouth Brooks/ Photo Researchers Inc.
33(R) Heather Angel
34(L) Kit Flannery/Bruce Coleman Inc.
35 Heather Angel
36 Clem Haagner/Bruce Coleman Inc.
37(TL) Dan Freeman/Bruce Coleman Ltd.
37(TR) James Simon/Bruce Coleman Ltd.
37(B) Alan Blank/Bruce Coleman Inc.
38 G. R. Roberts, Nelson, New Zealand
39(R) Dan Freeman/Bruce Coleman Ltd.
41 Anthony Bannister/NHPA
42 Lacey/Frank W. Lane
43(TR,BL) J.A.L. Cooke/Bruce Coleman Inc.
44(T)
44(B) Jane Burton/Bruce Coleman Ltd.
45(T) Anthony Bannister/NHPA
45(B) Oxford Scientific Films/Bruce Coleman Inc.
46(L) A. C. Kemp/Natural Science Photos
47 P. H. Ward/Natural Science Photos
48(T) Gianni Tortoli/Photo Researchers Inc.
48(B) D. B. Lewis/Natural Science Photos
49(B) P. H. Ward/Natural Science Photos
50 Christiansen/Frank W. Lane
51(TL) Picturepoint, London
51(TR) Stephen Dalton/NHPA
52(T, BR) Anthony Bannister/NHPA
52(BL) Peter Hill, A.R.P.S.
54-55 Anthony Bannister/NHPA
56-57 Dr. Edward S. Ross
60 Des Bartlett/Bruce Coleman Ltd.
62 Gianni Tortoli/Photo Researchers Inc.
63 F. Sauer/ZEFA
65 Rod Borland/Bruce Coleman Ltd.
67(T) Alan Blank/Bruce Coleman Inc.
67(B) Dan Freeman/Bruce Coleman Ltd.
68 B. R. Bringley/Natural Science Photos
70(T) Anthony Bannister/NHPA
70(BL) P. Morris Photographics
71 Alan Blank/Bruce Coleman Inc.
72(L) Tom Myers/Photo Researchers Inc.
72(R) Van Nostrand/Frank W. Lane
73(L) Norman Tomalin/Bruce Coleman Limited
73(R) Russ Kinne/Photo Researchers Inc.
74(TL) Anthony Bannister/NHPA
74(TR) J. R. Brownlie/Bruce Coleman Limited
74(B) Hans and Judy Beste/Ardea
77(T) Rod Allin/Bruce Coleman Ltd.
77(B) Rod Borland/Bruce Coleman Ltd.
78(L) Vial/Jacana
79 Kenneth W. Fink/Ardea
80 Alan Blank/Bruce Coleman Inc.
81(B) Tom McHugh/Photo Researchers Inc.
82(T) J. Van Wormer/Bruce Coleman Limited
82(B) J.-L. S. Dubois/Jacana
85 George Holton/Photo Researchers Inc.
86(L) Lee Battaglia/Colorific!
87 *Daily Telegraph* Color Library
88 Lee Lyon/Bruce Coleman Ltd.
92(L) Gohier/Pitch
93(L) Joe Van Wormer/Bruce Coleman Inc.
93(R) P. Morris Photographics
94 Clem Haagner/Bruce Coleman Inc.
95(T) J. Nuyten/Robert Harding Associates
95(B) P. A. Milwaukee/Jacana
96 G. D. Plage/Bruce Coleman Ltd.
97(L) G. Pizzey/Bruce Coleman Ltd.
97(R) J. R. Brownlie/Bruce Coleman Limited
98 Spectrum Color Library
99(R) Dick Robinson/Bruce Coleman Limited
101 Giorgio Gualco/U.P. Bruce Coleman Inc.
103 Peter Johnson/NHPA
104(L) Des Bartlett/Bruce Coleman Ltd.
104(R) Jen and Des Bartlett/Bruce Coleman Inc.
105(R) Bruce Coleman Limited
106 John Pearson/Bruce Coleman Limited
107(T) Clem Haagner/Bruce Coleman Inc.
107(B) Bavaria-Verlag, Gauting
108 Jack Dermid/Bruce Coleman Ltd.
109-10 P. Morris Photographics
111 Walker/Frank W. Lane
112(T) A. C. Kemp/Natural Science Photos
112(B) R. M. Bloomfield, Johannesburg
113(TR) R. M. Bloomfield/Bruce Coleman Inc.
113(BR) Peter Jackson/Bruce Coleman Limited
116(L) P. Morris Photographics
117 Giles Sholl/The John Hillelson Agency
119 Bourret/Pitch
120 Lee Lyon/Bruce Coleman Ltd.
121 Georg Gerster/The John Hillelson Agency
122(T) Dr. Edward S. Ross
122(B) Pierre Jaunet/Aspect
123(T) Simon Trevor/Bruce Coleman Inc.
123(B) Dr. Edward S. Ross
124 Simon Trevor/Bruce Coleman Ltd.
126(L) P. Curto/Bruce Coleman Inc.
127 David Attenborough
128(TL) Giorgio Gualco/U.P. Bruce Coleman Inc.
128(BL) Edmond Caprasse/A.A.A. Photo
129 D. Pike/Bruce Coleman Inc.
130 Georg Gerster/ The John Hillelson Agency
131(T) Leidmann/ZEFA
131(B) Harrison Forman
133 Su Gooders/Ardea
134 Giorgio Gualco/U.P. Bruce Coleman Inc.
135(TR) Karl Weidmann
135(BR) Georg Gerster/The John Hillelson Agency
136-7 Dr. Edward S. Ross
138(L) Giorgio Gualco/U.P. Bruce Coleman Inc.
139 Derek Bayes/Aspect

Artist Credits

© Aldus Books: David Nockels 14-15, 69, 76, 90-91; Joyce Tuhill 58-9, 114-5

Warmest thanks are due to my wife Anne, constant companion of our many desert journeys, and to my son Timothy, for their helpful suggestions; also to Mrs. V. G. Williams for kindly undertaking the typing of this manuscript.

DESERTS AND GRASSLANDS

Part 2

Grassland Life

by Eric Duffey

Series Coordinator	Geoffrey Rogers
Art Director	Frank Fry
Design Consultant	Guenther Radtke
Editorial Consultant	Donald Berwick
Series Consultant	Malcolm Ross-Macdonald
Art Editor	Susan Cook
Editor	Damian Grint
Copy Editor	Maureen Cartwright
Research	Jonathan Moore
	Enid Moore

Contents: Part 2

Editorial Advisers

DAVID ATTENBOROUGH. Naturalist and Broadcaster.

MICHAEL BOORER, B.SC. Author, Lecturer, and Broadcaster.

MATTHEW BRENNAN, ED.D. Director, Brentree Environmental Center, Professor of Conservation Education, Pennsylvania State University.

PHYLLIS BUSCH, ED.D. Author, Science Teacher, and Consultant in Environmental Education.

MICHAEL HASSELL, B.A., M.A. (OXON), D.PHIL. Lecturer in Ecology, Imperial College, London.

ANTHONY HUXLEY, M.A. Author and Editorial Consultant.

STUART MCNEILL, B.SC., PH.D. Lecturer in Ecology, Imperial College, London.

JAMES OLIVER, PH.D. Director of the New York Aquarium, former Director of the American Museum of Natural History, former Director of the New York Zoological Park, formerly Professor of Zoology, University of Florida.

Introduction

The town dweller—and this means most of us—
is likely to value the green fields of the countryside
mainly for their cool beauty. Yet even those who know
how vital the fields are for the production of food have
probably never realized just how much the primeval
grasslands have contributed to the development of
civilized man. In the dawn of history, the sheep, goats,
cattle, horses, and dogs of the open plains were the
first animals domesticated by man for food, transport,
and hunting. And when man found security in
permanent settlements, it was from the grasslike
ancestors of modern cereals, such as wheat, rice, and
corn, that he developed his earliest crops.

Today most grasslands have been changed by the
science of breeding and by other human activities. But
even though we shall never witness the vast buffalo
migrations of the North American prairies, we can
still see and admire the grand spectacle of wild game
on the African savannas and on other great
continental plains.

It is the biologist, of course, who is most aware of
the immense variety of life in grassland vegetation.
But everyone who enjoys a stroll on a sunny meadow,
bright with summer flowers, will find it even more
interesting if he takes note of the countless tiny
invertebrates that live among the flowers, leaves,
stems, and roots of plants, as well as in dead
vegetation on the soil surface. All have an important
function in the complex grassland community, and
every species, whether plant or animal, is profoundly
influenced by the others. This book is designed to help
us appreciate not only that community's complexity
but also its huge importance to our own species.

Origin and History of Grasslands

Of all vegetation types, grasslands are the kind we know best. Garden lawns, school playing fields, and meadows of the countryside are so much part of the everyday landscape that we take them for granted and perhaps never question their origin and development. In fact, we seldom think about grassland as a special vegetation type. Yet it has formed the basis of life for man ever since our ancestors learned how to make primitive stone tools about 2 million years ago. The birthplace of the first manlike primates is thought to be the forest edge of Africa, where the trees merge into plains of coarse grasses, scattered bushes, and small trees. It is there that early men would find shelter and abundant game. And they probably continued to live there throughout the slow, unfolding millennia of evolution until they learned to domesticate animals and to cultivate the ground.

Today's familiar garden lawns and urban parks are man-made, of course. But much of the world's fast-disappearing grassland is as natural a phenomenon as its forests or deserts or seas. We can define natural grassland as any region where only *herbaceous* (that is nonwoody) plants grow naturally and more or less abundantly. Woody plants—that is, bushes and trees—are either totally absent from grassland or are present in limited numbers. The main reason for this is that the type of soil, along with such factors as climate and low rainfall, will not permit unrestricted growth.

Grassland plants include not merely true grasses but also many flowering herbaceous plants that can tolerate conditions of soil and climate that woody plants cannot. There are two main ways in which they surmount such obstacles. Many grassland species are able to lie dormant for a long time, with most of the plant surviving below the ground surface as a root system, until conditions improve. Other species can survive as seed, ready to germinate whenever favorable weather occurs.

The tall, tufted orchard grass, or cock's-foot, is a valuable hay and pasture grass. Not only man's livestock feeds on grasses, but man himself receives over half of all his food energy from grasses—mainly the cereals rice, wheat, and corn.

It is estimated that 24 per cent of the vegetation cover in the world today—in other words, nearly 18 million square miles—consists of grasslands. Many of the well-known types that we shall be looking at in this book are believed to be of great antiquity, fashioned by a combination of weather and the slow development of particular types of soil. For example, the North American prairies are thought to date back to Miocene times, a geological epoch that began about 35 million years ago and lasted for some 28 million years. During this period the Rocky Mountains came into being, and in so doing they changed the climate, especially by reducing the amount of rainfall available to vast neighboring areas. The dry summers and drier winters that resulted favored the spread of grasslands in these regions, and the existing forests gradually disappeared. Similar weather patterns, of low rainfall and a short wet season followed by a longer period of drought had similar effects in other lowland areas of the world.

Many grasslands—particularly those in temperate Europe and North America—are of a much more recent origin, however, and have been created largely by the influence of man, who has destroyed the forest cover to provide more crop-producing and grazing land for himself and his domestic animals. Indeed, one of the most characteristic features of grasslands in developed countries (and increasingly so in other parts of the world) is their artificiality. Truly natural grasslands are now relatively scarce, and they are becoming more so as more land is utilized by man. In most lowland areas of the world, for instance, man has created grasslands to suit the needs of his grazing animals. The need for high productivity means that fast-growing species of grass must be sown. Thus, most artificial grasslands lack the variety of the natural grasslands,

A prairie in America's Middle West looking much as it did a century ago. Because their soils are rich and fertile, many prairies today are used for wheat-growing or stock-raising.

for they are created by sowing the seed of only a few selected varieties. The farmer is not interested in diversity. What he wants from his fields is the largest possible amount of vegetation to feed the stock or to store as hay. And where the farmer does not intervene directly, intensive grazing by cattle and sheep may reduce the variety of plants in natural grassland.

In upland regions of the world, grasslands are not treated in quite the same way as in the lowlands, because of the problems posed by slope and drainage, and by underlying rocks. Nevertheless, in recent years drainage methods have been improved, fertilizers applied, and other means used to stimulate growth and encourage those grasses of greatest value to the farmer. Thus the artificial grasslands of both upland and lowland regions are generally much poorer in insect and other wildlife species than are their natural counterparts. The main reason for this is that the many different plants that grow in a natural environment provide food or breeding sites for a far greater variety of insects and the other small creatures able to live on their leaves, flowers, and fruit, as well as in the *leaf litter* (the dead and decaying vegetation on the ground).

In the two centuries since the beginning of the Industrial Revolution, which gave an added boost to the development of modern agricultural technology, man's impact on the great plains of the world has been dramatic. The rapid growth in human populations has required an ever-increasing production of cereal crops and an improvement of rangelands for more beef, so that the completely natural grassland communities have shrunk to a small part of their original area. That is why the characteristic plants of the North American prairies survive today in only a few small areas. Throughout the world, native plants and animals have declined and agricultural activities have spread a green carpet of man-made grassland over innumerable acres where previously vegetation of a different type existed.

This is particularly true of places most recently colonized by immigration from the Old World. For example, in Australia 58 per cent and in New Zealand 47 per cent of the total land surface is pasture land, which maintains the enormous flocks of sheep and herds of cattle that are so vital to the economy of those countries. Even in the Old World, it is hard to tell where natural grassland ends and artificial begins. The vast,

Above: cattle at a water hole in the plains of western Texas. No trees could flourish in this dry climate even if the land were not being constantly trodden. Left: woody plants are eaten by grazing sheep before they can become established.

rolling *steppes* (the Russian name for the dry grassy continental plains) extending from the Hungarian plains to Siberia were long thought to be very ancient grasslands formed entirely by soil and climate. Some scientists, however, now believe that even these may once have been covered with a type of open forest, which was gradually cleared and the land brought down to its current arid state by man.

But before human beings had become powerful enough to change the natural environment, a remarkably rich fauna of *herbivores*, or plant-eating animals, able to exploit the type of vegetation characteristic of grasslands had developed. Abundant fossil remains show that the two great modern orders of herbivorous mammals existed in the early Tertiary period, nearly 65 million years ago. The ancestors of such one-toed animals as horses, rhinoceroses, and tapirs

13

(known as the Perissodactyla), and of those with two to four toes, such as pigs, camels, hippopotamuses, cattle, buffaloes, sheep, goats, deer, and antelopes (the Artiodactyla), once roamed the grasslands in all the major regions of the world except Australia, which was already isolated and evolving its own special fauna.

There must therefore have been extensive natural grasslands long ago in both the Old World and the New. These grasslands had to be exceedingly widespread in order to sustain the large number of grazing animals that are associated with them. And many thousands of years of continual cropping have profoundly affected the evolution of grassland vegetation. A number of plants have evolved mechanisms that enable them to keep up vigorous growth and seed production in spite of constant grazing and trampling. Only about 36 out of 7500 known species of grass have this degree of tolerance. Interestingly enough, these same 36 are also valued by farmers because of their high nutritive content for domestic animals. Some 24 of the 36 are native to Eurasia, 8 to eastern Africa, and 4 to subtropical Central or South America. It is worth remarking that temperate North America, eastern and southeastern Asia, and Australia have contributed little or nothing to the world pool of cultivated grasses. This strange fact appears to indicate that a relatively poor fauna of herbivorous mammals evolved in those regions.

The effect of climate on vegetation—that is, the development of grassland where rainfall is low, usually between 10 and 30 inches a year—can be seen in many parts of the world where there are large land masses. Good examples of the gradual descent from thickly wooded country down to sparse grassland as a result of decreasing rainfall are apparent in the United States, for instance, in the region stretching westward from the Appalachians. In this region, within the humid climate of the mountains, you may find yourself in a rich deciduous forest. As you travel westward into drier country, the species of trees may change; and they are generally not so tall as the ones farther east. Eventually the

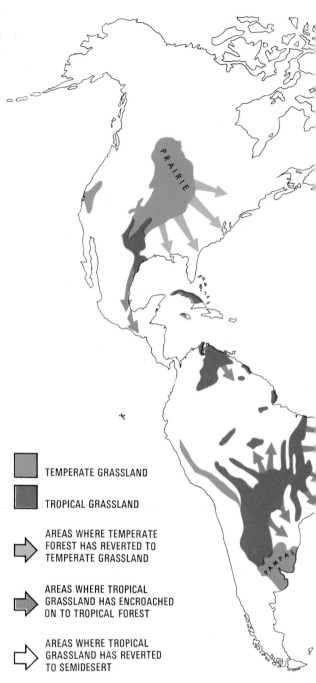

TEMPERATE GRASSLAND

TROPICAL GRASSLAND

AREAS WHERE TEMPERATE FOREST HAS REVERTED TO TEMPERATE GRASSLAND

AREAS WHERE TROPICAL GRASSLAND HAS ENCROACHED ON TO TROPICAL FOREST

AREAS WHERE TROPICAL GRASSLAND HAS REVERTED TO SEMIDESERT

trees give way to a tall-grass prairie, which in turn merges into short-grass plains, and eventually into grassland so arid that it can be called steppe, or desert grassland.

Similar gradations can be found in tropical South America and Africa, with extensive areas of scrubland sometimes occurring between the forest and the true grassland plains. Tropical grasslands with scattered bushes and small trees, which are known as *savannas*, are particularly

widespread in Africa, where a richer fauna of grazing and browsing animals has evolved than on any other continent. The human inhabitants of both savannas and temperate grasslands often burn off the old cover of grasses in order to provide new grazing for their domestic animals. This usually results in a change in the variety of species that make up the plant life, and it also extends the savanna grassland into areas that would otherwise support forest.

The practice of burning grassland is a very ancient one. Many American ecologists believe that for hundreds of years before the arrival of Europeans, the Indians regularly burned the prairies. No one is quite sure why they should have done this, because the chief purpose of burning is to encourage fresh, new grass growth for domestic stock, and the Indians, of course, were not pastoral farmers. Quite possibly they used fire to drive game out into the open.

15

Lightning without rain sometimes causes forest fires, and so we cannot claim that all grassland burning has been done by human beings. But it is no doubt true that, because of both their frequency and their location, man-made fires are far more likely to affect vegetation permanently than are natural ones. During the course of many centuries, nomadic and pastoral man has pushed back the edge of the forest or even destroyed it altogether in order to get more food for his stock. Thus, almost everywhere today vegetation patterns have been greatly modified by human activities, and so they seldom reflect only natural climatic change.

At any rate, in whatever way they originated, grasslands are found in all parts of the world, from the tropics to the Arctic and from the lowlands to the highest point on mountains where life can survive. And, as we have seen, they can include many kinds of plants other than grasses. In a typical agricultural region, however, this latter fact may not be very obvious. Where pasture management is concerned, the modern farmer is primarily interested in plants that grow fast, have high nutritive content, and can withstand heavy grazing. Some grasses are ideal for these purposes. A typical grass plant has a well-developed root system and numerous stems called *tillers*, which are continually growing from the base, not from the tip of the shoot, as with other

plants. This means that even when a grazing animal bites off most of the green growth above the ground, the plant can continue to grow. In fact, grazing or cutting very often stimulates the production of new tillers, so that the sward or turf becomes thicker and denser.

It is this characteristic of grasses that enables those of us who live in cool, temperate climates to maintain our beautiful green lawns. Cutting, grazing, and trampling also tend to eliminate some of the broad-leaved plants that might otherwise run riot. The farmer assists the process of decreasing diversity by using fertilizers and weedkillers (or *herbicides*), which promote rapid grass growth and eliminate competitive vegeta-

tion. It is small wonder, then, that many people are surprised and delighted when they first see the marvelous variety of colorful flowers in an alpine meadow, whether in the Old or the New World. In such meadows, no agricultural activity, apart from occasional grazing, has interfered with the natural richness of the flora.

Lovely as flowers may be, it is the grasses that man finds most useful. Their ecological characteristics and the possibility of adapting them to new situations have long been recognized and put to good use. In many parts of the world where overgrazing or bad land management has caused erosion, for instance, grasses may be sown to stabilize the bare soil. Special techniques for

Fire has been used by man for centuries in both temperate grasslands and tropical savannas to improve pasture for his domestic stock. Left: the grass in this area has been recently burned. In about four weeks a flush of young, fresh green grass will appear, as it has around the pale triangle of unburned grass in the picture above. Right: over-exploitation of pastureland, on the other hand, such as the intensively grazed area to the right of the fence in this picture, means that the soil becomes dry and barren, here supporting only thorn scrub and acacia trees.

Man has other uses for grasses besides food for himself or his livestock. The man above is gathering reeds in a Romanian marsh, but it could be almost anywhere, for these sturdy grasses are a common shallow-water sight in many parts of the world. Because reeds are both waterproof and excellent insulators, many Europeans still use them for thatching roofs (below right). Another useful plant is marram grass (below left); it helps to stabilize dune areas with its long roots, which bind the particles of sand together and keep them from blowing away.

doing this have been developed in the European Alps, where massive soil disturbance can result from the construction of ski lifts and cable cars. On North American and European coasts, where sand dunes form a natural defense against winter storms, marram grass is commonly planted to bind the sand and prevent erosion. Marram grass is especially well adapted for growth in the unstable dune situation, because it has an extensive root system that is ideal for holding the sand together, and tall, stiff leaves that help to trap windblown sand. Moreover, it grows rapidly upward and can thus keep pace with the accumulation of sand.

Another remarkable plant has had a significant effect on many unexploited salt marshes in the temperate regions: the cord grass *Spartina anglica*. This grass, which developed from a hybrid between a European and an American species of cord grass, is much more vigorous than either of the parent species; it has proved so effective in consolidating salt marshes that it has been widely planted around the world's coastlines. *Spartina anglica* helps to trap the suspended silt in tidal water, and other plants are able to establish themselves as the level of the marsh builds up, until the mud flats become covered with vegetation. In this way a number of salt marshes are being developed into valuable grazing areas for sheep, horses, and cattle.

Still another member of the grass family that is of great value to man is the tall and handsome common reed, which grows all over the world in marshy places or in shallow water. In winter, when the leaves have fallen and only the hard, stiff stem (reaching six feet or more in height) remains, the reed crop is ready for use. The picturesque thatched roofs to be seen in many European villages are frequently made of reed, for it is not only waterproof but also a very efficient insulator. In Argentina, it is cut green for fodder or is used, when dead, as stable litter for domestic animals. It is regarded as valuable material for fence-making in some countries, and provides a source of cellulose in the hardboard, paper, and synthetic-textile industries. The Dutch plant it to stabilize river and canal banks, and Dutch airplanes sow enormous quantities of the seed onto the bare land that is being reclaimed from the sea; the reed's *rhizomes* (thick underground stems) help to bind together the mud particles and prepare Holland's new-made soil for future cultivation.

We must also mention a few other members of the grass family—grasses that play an especially vital part in the well-being of all of us, wherever we live. These are the plants that we call *cereals*, and about a dozen of them are of major importance to man.

Cereals are the main source of food for all races of mankind, either directly as part of the daily diet, or indirectly in the form of protein after being fed to animals to produce meat, milk, and eggs. About 70 per cent of the harvested land area of the world is sown with cereals. Over half of this total is given over to wheat, rice, or corn (maize); among them, these plants account for about three quarters of the world's cereal production. And upon them largely depends the fortunes of mankind—in fact, our very survival.

Wheat is the foremost cereal of the temperate zone, requiring moisture and moderate temperatures during growth, followed by dry and warm conditions for harvesting. It is also one of the most ancient of cultivated plants; even 4500 years ago the Egyptians had learned how to grind the grain and produce leavened bread from it. Rice, which forms the staple diet of millions of people in Asia and parts of Africa and South America, has also been cultivated for thousands of years. It is essentially a crop of tropical and subtropical regions, although some modern varieties grow well in more temperate parts of southern Europe and the United States.

Corn, a grass of the New World, is known to have grown as a wild plant in Mexico 80,000 years ago. Now a valuable crop all over the world, it has been described as a more precious gift to the Old World from the New than all the gold brought back by the European conquerors of the Americas. Over half the world's crop is now grown in the United States, but it is being increasingly cultivated in Europe, mainly as a fodder or silage crop, even in areas where the climate is not warm enough for the grain to ripen.

Among the other important cereals are sorghum, millet, oats, rye, and barley. Sorghum is cultivated chiefly in Africa. It grows well in areas where the climate is too dry for other cereals. Although they use it mainly as an animal foodstuff, Africans sometimes eat it in place of rice. Millet is also a basic food for animals, particularly in India and Africa. Millet is another ancient cereal and has been found at Neolithic sites in Europe; a different kind of this grain was a main crop in the Far East in pre-historic times, and it thereby ranks in importance with corn as a basis of early civilization.

Oats and rye, which are cereals of cool, moist climates, are commonly used for feeding livestock, although many people like to eat oats in a variety of forms and rye as bread. Another use for rye is in the distilling of whiskey. And barley, too, is not merely an animal food but a tasty ingredient in a number of alcoholic beverages, such as beer.

In the preceding pages we have glanced at the general outlines of the grassland picture in order to get an idea of what grasslands actually are and to see some of the ways in which they have been farmed, both by nature and by man. It should now be clear that "grassland" is not just a single environment. There are several kinds of grassland, and each of them is inhabited by its own type of animal community. What are those several kinds of grassland? What distinguishes them from one another? Where are they to be found? We shall take up these and a few related questions in the next chapter.

Many of the world's grasslands have been taken over and cultivated by man—but not always for the "useful" grasses such as the cereals wheat (below left) and barley (below right). Some are planted with trees for fruit crops such as these orange groves (above), which grow best in good grassland conditions—a warm, but not tropical, and not too moist climate.

Right: in those areas of the world too wet for wheat and corn, rice is the staple food. Below: a bird's-eye view of Philippine rice paddies, and (above) a close-up view of growing rice.

Types of Grassland

Precise definitions in almost any field of human knowledge are seldom easy to come by, and this is especially true for the student of grassland ecology. Once we have made the obvious distinction between natural and man-made grasslands, we must hasten to add that the borderline between the natural and the artificial is sometimes very much blurred. Vast areas of grassland are quite obviously man-made. In Europe, for instance, the most fertile land under cultivation is land that was once covered by deciduous forest (and that might again become forest if civilization as we know it ever ends). Similarly, millions of acres of American forest have been cleared since the 17th century. But the distinction is not always so apparent. In many places—the American prairie, for instance—farmers have tended to cultivate already existing fertile grasslands and to extend them rather than create new fields out of heavily wooded areas.

On the other side of the picture, many of the world's government-controlled national parks and nature reserves include grassland areas that, since they are theoretically "protected" from the depredations of human intruders, we can justifiably think of as natural. Yet the activities of tourists, picnickers, and sportsmen may well have a permanent effect upon the vegetation. Are they, then, still natural, or are they merely *almost* natural?

For our purposes it is perhaps best to agree that natural grassland may be much influenced by pastoral or agricultural man, but it can nonetheless be considered natural if it conforms roughly to one of three general types: mountain grassland, continental plains, and savannas. All of these would, in other words, remain grassland even if no man ever set foot upon them, or at least they would be more likely than not to do so, as a result of climatic and geographical conditions.

There is probably no place in the modern world where we can find either grassland itself, or the wildlife within the grassland, completely

The grassy hummocks in this sunbathed pasture have been shaped by the trampling hooves of generations of cattle.

unaffected by past or present man. But we can get fairly close to untouched nature by climbing up to the mountain pastures that lie high above the timberline. There, whether in the Rockies, the Andes, or the Urals, we are beyond the reach of agriculture, up where rocky peaks and snowfields thrust through the broad patches of green grass. And we soon see that what most distinguishes mountain grassland from other types is its array of different flowering plants.

There are alpine regions in every continent, but the most famous such region is no doubt the one that gave its name to all the rest: the Alps of Central Europe. A trip above the timberline in the Alps is an experience that nobody who has an interest in natural history should miss,

especially in the early summer, when the plant life of the meadows is at its richest. Among the limestone rocks of the Swiss Jura, sheets of blue gentians carpet the ground, and meadows of yellow and pink primulas of many species adjoin hillsides white with narcissus, filling the mountain air with their sweet scent. Among other flowers to be found in the same area are pasque-flowers (both yellow and white), saxifrages, orchids, and crocuses, which spring up even before the melting snowbeds have disappeared.

In some ways the alpine pastures of the Pyrenees, which lie partly in Spain and partly in France, are even more colorful than those of the Alps. Early springtime in the Pyrenees brings forth a crop of wave after wave of unusual daffodil species, flowering in succession and bathing the mountain pastures and hillsides in color. And only in the Pyrenees can you see the huge white spire of the so-called Pyrenean saxifrage, and the high, rock-strewn slopes ablaze with the golden

Nature remains unspoiled above the timberline, both in New Zealand (below), where stout tussock grass carpets the mountain areas, and in the Swiss Alps (right), where snowy peaks look down on rolling fields of many kinds of late-spring flowers.

flowers of the Pyrenean pheasant-eye. Comparable, if often less spectacular, mountain meadows exist above the timberline in most parts of the world. It is because of their inaccessibility that they remain so nearly unspoiled.

Other types of natural grassland are far more common, particularly the continental plains. These developed long ago on most continents, in lowland regions where rainfall was relatively little and the dry season relatively long, both of which make an environment that is unsuitable for woody plants. Such great open plains are identified by various names in various places— the *prairies* of North America, the *pampas* of South America, the *puszta* of Hungary and eastern Europe, the *veldt* (an Africaans word meaning "field") of South Africa, and so on. Although all of them are alike in being great open plains, each has a distinctive fauna adapted to local conditions of climate, vegetation, and soil. And they have also been influenced dif-

ferently throughout their long histories by the immigration of some living creatures and the extinction of others, as well as by many unknown factors of geological time.

The richest assemblage of large grazing animals has developed in the plains of Africa, which extend for vast distances both north and south of the equator. But before we move on to Africa, let us take a preliminary look at the grasslands of North America and Eurasia, where the continental plains stretch across the temperate zone. (Interestingly enough, the vast semiarid lowlands of Australia do not form the same sort of extensive grass plain that we find in comparable climates of temperate America and Eurasia. In Australia the natural grassland was studded with eucalyptus trees, which are able to grow very successfully in areas of low rainfall. And so it would probably be more truly descriptive to speak of Australia as having savannalike

"grassy woodlands" rather than pure grasslands.)

Temperate grasslands include not only fertile prairies and savannas but desert grassland and steppeland. Desert grassland, of which there is a great deal in America, is just one stage above true desert, for it exists in areas where there is so little rain that only the most hardy of grasses manage to survive. The steppes are also low-rainfall continental areas in which desert conditions may sometimes prevail, but they tend to be somewhat less arid than the desert grasslands.

Many people think of steppeland as peculiar to Russia. This is a misconception, however. The word is generally applied to dry grasslands wherever they occur; there is, for instance, a large area of steppeland at the foot of the American Rockies (although it is sometimes given the more colloquial American name of "short-grass prairie").

The largest of the world's continental plains, the steppe grassland of Eurasia, occupies a belt of some 2500 miles from the Ukraine in the southern part of Russia eastward to the Chinese Altai Mountain region in the heart of Asia. Of this vast area, about 1200 miles lie west of the Ural River, extending as far as the Carpathian Mountains; this portion of the great plain, which stretches through Hungary into Austria, can be described as European.

The Eurasian steppeland belt, like the North American prairies, consists of open, undulating, grassy plains stretching as far as the eye can see to the flat, distant horizon. It owes its origin to deposits of sandy soils and, in places, clay soils laid down after the last glaciation (about 10,000 years ago), and it has what is known as a "continental climate"—that is, great daily and yearly ranges of temperature, with hot, dry summers and very cold winters. The expanse of steppeland whose geological history is perhaps best known to us, the Ukrainian steppes, survived virtually unaltered for many thousands of years after the retreat of the ice when the Ice Age ended, and only during the last half century has most of this land been converted to farmland. Here and there fragments of the natural steppes remain in the form of nature reserves established by the Soviet Union; but the greater part has been plowed and is cultivated and irrigated.

For a time after the last glaciation, most of Europe became a type of steppe landscape. During the Ice Age, a vast, treeless, frozen region called *tundra* existed all around the icecaps, and the tundra developed into steppeland as runoff water from melting ice deposited large quantities of silt and debris. There is fossil evidence that herds of wild horses, saiga antelopes, European bison, and many other grass-eating

Left: typical of the vast pasturelands in the sheep country of New Zealand's North Island are these rolling green hills. Temperate grasslands of this type are often potentially very fertile, but heavy grazing keeps high growth of the grasses permanently in check.

Right: around this tiny village in the Uzbekistan steppelands of south central Asia stretch endless miles of open grassy plains, where the sheep, goats, and cattle of herdsmen, such as those who live in the primitive huts shown here, have grazed for centuries. The soil is too sandy, summers are too dry, and winters are too cold for cultivation of the land.

The tree-shadowed lake in the background and the obviously flourishing tree near the camera help us recognize this spot as a man-made bit of grassland. It is, in fact, an English meadow, typical of thousands of carefully managed grazing areas in the highly cultivated Western world.

The field below is clearly natural—just as clearly as the meadow to the left is not. On the edge of the barren Mojave Desert in California, near-total aridity merges into this dry grassland, where bright red poppies thrive.

animals roamed freely over the grasslands during this period. But the steppe landscape did not last. Warmer weather led to a succession of plants, and eventually forest grew over most of what is now known as Europe. Only in the more easterly parts of the continent, where the rainfall was too light for the growth of trees, did the dry grassland remain; it was there that the steppe fauna survived until historic times. As late as the 19th century, wild horses were still living on the steppes of the Ukraine, but increased hunting and destruction of the habitat killed them off.

Before these great plains were converted to agricultural use, they must have presented a magnificent sight to the visitor in early summer, with mile after mile of waving grass disappearing into the brilliant blue of the horizon. The dominant species of grass in the natural Eurasian steppe belongs to the genus *Stipa*, of which there are four species. One of these is a very large plant as tall as a man, but the others are quite short. More striking than the *Stipa* are the numerous flowering plants that carpet the steppes in the spring—a kaleidoscopic scene of bright colors that keep changing as the season advances.

Wild tulips are one of the most characteristic steppe flowers; they form a mosaic of red and yellow in the months of May and June. There are also two species of anemone, gageas, spring drabas, the adonis, the blue and the yellow dwarf iris, and great stretches of dark-red peonies, all mingled with occasional patches of blue sage. In the extreme westerly steppelands, or puszta, of Hungary and Austria, the rich flora has disappeared with the advance of agriculture; you have to go to government-sponsored nature reserves to see, for example, the pale-blue flowers of the spiked speedwell, which used to be a very distinctive feature of the puszta.

Steppeland and desert have many characteristics in common, and both demand great adaptability from the animals that live in them. There is no escape from the hot summer sun, and the moisture content of the atmosphere can vary enormously from low humidity in daytime to high humidity at night. In the winter bitter winds blow over the exposed, treeless Eurasian plains, and there is virtually no protection for animals that do not migrate elsewhere to escape the cold. Small mammals and reptiles protect themselves from the weather and from predators by going underground and living in extensive burrows. Greater mole rats, for example, spend almost their entire life underground (escaping the heat in summer, the cold in winter, and animal enemies that cannot pursue them into their burrows).

Only two hoofed herbivores have survived to modern times in the Eurasian steppes: a few wild horses in Asia, and—after being rescued by Russian conservationists—the saiga antelope, which is fairly widely distributed. The saiga

antelopes' only protection against the elements is a layer of fat under the skin. And so they herd together for warmth in the winter and search out areas where the cold is not too extreme. We shall take a closer look at them, as at other steppeland creatures, in later chapters.

In spite of the rather narrow range of habitats in flat grassland, numerous species of rodents have evolved in the course of time. Also, the Eurasian steppes are a favorite area for large numbers of ground-nesting birds, particularly bustards, larks, pipits, wheatears, and game birds, and their predators, the eagles and falcons. Because of the immense distances, different types of animals can find suitable homes in widely separated areas. As with the continental plain of North America, there is a gradual transition from one sort of environment through several stages to a contrasting one. In Eurasia the gradation moves slowly from desertlike conditions, through steppe where the grasses provide an almost continuous cover, then into a landscape with scattered trees, which finally merges with deciduous and mixed forest. This transitional zone runs from south to north and from the deserts of Asia westward to the Caspian Sea and the heavily wooded land of central Europe.

There are extensive dry-grass plains in Africa, too, many of which are classed under the general heading *savanna*. The climatic regions that extend southward from the northern part of Africa to the equator and on down toward the southern part of the continent are represented by a series of long belts of vegetation across the continent from the Atlantic to the Nile Valley. The transition from one zone to another is not generally marked by a sharp dividing line, but no one standing in the heart of one vegetation belt could confuse it with another. As we move southward from the Sahara Desert toward the Gulf of Guinea, the amount of rainfall steadily increases; after 1000 miles of unbroken desert with perhaps less than five inches of rain a year, the annual precipitation increases over the next 800 miles to well over 100 inches in some places, and the type and degree of vegetation change accordingly. On the coast barren rocks and sand give way to steaming mangrove swamps and

In contrast with the fertile valleys and lower slopes, the grasses of Morocco's Atlas Mountains are so sparse that Bedouin flocks such as this one must be kept on the move.

31

raffia palms, with an occasional patch of nearly impenetrable tropical forest.

In spite of the great variety of landscape, we can distinguish the main zones of vegetation. There is a marked transition from the barren desert, through desert-grass savanna, to relatively lush tropical savanna with good-size trees and perennial grasses. This savanna eventually merges into thickly wooded areas. And then, as we continue southward away from the equator toward a more temperate and less rainy climate, the order reverses. Southward to Cape Province the vegetation belts are not as clearly defined, and there is more variation because of special geographic and climatic conditions. But in general we can see a reversal of the situation that prevails farther north: the forest gives way to savanna, then to desert-grass savanna, then (in southwest coastal areas) to desert.

In South Africa much of the coastal region is fertile land, and in the eastern parts of the interior of Cape Province are the extensive, mainly treeless grasslands known as the *veldt*. These lush grasslands of eastern mountain slopes and high plateaus are particularly well suited to grazing, but large areas have been brought under cultivation, and cereals and potatoes are now grown.

Both north and south of the equator, then, we find seemingly endless savanna stretching across almost completely flat plains, broken only by trees and bushes or by an occasional hill. A good deal of this land is heavily populated by men and their herds of cattle, goats, and sheep. As a result, the vegetation has often been greatly modified, nearly always for the worse. But there are some areas that, possibly because of lack of water, remain more or less in their natural state.

It is characteristic of the savannas that they vary considerably in appearance from area to area and from year to year. As is often true of low-rainfall areas, the less rain there is, the more erratic it is in its occurrence. An average rainfall of 5 inches a year may fluctuate from 0 to 15 or even 20 inches in successive years.

Where the grasslands fringe the desert, perennial grasses are scarce, and most of the grass cover consists of annual plants—that is, plants that fulfill their life cycle in a single short season. This is because many semidesert plants must sometimes lie dormant, as seeds, through several years of drought; and they must then be able to germinate quickly when there is adequate rain

Savanna grassland varies widely in type. Above: lush tropical savanna in the Central African Republic where up to 30 inches of rain permits the growth of palm trees and perennial grasses. Below right: dry grassland supporting flat-topped acacia trees, is characteristic of the majority of African savanna. Top right: typical Australian savanna scattered with eucalyptus trees, some of which have had a ring of bark removed to kill them to provide more open grazing land for sheep.

and to set seed in the minimum time possible in order to await the next rainfall. Thus, the grasses in these semiarid areas produce a flush of green for perhaps two months in a good year—that is, after the rain. For the rest of the time the landscape looks brown and parched. But animals can sometimes graze on the grass even when it is not green. After a period of growth, for instance, just when the fierce sun of the dry season is turning the grassland to a pale brown color, a type of hay of a surprisingly good food value is produced, and this is exploited by various species of antelope and other herbivorous mammals.

No preliminary account of the African savannas would be complete without some reference to the acacia trees. The genus *Acacia* includes a large number of different species of *leguminous* (protein-rich) trees with feathery leaves, thorns, and sweet-scented flowers. Woody plants, as we

know, do not usually grow in grasslands, but the acacias do. They colonize almost every part of Africa except forest land, and they are found in their greatest variety where the rainfall is between 10 and 30 inches a year (i.e. in grassland areas). On the fringes of the desert they are usually little bushes shaped like inverted cones, but their size increases as climatic conditions improve, and in some regions they grow to be majestic flat-topped trees 60 feet high, with umbrellalike crowns as much as 120 feet across. Acacias seem to have become adapted to almost every variety of African soil and climate, and it would be easy for a trained ecologist to describe reasonably accurately the climate of the place where he stood if he knew the type of soil and the species of acacia growing on it.

Most African acacias are armed with hooked thorns or long spikes, which protect them against browsing animals (those that feed on the bark and foliage of trees and shrubs). The conical form of growth also protects the central growing point by means of an outer ring of thorny branches, so that the tree is able to grow even when many animals are trying to browse its shoots. Its fruit is a pealike pod, in certain cases spirally twisted, which falls to the ground and is greatly relished by wild and domestic animals.

One species of African acacia has an unusual form of self-protection. A hollow, egg-shaped ball develops at the base of each pair of long spiky thorns. The ball hardens as it dries out, and becomes a cozy home for a colony of a special type of small ant. If a browsing animal comes along to feed on the growing tips of the branches, the ants swarm out and fiercely attack the animal, thus saving the tree from serious damage.

In the dry grassland areas a tree must be able to survive drought. Usually when a drought comes, the acacias shed their leaves, and the bark—which is corky or protected by a waxy skin—helps to minimize water loss. Some of the trees are deep-rooted and can tap water stored in the ground out of reach of the shallow-rooted grasses. Others have a long, spreading root system that draws water from a wide area. But generally dry-grassland acacias remain stunted because their water requirement increases as they grow; then, when a prolonged drought occurs, the bigger trees simply die of thirst.

Savanna exists not only in Africa but also in other tropical and subtropical regions, particu-

larly in South America and Australia. Savannas differ from other types of grassland in that, having more rainfall, the soil can support scattered trees or shrubs, or both. In addition, in some savannas we actually find a higher proportion of *forbs* (that is, nonwoody plants that are not grasses) than of grass. Because of the presence of trees and shrubs, browsing and grazing animals can coexist in savannas. And even the bird and insect life is different from that of other grasslands, because birds can nest in bushes instead of on the ground, and insects—such as the ants in acacia trees—can find homes in wood or on bush foliage.

Savannas are therefore remarkably rich in

Left: although wild pigs are thought of as creatures of woodlands and forests, the African warthog is more frequently found on savannas, where it lives in holes abandoned by other animals. Its large, ungainly head, four tusks, and the wart-like pads on its face serve to make the warthog one of the ugliest creatures of the African plains. The Thomson's gazelle (right), in contrast, has been described as "without doubt the most beautiful grass-eating animal of the African savanna." Suprisingly, this graceful animal shares a common ancestor with goats and sheep. Like other species of gazelle it eats the coarser grasses of the savanna and foliage of thorn bushes.

both plant and animal species. But this is not to say that there is little wildlife to be found in other kinds of grassland. As we shall see in the following chapters, a surprising variety of plant and animal life can survive even in semidesert areas. And although, for obvious reasons, herbivorous mammals predominate in all grasslands, it is fascinating to observe the differences between, say, the fauna of one continental plain and that of another.

In the prairies of North America, for example, the jackrabbit is one of the most important small grazing animals; but this species is not found in the pampas of Argentina, where the equivalent ecological niche is occupied by the Patagonian cavy—a rodent that, although related to the guinea pig, has long hind legs and large ears and behaves very much like the jackrabbit. The bison and pronghorn are (or perhaps we should say "were") further examples of typical large herbivores of North America; their role is filled in Eurasia by the saiga antelope, wild horse, and wild ass. And the large landmass of Australia has an entirely different group of animals from those of any other continent; the kangaroos and wallabies are the ecological equivalent of America's bison and pronghorn.

Now let us look more closely at these creatures and many others that make their homes in the world's vast and varied grasslands.

Large Animals

As human populations expand, the world's wildernesses contract. But occasional herds of wild animals, such as these zebras of the Tanzanian savanna, still manage to survive in the shrinking grassland regions of every continent.

So much of grassland has been settled by man or is man-made that it is becoming an increasingly inhospitable habitat for many wild animals. Yet it is still possible to find areas where, beyond the reach of agriculture, undomesticated creatures large and small can roam freely. There are mountain pastures above the timberline in every continent where solitary eagles soar over grassland inhabited by cold-country mammals. The Eurasian steppelands remain largely unaffected by

man's activities in some areas. And in the vast open spaces of Africa we still find arid desert places merging first into dry grassland, then into more typical savanna where zebras, elephants, and giraffes graze or browse at will.

Let us begin our figurative hunt for grassland wildlife by climbing high up into the mountains. Only a limited number of large animals can thrive in such places. Vegetation above the timberline is likely to be too scarce to support many species, and the climate is too rough for most. Still, there are hardy animals whose natural habitat is the mountain grassland, and these we shall look at very briefly. Typical of all such ecosystems, as we have seen, are the Alps, which for centuries have captured the imagination of travelers from every part of the globe. There, at the top of the European world, live the ibex and the chamois, two mammals that have a fascination for both naturalists and hunters.

The graceful chamois, a distant relative of the goats, is one of the most frequently observed large animals of the Alps. A large male may weigh up to 22 or 23 pounds and stand something over 2½ feet tall at the shoulder. Its horns are short and erect, with the tips curving backward. It is essentially European in distribution (though it extends into eastern Asia) and has been introduced into the mountains of New Zealand, where it thrives. But wherever they live, these animals are much sought after by human hunters. That may be one reason why there are such limited numbers of them. Biologists in Switzerland seem unable to suggest any other explanation; it *is* surprising that the population of chamois in the Alps has remained quite stable instead of increasing during the past century, because the bigger animals that once preyed on them—such as bear, wolf, lynx, and wildcat—have all been exterminated.

Perhaps the most romantic and exciting animal to be seen on the alpine pastures above the timberline is the ibex. This majestic animal is larger and heavier than the chamois, standing nearly 3 feet high at the shoulder and weighing up to 55 pounds—more than twice as much as the chamois. It has long, curved horns, often of impressive size. It is this last feature, together with its shyness and the fact that the hunter must climb up to the highest and most remote parts of the mountains to find it, that has made the ibex one of the most desirable of game animals.

The hunting of wild animals often arouses strong feelings in people. When natural predators have been exterminated, hunting by man is sometimes the only way to keep animal populations from growing too fast and overgrazing the land that feeds them. But if the hunter's gun is not controlled, it can do irreparable damage to grassland fauna.

If we move down from the mountain heights to the grasslands below, and turn specifically to the North American grasslands—the prairies—we can see rather graphically the results of hunting and other types of human activity.

The North American prairies are much more diverse than is sometimes thought. Before the arrival of European man, they formed a wild land of striking beauty. There are still a few places left with open landscapes of softly undulating hillocks—brown and featureless, to be sure, but nonetheless strangely charming because of their curious geometrical patterns. The prairie sky, too, has unusual beauty and character. On one side there may be a great, dark blanket of cloud, while on the other there is brilliant sunshine from a wide blue sky. The weather can also be changeable, with calm sunshine suddenly broken by a hailstorm or a downpour of rain of tropical intensity in an arctic temperature. The treeless plains are dotted with scores of shallow lakes, and melting snow can temporarily create other wet places. Some of these are strongly alkaline and attract a distinctive range of bird life. In general, prairie birds tend to be paler and smaller than their counterparts on the humid west coast of the continent.

Such differences have been brought about to some extent by the great barrier of the Rocky Mountains, which run from north to south. In the course of evolution, this barrier has prevented interchange between wildlife populations on either side. Game birds such as the prairie chicken and the sharp-tailed grouse are not, therefore, west-coast animals; but they were once very much a feature of the prairie belt. Their numbers declined rapidly throughout the 19th century because of increasingly heavy hunting. Often the hunting was carried on in organized groups, for its object was not primarily sport but the harvesting of large numbers of game birds as food for the expanding human population.

But the main reason for the scarcity of game birds today is the gradual disappearance of their typical habitat as a result of the systematic destruction of the natural prairies for cultivation. In the same way, the birds' natural predators—coyotes, skunks, and hawks—have also declined with the destruction of their prey and the shrinking of suitable habitat. We shall return to a discussion of the remaining birds and smaller prairie animals in a later chapter.

The most characteristic beast of the untouched prairie is the mighty bison. Bison once roamed from the spruce forests of the Canadian lakes to the center of Mexico, and from the Rockies to the eastern seaboard. They may even have inhabited the prairies of the Pacific coastal lowlands. Of the several varieties known to have existed in pre-European North America, only two remain:

The long, thick, ridged horns of the extremely rare alpine ibex are especially attractive to trophy hunters.

By the time the American artist William Jacob Hays (1830–75) painted this picture, the great bison herds of America's prairies were being slaughtered to near extinction by European settlers.

the woodland bison of Canada's Great Slave Lake area, and the plains bison, perhaps better known as the buffalo.

The bison migrated seasonally along fixed routes within the enormous territory of central North America. It is thought that there were once some 50 to 60 million in the prairies and perhaps another 5 million in the woodlands. The first European colonists were , staggered by the number of these animals, and there are several

contemporary descriptions of bison migrations, when the prairies were dark with moving animals as far as the eye could see. The Indians were already exploiting them for their meat and hides, but the Europeans (who introduced both firearms and the horse) were far more efficient killers than the Indians. Later on, as the great railroads spread across the western part of America, a tremendous and largely irresponsible slaughter took place, partly to supply food to construction workers, but mainly as a sport for travelers. It was during this period, in the latter half of the 19th century, that William F. Cody (Buffalo Bill) shot 4280 bison in 18 months.

And so the great herds vanished without people realizing what was happening. Many Americans thought at the time that most buffaloes had simply emigrated to Canada and would soon return in large numbers. This was far from the truth, for the bison was close to extinction in Canada too.

Since the beginning of the 20th century, herds in both the United States and Canada have again been built up under government protection, and the bison has been saved from total extermination—but only just saved. In recent years there has been a growing interest among some ranchers to raise bison together with cattle. This contri-

butes toward national conservation programs; and ranchers are finding that the market value of buffalo meat compares quite favorably with that of cattle. Bison are much more robust than cattle. They generally have a lower mortality rate during the cold, hard winters, and they can eat many plants that cattle tend to avoid. In protected areas it has now become necessary to crop some of the herds (that is, to keep their numbers down artificially) in order to keep them from overgrazing range lands. The United States and Canadian governments issue a limited number of hunting licenses, so that bison populations are reduced to the capacity of range

Left: a female pronghorn of the North American prairie with her young. Indiscriminate hunting in the 19th century brought these swift and lovely creatures to the brink of extinction, but emergency protective measures have saved them.

Below: an African white rhino guards her drinking calf. White rhinos, the largest living land mammals after elephants, have long necks and squared mouths, both adaptations to grazing.

lands to support them, and the health of the herds is thereby maintained.

As the numbers of bison declined on the prairies, America's hunters turned their attention to smaller game, particularly the pronghorn (sometimes called the "pronghorn antelope," although it is not a true antelope). Extremely well adapted to life in the prairies, pronghorns used to be widespread throughout North America, from Alberta in Canada south to the plateaus of northern Mexico and westward to the Pacific. By 1910 only small, scattered groups survived, and again the species has been saved from extinction only by emergency protective measures. The measures have worked so well that pronghorns are now fairly numerous in parts of the prairie belt, particularly Wyoming and Montana. In some places they can even be seen grazing placidly along the fringes of main roads.

These white-and-chestnut-colored animals have long been famous for their great speed—a speed that used to be a severe test of the skill of Indian hunters. Nineteenth-century accounts describe the pronghorn as having such extraordinary fleetness that no horse had a chance of outrunning or even tiring it, so that the Indians were unable to chase it on horseback. One hunting technique was to form a scattered circle around the herd, so that it was possible to chase the pronghorns to and fro over a wide but limited area, with each group of Indians turning the herd and sending it back toward hunters waiting at another part of the circumference. The idea was to get the pronghorns so tired that the circle could gradually tighten, enabling the horses to come close enough for the Indians to use their bows and arrows.

The pronghorn, whether male or female, has hollow horns that are shed annually. Each of the two horns has a projecting part—the prong—jutting forth from the main branch (called the *tine*). During the growth season, new skin starts to rise from the bony core base inside the old horny covering. When the skin reaches the tips of both the main tine and the prong, it splits the old horn, which drops off. The pronghorn also has a patch of white hair on its rump. It is believed that these long, stiff white hairs are fluffed up by the animal as an alarm signal.

In spite of the enormous variety of landscapes and climates in North America, the numbers and

Overleaf: *the large plant-eating animals are the dominant members of the African grassland community and fall into two categories: the browsers, such as elephants, giraffes, and rhinos, which feed on trees and shrubs and have a constant high-quality food supply with no need to migrate seasonally, and the grazers, which are faced with the problem of very poor food in the dry season and must therefore migrate to richer pastures. Predators and scavengers follow the movement of the grazing herds. Termites are responsible, with the fungi, for the breakdown of much of the living and dead plant material.*

kinds of wildlife in the continent's extensive grasslands do not compare with the richness of grassland animals in Africa. For instance, North America has about 20 species of land mammal larger than a dog, but Africa has a total of over 80 such species. Apart from elephants, hippopotamuses, and rhinoceroses, there are also four species of relatives of the horse (zebras and wild asses)—none of which is found in

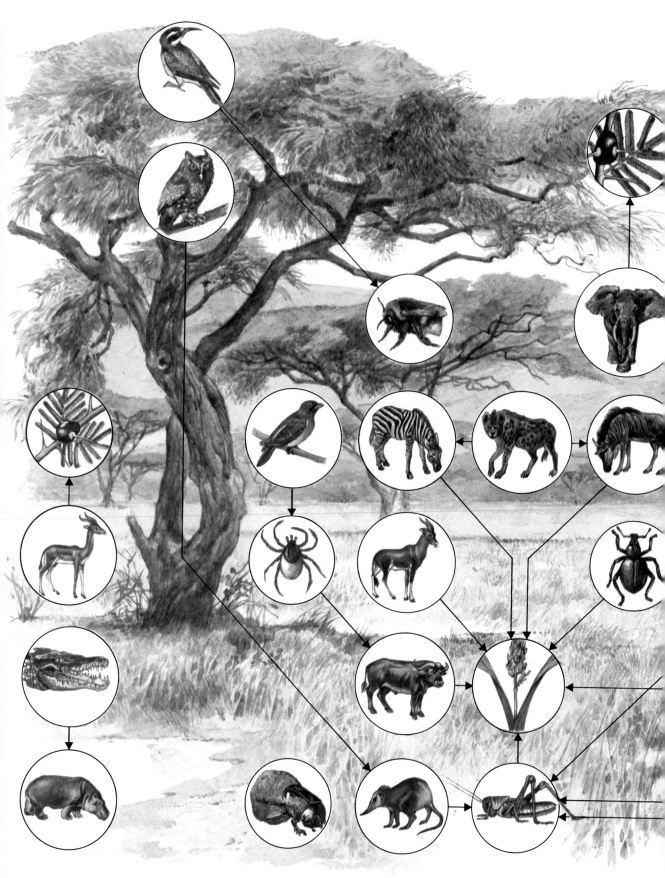

A Simple Food Web for the African Grasslands

1 Bee eater
2 Scops owl
3 Acacia leaves
4 Bee
5 Elephant
6 Giraffe
7 Vulture
8 Weaver bird
9 Acacia leaves
10 Oxpecker
11 Zebra
12 Hyena

13 Wildebeest
14 Lion
15 Marabou stork
16 Gerenuk
17 Tick
18 Topi
19 Weevil
20 Chameleon
21 Thomson's gazelle
22 Flesh-fly
23 Dead gazelle
24 Jackal

25 Crocodile
26 Water buffalo
27 Grass
28 Click beetle
29 Mantid
30 Termite
31 Carrion beetle
32 Hippopotamus
33 Dung beetle
34 Elephant shrew
35 Grasshopper
36 Baboon
37 Termite fungus

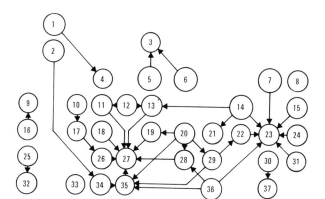

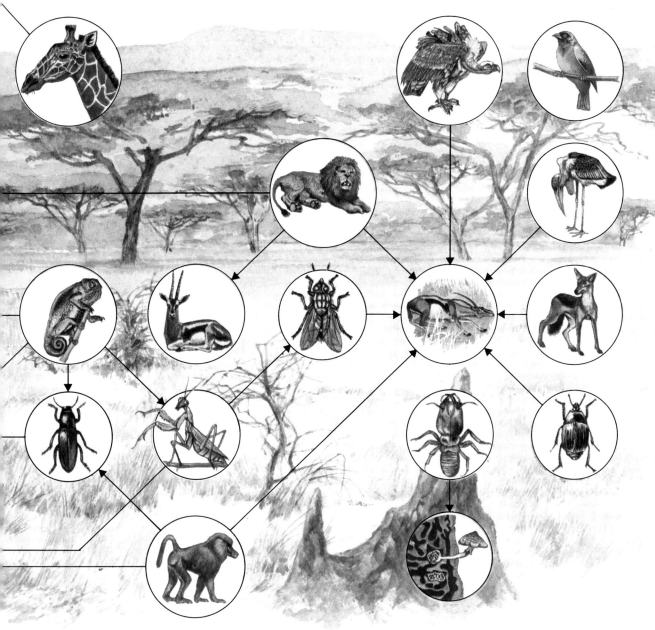

Elephants at a water hole in Kenya. Unlike their Asiatic relatives, which are grass-eaters, African elephants include a large amount of foliage and bark in their diet. Because of their enormous appetites and outstanding strength they have had a considerable effect on the vegetation within their ranges and, in consequence, upon the habitats of many other animals.

North America. In addition, Africa can claim more than 60 species of antelope, varying from the huge eland, which weighs almost a ton, to the pygmy antelope, which weighs less than 10 pounds.

Some of the differences between the wealth of Africa and the relative poverty of America (in this one respect) is no doubt due to the greater depredations of industrial and agricultural man in the New World. We must also remember that North America lies in the temperate-to-frigid Northern Hemisphere, whereas Africa spans enormous areas both north and south of the equator, providing a more complex range of habitable climatic zones. And it is the savannas and the moister grasslands that support the greatest number and variety of animals.

The large-mammal fauna of Africa makes the continent unique, but it is a tragic commentary on present-day events that a good part of even this fauna has already disappeared from large areas. As the human population has increased, much unspoiled country has been converted to agriculture and urban development, and great numbers of animals have been killed by commercial exploitation. That these changes have taken place in a remarkably short time becomes abundantly evident when we consider that only a little over a century has passed since the first Europeans began to explore systematically the interior of the continent. This means that most of the animals displaced by the rapid expansion of settlements and the changes arising from modern technology have been inadequately studied. There is a danger, indeed, that many species will be lost completely before we have learned much about their biology and habits.

The majority of grassland areas as they exist in Africa north of the equator have been produced by a combination of grazing and burning, as well as by the kind of soil and climate. It is certainly a fact that in most places, except where the rainfall is very low, the grasses would be rapidly succeeded by woody bushes and trees if it were not for grazing and fire. Much of the grassland in Africa's low-rainfall regions is burned by man during the dry season every year, in order to promote a fresh growth of green shoots as soon as rain reaches the ground. If the traditional time of burning is changed, the dominant varieties of grass species alter very quickly. Also, large grazing animals have an immediate effect on the pasture, partly by

rampling and partly by cropping. This effect has been regulating the pattern of vegetation for millions of years, so that the feeding behavior and migratory movements of some herbivores have become adapted to take advantage of pasture changes that are most favorable to them.

It is this sort of adaptation that enables many different species of grazing and browsing animals to live together in the same area without being threatened by too much competition for available resources. Adaptation to the grassland environment also seems to have permitted the evolution of relatively large, highly mobile herbivores, which, because they can wander extensively, are able to exploit fully the natural potential of a wide area. Each species of grass-eater tends to favor certain types of grasses, and in some cases the animals have developed the capacity to get all the moisture necessary for their survival from green leaves, so that they do not require easy access to open water. Zebras, gnus, gazelles, buffaloes, kongonis, and reedbucks are just a small sample of the wide range of shapes and sizes that has evolved in the grassland habitat.

During the dry season, many large herbivores congregate in well-watered or shady places. With the arrival of the rains, however, good grazing conditions return to the brown dusty plains, and the herds disperse. South of the equator, in the Rukwa valley of southern Tanzania, the elephant, buffalo, and hippo start to feed on tall marsh grass at the end of the rainy season. Feeding and trampling by such large animals has a tremendous physical impact on the vegetation; the thick grass, 10 feet high, is chewed, stripped, pulped, and trodden flat. When bulky food of this type becomes scarce and surface water begins to dry up, these very big animals (excepting the nonnomadic hippos) move on to other areas. In their absence the grass puts out new shoots, and these in turn attract smaller animals: eland, zebra, and hartebeest.

After the rainy season, the topis also come down from the higher ground where they have concentrated while the valley pastures were flooded. Once flood water has disappeared, the fresh green shoots make attractive grazing for these silky-coated antelopes. Constant grazing keeps the grass short and green; and before it can dry up completely, showers that usually fall toward the end of the dry season bring on a flush of growth—a convenient phenomenon, for it happens shortly after the birth of the topi calves. The dependence of the topis on this cycle of events was dramatically illustrated a few years ago, when unprecedented rains resulted

Impalas (left) are among the larger of the 60-odd antelope species that inhabit Africa's grasslands. Very different from these timid beasts are the Cape buffaloes of southeastern Africa (below), which are famous for their unpredictability and ferocity.

in extensive flooding around Lake Rukwa. When, at the end of the rainy season, the topis moved down from the high ground as usual, they found the plains covered with water, and large numbers died as they stood around unable to feed.

Grant's gazelle in the Serengeti area of Northern Tanzania does not need access to open water. During the dry season these animals disperse over the empty plains, feeding on the dry grass stubble or browsing on whatever scrub foliage is available, while larger animals are concentrated in the lusher valleys. With the arrival of the rains, the bigger mammals move on to richer pastures, and the gazelles come into the vacated area, where they feed on the short, fresh cushion grass. This type of dependence of one animal on the behavior of others is part of a very complex system. How could it not be complex, considering that there are so many species of herbivores and so many hundreds of different grasses, which grow, flower, and wither at such different times!

A good example of the delicate balance between animals and the vegetation on which they must depend is the spread of an attractive species of antelope, the lesser kudu, in the Karamoja region of Uganda. In the early years of this century, this area was populated by elephants, which devoured so much of the vegetation that the kudu could not survive there. But a heavy demand for ivory resulted in overhunting of the elephants, which eventually disappeared from Karamoja. The Ugandans traded the ivory for cattle, which multiplied rapidly and soon overgrazed the rangeland. Because cattle graze very selectively, overexploiting herbaceous vegetation but rejecting less palatable bushes, they created conditions for the spread of a dense thicket of bush—a habitat that was ideal for the bush-hungry lesser kudu.

Of course, where large numbers of plant-eating animals live, as in the dry grasslands and relatively lush savannas that abound in Africa, they inevitably attract predators of many types: lions, cheetahs, hyenas, hunting dogs, jackals, and many smaller carnivores, all well adapted to exploiting the young or adults of the more numerous herbivores.

As has been said, fleet-footedness is a common characteristic of both predators and potential prey in grassland. And no animal can run faster than the cheetah. This animal occurs over a very wide region from Mauritania to the Sudan and

There are many animals of Africa's dry grasslands and savannas that look alike but they are not necessarily members of the same family. Left: Cape hunting dogs (top), which hunt their live prey in packs, are as unattractive as—but unrelated to—the spotted hyenas (bottom), which are mainly nocturnal carrion-eaters. Above: the gerenuk, a long-necked browsing antelope, is not related to the giraffe, although they look rather similar.

on into southern Asia, but it is much less common than it used to be. The cheetah preys mainly on small or medium-sized gazelles and antelopes. When hunting, it often stalks to within a short distance of its prey, trying to hide between tufts of vegetation as it gets closer. Although it has been timed running at between 60 and 70 miles an hour, which is much faster than any antelope can run, it can keep up such high speeds for only about a quarter to half a mile, and so once it has started to sprint, it has no more than perhaps 20 seconds in which to catch its prey. Thus, to launch a successful attack, it must start its run from a distance of not more than 200 yards. At full speed it covers the ground in great bounds. Although the prey may swerve from one side to another, the cheetah usually catches up with it, trips it with a paw, and instantly seizes it by the throat.

Cheetahs are less ferocious than lions and leopards and are quite easily tamed. In fact, for many centuries chieftains in the Sudan and elsewhere have trained them for the hunt or kept them as pets. They do not roar or growl like lions or leopards, but purr and mew like cats. And, like so many other members of the cat family, they are extremely handsome creatures —as is also the caracal (or desert lynx of Africa and southwest Asia). This is a cat slightly over three feet long from nose to tail, golden brown in color, with long black hair on the tips of its ears and a short, black-tufted tail. It preys upon hares and large rodents, and also upon birds, which it is able to catch even when they are in flight, by leaping up and plucking them from the air with its front paws.

In the acacia bushlands and savannas of the vast continent, we find a different type of large herbivore from the animals that graze the dry-grassland pastures. Giraffes, for instance, are browsers and would not be at home in open grassland without trees or bushes; they are found particularly in East Africa, Uganda and Tanzania. Here, too, is the red-fronted gazelle and in the moister savannas there are elephants, and a number of antelope species, including—probably the most characteristic antelope of the moist grasslands—the korrigum, which is nomadic.

Cheetahs hunt their prey mainly by chasing, unlike most other cats, which hunt by stealth. In this picture, an adult cheetah rests, while an adolescent finishes its meal.

Great herds of korrigums are on the move as the rainy season ends, their sole purpose being to find the new green pastures that spring up immediately after the rains. It is at this time that the females produce their calves—and, remarkably, the newborn calves are capable of migrating along with the herd within hours of their birth.

Many grassland herbivores are forced, like the korrigum, to be wanderers. Grassland that consists mainly of annual plants can never support large numbers of animals for more than a short period. This is because the plants soon die in the dry season and only the seeds survive, to lie dormant until it rains again. The nomadic behavior of so many of the large herbivores is therefore an adaptation for finding food during different seasons of the year. For example, from time to time there are large concentrations of Grant's gazelles, zebras, and oryxes in the highlands of eastern Africa. This may seem to indicate a rich, practically permanent grazing potential, but it is a misleading impression. The animal populations have undoubtedly gathered here from far afield and will soon move off in search of fresh pastures.

In areas where rainfall is irregular and scanty, but where the soil is deep enough for trees and bushes to grow among the grasses, the shrub foliage manages to stay green for much longer than the shallow-rooted grass. It is not surprising, therefore, that browsing animals may well be more common in bushlands and savannas than are the grazers.

Elephants, which are fairly numerous in the southern parts of eastern Africa, eat tall grass as well as tree and bush vegetation. But there are three common animals that concentrate on browsing only: the giraffe; the gerenuk, which is a rather strange, long-necked, antelope able to stand upright on its hind legs when feeding; and the dik-dik, a small antelope. Among them, these three very different animals are able to exploit the acacia foliage from the lowest branches to as high as a giraffe can reach (18 feet or more). By standing on its hind legs, the gerenuk can browse up to about eight feet, and the dik-diks crop the tangle of low branches and small shrubs. The dik-diks and gerenuks can go for very long periods without water. Indeed, the gerenuk appears to get almost all the water it needs either from the vegetation it eats or from drinking the urine of its own species.

The bush is also sometimes browsed by the

CHEETAH

GRANT'S GAZELLE

ORIBI

SABLE ANTELOPE

OSTRICH

The artist has collected together many of the animals that are likely to fall prey to the cheetahs of East Africa during the course of their lifetime. To the 25 species pictured here may be added a large number of others from grasslands ranged by cheetahs throughout other parts of Africa, western Asia, and India.

54

A Cheetah and Its Prey

THOMSON'S GAZELLE

LESSER KUDU

COMMON ZEBRA

TOPI

STEINBOK

BEISA ORYX

KONGONI

BRINDLED GNU

IMPALA

GERENUK

KOB

DIK-DIK

DUIKER

KORI BUSTARD

CAPE HARE

GREVY'S ZEBRA

BLACK-BACKED JACKAL

GUINEA FOWL

HARNESSED ANTELOPE

WARTHOG

MOLE RAT

A herd of giraffes near the Niger River in southern Mali. Although giraffes were much hunted in the past, large herds can still be found browsing in some dry savanna woodlands.

greater and lesser kudus. But these graceful antelopes—valued by some hunters because of the male's long, spiral horns—really prefer the impenetrable thickets to be found on rocky hills. Two other small browsing animals can be quite numerous in eastern Africa: the dibatag, a gazellelike creature, and the beira antelope. Like most browsers, these animals are not noma-

dic but can stay in one place because of the ample supply of bushy vegetation. Although the dibatag looks like a long-necked gazelle, it is actually related to the reedbucks, which are small antelopes. It trots with its long neck raised high, and it browses on spiny, semisucculent tree foliage of a type that most other animals seem to find unpalatable.

Savannas and shrublands are generally much less arid than most natural grassland areas, and can support larger animal populations, with grazing and browsing species coexisting com-

fortably. The shrublands of Kenya, for example, are the habitat of many species of antelope and zebra, along with the browsers already mentioned. The commonest grazers there are the oryx, the gnu, the common zebra, Grevy's zebra, and two groups of *very* adaptable gazelles (although living ordinarily in the moist savanna, they sometimes penetrate into the desert, where only scattered shrubs and a few blades of annual grass survive). Grevy's zebra is larger than the common zebra. It has many narrow black stripes, and although at close range it is unmistakably black and white in color, as with other zebras, at a distance it seems to be brownish and merges beautifully into the landscape.

Before leaving Africa, let us look at two other species of antelope that are quite rare and are becoming rarer. The first is the giant sable antelope, which is among the largest of the African antelopes. The bulls of the species are black, with white markings on the face and white underparts, whereas the females and nonbreeding males are lighter, the males having black faces. Unfortunately for the giant sable antelope, it is the possessor of a pair of magnificent scimitar-shaped horns that in some cases grow to more than five feet long, and it is these much-sought-after trophies that in the past have contributed to its decline. The giant sable antelope is now restricted to a small area of tree-scattered savanna on the Luanda Reserve in northern Angola, the total population being estimated at between 500 and 700 animals.

The second example is a species of eland, the largest of the living antelopes, called the western giant eland. It is a sturdy, mahogany-colored animal with 14 or 15 vertical white stripes along its back. Both male and female have long, spiral horns. The western giant eland grazes partly forested lands and open plains on the borders of Mali, Senegal, and Guinea, and because of the excellence of its meat and the high quality of its leather, it has been ruthlessly hunted. The remaining small herds have been further decimated by rinderpest, a plague to which elands are particularly susceptible and which is usually fatal. The western giant eland's numbers are now so reduced that it is unlikely to survive in the wild for many more years.

Although we have ranged widely over the immensely rich African continent, we have glimpsed only a fragment of Africa's vast complex of animal communities and habitats (many of which are still largely unstudied). In later chapters we shall consider bird life and the life of smaller animals, as well as their interrelationships within the grassland ecosystems. Now, though, let us meet some of the larger animals that inhabit the grasslands of South America, Australia, and Eurasia. A good starting place is South America, whose fauna is remarkably distinctive. Most people, asked to name the animal that comes to mind when the pampas of South America are mentioned, immediately think of the gaucho seated jauntily on his horse, and answer "horses."

The earliest known member of the horse family appeared in the Eocene period, about 65 million years ago, and has been appropriately named *Eohippus*, meaning "dawn horse." It was a small animal about the size of a dog, and it had toes with claws rather than a hoof on each foot. It probably browsed on the leaves and fruits of bushes as well as on grasses, but its descendants grew gradually larger and more horselike. The toenails became hooves, and the mouth changed

so that the lips became more mobile and the teeth more efficient for cropping grass. During the Pliocene period, from 7 to 2 million years ago, there were six genera of horses, all typical grazing animals. But only the genus *Equus* has survived to modern times.

In North America a primitive horse named *Merychippus* developed the physique and physiology needed for feeding specifically on grasses. This in turn led to a more highly developed group, *Hipparion*, which colonized almost the whole world by dispersal from America and Asia and into Africa before changes of climate and vegetation, or possibly competition from other mammalian species, somehow caused its extinction. Later the genus *Equus* (the true horse) moved out from North America into Asia and other parts of the Old World as well as into South America. Our present-day horses and zebras

are remnants of this worldwide dispersion.

Yet, for reasons we do not understand, the horse became extinct in the Western Hemisphere about 10,000 years ago, having survived for millions of years. Other grazing animals also disappeared at the same time, and some scientists believe that man, who had recently reached North America from Asia, was the culprit. Horses did not come back to America until they were brought in by the Spaniards in the 16th century. Today only one wild species of true horse is known in the world. This is a pony-sized animal called Przewalski's horse in honor of the Russian explorer who first described it.

The coat of Przewalski's horse is rather shaggy, especially in the winter, when its color changes from light yellow to yellowish brown. The species survives precariously in only one area— an open, windswept plain in southwestern

Above: a pair of black rhinos feeding in the Masai Amboseli Game Reserve, Kenya. The pointed lips of black rhinos finish in a "hook," which helps make the rhinos efficient browsers of leaves and twigs of bushes in their dry savanna and scrubland ranges. Once widely distributed throughout Africa, the black rhinos, like their white and Asiatic relatives, have been much reduced in numbers in the wild by hunting, poaching, and the reclamation for agriculture of their natural habitat.

Mongolia close to the frontier with China. It is a very shy animal, and few people have been fortunate enough to get a close view of it in its natural habitat. Most of us can still have the pleasure of seeing this splendid little horse, however, because at least 150 are held in zoos— more, indeed, than survive in the wild.

The horse is not the only common beast of burden that had its earliest home in the Americas. Strangely enough, the camel family seems to have originated in North America during the

Eocene period. No camels survive there now, apart from those in zoos. But a unique group of animals that live mainly in the extensive dry grasslands of South America's Andean plateaus are clearly related to camels; although they are smaller and have no humps, you cannot fail to see the family resemblance if you take a good look at any of the four species that represent this South American branch of the camel family.

Two of the four species have been domesticated for many centuries. The larger is the llama, widely used as a beast of burden. The other domestic species, the alpaca, is much valued for its fine wool. Two further species still exist in the wild state: the guanaco, and the vicuna. The guanaco is less endangered by the activities of man, chiefly because it is less economically "useful." It is the most widespread of the South American relatives of the camel. Although typically a high-altitude plateau animal, small herds of guanacos range throughout the southern part of the continent, from the highest points where vegetation can grow all the way down to sea level. The fourth species, the vicuna, has the misfortune to be very valuable to man, who covets its meat, its hide, and particularly its

60

wool, which is the finest in the world. Although vicunas have been under government protection for many years, such protection has been ineffectual, and the species is close to extinction.

The predators in these high-altitude grasslands include the Andean fox, the condor (one of the largest of all birds of prey), the puma, the wildcat, and, of course, man.

Below the mountains, on the dry grassy plains of Patagonia, in southern Argentina, where there are extensive areas of low scrub, there lives a large rodent called the Patagonian cavy (or mara)—a creature some $2\frac{1}{2}$ feet long—which is

entirely adapted to what is known as a *cursorial* way of life; this simply means that, unlike most rodents, it depends for its survival on its ability to run speedily. Thus it fills the same sort of ecological niche as middle-sized antelopes in Africa, such as an impala or gazelle, for there are no true antelopes in the New World. In both habits and appearance, Patagonian cavies are a curious combination of rodents and small hoofed animals (the *ungulates*). Their hind legs are long and powerful, with three-toed feet that, with their heavy pads and claws, somewhat resemble hooves. The forelimbs are much more lightly

61

A female Patagonian cavy with one of her young. On the dry South American pampas, cavies have adapted to fill the niche occupied in other areas by rodents and antelopes.

built, with four toes and sharp claws, and are held quite straight, like a small antelope's, when the animal is motionless.

These strange creatures run extremely swiftly in a series of bounces, leaping over bushes and other obstacles. Their sharp claws are useful for digging the large burrows in which they live. These are usually dug in the gentle slopes of hillsides where there is scattered scrub with grassy clearings. Here the Patagonian cavies graze and their young play; the scrub provides shelter and a hiding-place, where the adult female can safely suckle her young, which she does by squatting on her haunches while her babies feed in the standing position.

The adult Patagonian cavy has a number of natural enemies on the plains. There are two common species of fox—the pampas fox and the Patagonian fox—as well as the puma, the pampas cat, and others that are rather rare at the present time. Smaller predators such as weasels, the buzzard eagle, and the red-backed hawk feed on the young cavies. Human hunters also seek out the Patagonian cavy because of the excellent quality of its meat, and there is no doubt that domestic dogs take a heavy toll of the young ones. And so, in spite of its fairly wide

distribution in the scrubby dry-grass country of Patagonia, and northward up to midwestern Argentina, the numbers of Patagonian cavies are steadily declining; in fact, some zoologists believe that its day of extinction may not be far off. One very important additional threat to its existence is competition from European rabbits, which have multiplied rapidly since their introduction to South America by man. Because their distribution more or less coincides with the range of the Patagonian cavy, they naturally compete for the same limited food supply.

The South American pampas are subject to frequent periods of drought that in turn affect the wildlife population. Because of this, the larger predators of the plains have to be almost omnivorous. Few of these larger predators are specialized feeders—the termite-eating giant anteater is one of the exceptions, perhaps—and most, such as the maned wolf and the pampas fox, will eat anything they can find. Not a great deal is known about the foxlike maned wolf. Although adapted to grassland life (its stiltlike legs give it a wide visual range over the flat pampas and make it a very fleet runner), like other wolves it prefers to shelter in the woodland. Unlike them, however, it does not hunt in packs. Small mammals such as cuis (wild guinea pigs), young viscachas (medium-dog-sized rodents related to the chinchilla), and rabbits are its main prey, but it will also eat birds, reptiles, insects, and even fruit. The diet of the pampas fox is similar to that of the maned wolf. Curiously, it often makes its home in viscacha burrows, living peaceably alongside its hosts and catching other rodents until the young viscachas are weaned and leave their burrows in the spring. It is then that the fox turns to this new, abundant, easily caught meal.

The termite-eating giant anteater, mentioned earlier, is another of the larger mammals of the pampas, measuring up to seven feet long from the tip of its tail to the end of its long tapering snout. It is nomadic, unlike most of the creatures of the plains, making neither nest nor burrow. At night it merely curls up on the ground and covers itself with its long bushy tail. Most of the giant anteater's waking hours are spent with its head bent close to the ground in a perpetual search for food. When it comes to a termite nest it rips it apart with the large powerful claws on its forepaws and sucks up the termites, eggs, and pupae with its long sticky tongue.

A seven-foot-long giant anteater roams the pampas in search of its termite prey. It uses its powerful claws to rip open the nests of termites and also to defend itself if cornered in a fight.

We turn now to the third large grassland area in the Southern Hemisphere, after Southern Africa and South America, and take a look at the larger animals of Australia. The great continental plains of Australia have been modified by man in an attempt to increase and improve pasturage for sheep; and this effort to squeeze more out of the grassland ecosystem than it can produce has had some interesting effects. Kangaroos and wallabies are the characteristic marsupial herbivores of this habitat, with each of the many species adapted to its own special niche. For example, the gray kangaroo prefers to feed on grasses that grow in the shade of scattered trees in a type of savanna. But because much of this sort of land has been cleared of its woody growth by sheep farmers, the number of gray kangaroos has sharply declined. At the same time, the habitat has become favorable for the red kangaroo, which grazes in open grassland.

The red kangaroo has actually profited from the sort of land "reclamation" that makes the habitat better for sheep-grazing. When pasture is improved in this way, water for domestic animals must usually be provided by wells and tanks, because rainfall is often low and may be very seasonal, but the kangaroo is not dependent on such man-made resources. In the hot, arid northwestern corner of Australia, for example, where there have been several long periods of drought during the past 50 years, both sheep and the euro kangaroo, or wallaroo, which inhabits rock-strewn areas, have temporarily declined in numbers as a result of the scarcity of water, but the better-adapted kangaroos have always recovered quickly, whereas the sheep have not. Today the population density of the euro far exceeds that of sheep. Part of the reason for this is that the euro can survive on plants that sheep are unable to eat. And the kangaroos can also exist without water for long periods by making use of rock shelters, where they escape the heat of the day during the dry season.

Overgrazing and trampling by sheep in dry vulnerable Australian grasslands degrades the pasture so that the most palatable and useful species of grasses decline in number and the species that the sheep reject are the ones that survive or even increase. After a time the pastures become less and less suitable for sheep, but the better-adapted kangaroos, feeding on a wider range of plants, continue to thrive.

From the great open spaces of Australia we turn to the similarly vast steppelands of Europe and Asia, where the most characteristic large herbivore is the saiga antelope. About two and a half feet high, this curious creature, which looks rather like a swollen-nosed cross between a sheep and an antelope, lives in the dry grasslands and semidesert country stretching from European Russia eastward into Mongolia and China. Essentially a plains animal, it avoids not only mountains and hills but even regions that are crossed by ravines and valleys.

As an adaptation to the smooth-plains topography, the saiga habitually runs at a trot. Thus its body is held level and does not move up and down, as does that of a galloping animal; its head is usually held low. Nevertheless, it can move very fast: up to 50 miles an hour on a level surface, according to some observers. In broken country, however, it is so much at a disadvantage that it cannot normally jump across even a very narrow ditch.

The saiga antelope feeds on all the steppe grasses, including some that are poisonous to domestic stock, and thus resembles the Australian marsupials in its ability to thrive in areas where domestic stock would starve. Even so, it roams over a very wide area in search of pasture and in response to the seasons. In the winter it moves southward to less severe climates, returning north in the spring, just as the fresh green shoots are beginning to appear. Summer in the Eurasian steppes can be very dry and hot, with good grazing hard to find; and so, from June through August, when its habitat is parched by the sun and no rain falls, the saiga migrates to areas where there are lakes and rivers. As soon as the rains come, however, it moves back into the vast plains.

A good deal of the dry steppeland is now artificially irrigated and is used for growing crops of wheat, corn, and alfalfa (lucerne). Saiga antelopes avoid agricultural crops, because the tall growth impedes the vision and free movement afforded by their preferred habitat, and so they are not a nuisance to farmers. Until quite recently, however, human beings were a very great nuisance to *them*.

Some 5000 years ago, the saiga was a remarkably widespread animal; it flourished not only throughout the whole of Europe and Asia, from the British Isles to China, but also in North America, where its remains have been found in Alaska. It was obviously an important source of food for prehistoric man, for the remains of its bones have often been found in the excavations of Paleolithic and Neolithic dwellings. Even as late as the 18th century, very large numbers of

these animals evidently inhabited a wide area of the Eurasian steppes. During the second half of the 19th century, the steppelands of European Russia were rapidly settled by man, who cultivated the soil and drove off or killed much of the wildlife. It was around this time that man's activities brought about such catastrophes as the extermination of Europe's wild horses. The saiga was not exterminated, but their numbers declined, and many herds retreated eastward.

Even in the Asian steppes, however, hunting was intensified. Not only did the Chinese regard the meat very highly, but they also used powdered horns in medicinal preparations. Russia also

A red kangaroo mother and her baby—called a "joey" by Australians. The red kangaroos inhabit the open plains of the central regions of Australia, where grass grows only sparsely.

valued the horns, which could be used for many purposes, both functional and decorative. Hundreds of thousands of pairs of horns were exported every year, and so saiga-hunting became a very lucrative occupation.

It is hardly surprising that by the 20th century the total number of saigas had fallen dramatically. By 1919 the species was on the verge of extinction—at which point the Russian government passed a law prohibiting all hunting of the saiga. No more than a few hundred of these animals now survived, and they seem to have been confined to the remotest parts of the lower basin of the Volga River and to one or two places in Asia.

For some 15 or 20 years after the hunting ban was instituted, there appeared to be no rise in numbers. This may have been partly because the saiga population was scattered in small groups and susceptible to predation by wolves, and partly because of a succession of severe winters, which must have caused heavy mortality.

Around the 1940s, however, the saiga began to appear in places where its presence had not been recorded for a very long time. A rough count

65

soon indicated that about 700,000 now lived in the Asian steppes, with another 50,000 or so in the European part of their range. This was the start of a population explosion. Certainly one important factor leading to their recovery was the Russian government's effort to wipe out wolves, the saigas' main predators. In 1946, over 42,000 wolves were killed, and by as late as 1963 there were some 17,600 people employed on wolf-extermination. A 1960 estimate suggested that the number of saiga antelopes had reached 2 million and that they now roamed through over $1\frac{1}{2}$ million square miles. Although it was protection

from predation and hunting that largely enabled this recovery to take place, the recovery could not have occurred so swiftly if the saiga were not so well adapted to their harsh environment.

The saiga is also an unusually fertile animal. While still a yearling it produces its first two young, and thereafter it has two more every spring, so the population can increase rapidly if hunting is controlled. The females usually have their offspring in rather bare places, where the grass cover is sparse and there is no water supply. Consequently, they are relatively free from the attentions of wolves (which, though to

the adult males fight for possession of a harem.

Even in the southern part of the saigas' range, where they spend the winter, severe weather is likely to occur about once every 10 or 12 years. Freezing winds blow across the open plains, and snow may lie deep over the sparse vegetation. In such winters many saigas die—particularly the adult males, which seem to suffer more than the females. But because of their high fertility, the population generally makes a rapid recovery.

The Russian government has relaxed its no-hunting rule, to permit controlled exploitation of the no-longer-endangered saiga herds. Russian scientists, who have made detailed studies of the saiga, estimate (by calculating its rapid growth rate and its natural death rate) that it is safe to crop some 40 per cent of the population in any one hunting season. Of course, hunting is regulated, so that a smaller quota is taken whenever there has been a hard winter or a bad summer drought. In a good year, between 200,000 and 300,000 animals are killed in the Soviet Union, providing Russia with substantial amounts of meat, hides, and bones, and providing an occupation for many people who live in the more remote parts of the steppes.

The number of saigas in the Eurasian steppes has fallen from the peak of 2 million in 1960 to around 1 million today. This drop does not seem to be due to hunting, but rather to an extension of agriculture, which destroys the saiga's food and creates such barriers to wildlife as irrigation canals, rice fields, and so on. In addition, increasing numbers of sheep are pastured on the steppes, and this further contracts the saiga's range. Almost certainly, its habitat will grow even more restricted as the human populations of Russia and China increase. Nevertheless, because the saiga can find food in areas that are unsuitable for agriculture, it should continue to thrive in sizable numbers for many years to come. Indeed, the people of the steppelands are coming to realize that the preservation of the saiga herds is the best possible means of using the dry grasslands that cannot support domestic stock or agriculture.

Grassland unsuitable for farming exists in every continent. And there is surely no better way to use it than to preserve its wildlife.

some extent forest animals, do range into the northern steppeland). The spring sunshine warms up the bare soil on which the newly born young lie; and because they have the same color as the pale sand, they are nicely camouflaged. In some saiga nurseries there may be from two to three newborn young per acre over a large area.

As soon as the babies are strong enough, the herds move on to their summer pastures. At such times many thousands of saiga antelopes can be seen advancing across the dusty Eurasian plains. In late autumn they begin the long trek southward again. And in December they mate, and

Small Animals

No other grassland vertebrates are more prolific —and therefore more available as a food supply for predators—than the rodents and the rodent-like rabbits. They abound in dry grassland all over the world. Africa has its jerboas and gerbils, America has its kangaroo rats and pocket mice, Europe has its gerbils, hamsters, and suchlike, and rabbits and hares abound almost everywhere. In spite of their many enemies, they survive and multiply because they are so splendidly fitted for grassland living. Some rodents have evolved a mainly bipedal movement—that is, they hop rather than run on four feet. Similarly, bipedal animals are found among the native *marsupial* fauna (animals that carry their young in pouches on their abdomen) of Australia— which seems to suggest that hopping is a more efficient means of getting around the sparse grasslands than running. Wherever they live, too, the dry-grassland rodents are rather pale in color—an adaptation to the environment in which they live, because their coloring not only helps to conceal them from predators, but also serves as a heat reflector. They feed mostly on such generally available grassland foods as weeds, seeds, roots, and tubers. And a number of them accumulate underground stores of food material, such as hay, to tide them over unfavorable seasons.

Another useful adaptation is the ability to go for long periods without drinking water. Some species, as in the case of the large herbivores that we looked at in an earlier chapter, are able to get all their water requirements from the seeds and other plant materials that they eat. Most rodents are nocturnal, and this enables them to hide from daytime predators and to avoid the heat of the day by remaining in their burrows. The daytime visitor to a grassland habitat may think that small mammals are very scarce, but a drive through the area at nighttime, when their eyes glow in the headlights, shows that they are present in considerable numbers.

Some parts of the Eurasian steppes are a good deal drier than others, and the small animals of these drier types of steppeland are rather different from those that live where the vegetation is thicker and forms a continuous cover. Small mammals of the very dry steppes include the midday gerbil, the tamarisk gerbil, the northern three-toed jerboa, Everman's hamster, and the long-eared hedgehog (an insect-eater, not a herbivore), most of which are able to live for exceptionally long periods without drinking water. Among the several kinds of predatory animal that hunt them are the Corsac fox (which changes its color from a summertime reddish yellow to a winter gray), the wolf (which still survives in a few places), the steppe polecat, and the marbled polecat. Birds of prey are quite scarce in the drier areas of the Eurasian steppes, but to the north, where the vegetation becomes denser, the population of small mammals increases enormously, and there is a corresponding increase in the number of predatory birds. One of the most characteristic species here is the tawny eagle, an unusual species of eagle in that it builds its nest on the ground.

In the thicker grasses of the wetter type of steppe we find—in addition to several species of jerboa and a variety of shrews and mice—the very interesting common hamster, which, though a native chiefly of western Asia, appears to be extending its breeding grounds westward into the Hungarian puszta and the cultivated plains of central Europe. The common hamster is a little smaller than a guinea pig, and has a short, barely visible tail. The hamster is conspicuous for its habit of hoarding uncommonly large quantities of food in its burrow. It picks up many different kinds of vegetable material, filling the large pouches inside its cheeks to carry the stuff back to its nest. In cultivated land it hoards grain, wheat, pieces of turnip, potatoes, beans, peas, carrots, cabbage, and fruit. In uncultivated land it takes what it can get, even including (not uncommonly among many primarily herbivorous rodents) a certain amount of animal food. In the case of the hamster, the animal food includes perhaps shrews, and the young of rats, mice, and birds, as well as reptiles, frogs, and worms.

A single acre of grassland may be the habitat of many hundreds of rodents. This close-up photograph of a field vole (or meadow mouse) clearly illustrates their constant preoccupation: food.

The stored food enables it to survive the long winter months, when it hibernates. Although it sleeps during most of the winter, with a body temperature down to only 43°F from a normal 110°F, it wakes from time to time in order to have a nourishing snack. In preparation, it sometimes hoards as much as 25 pounds of food—which seems a great deal for an animal whose maximum weight is only about 14 ounces!

The steppelands on the clay soils of northwestern Asia and northeastern Europe provide a richer environment for small animals to live in than do the steppes on sandy soils. Because clay

Left: young American cottontail rabbits. Their instinctive habit of remaining motionless while mother is away gives the slower-moving youngsters some slight protection against their natural enemies—such as the crouching red fox shown below.

has more nutrients, it provides a richer plant growth and the ground is firmer for burrowing. Here the most common mammal is a small ground squirrel called the *suslik*, represented by two species, the yellow suslik and the pygmy suslik. Both of these hibernate underground for as much as nine months of the year in order to survive the dry falls and the icy winters. They must therefore breed during the short spring and summer season, during which time they must also build up enough fat to last the long winter.

When susliks wake toward the end of March or the beginning of April from their nine-months-long sleep, mating takes place, and the young are born 25 to 28 days later. After another month or so, they all leave their underground burrows and become very active food-gatherers. During this time they are hunted by one of the susliks' most dangerous enemies, the black kite. A widely

distributed bird, the black kite will eat almost any kind of animal food, including carrion, insects, fish, and offal, as well as rodents. It seems to be especially adept at picking off unwary susliks as it flies low and silently over the land.

By the end of June, when the vegetation begins to wither and lose its food value, the susliks go underground again for their long nap. At this period the suslik weighs 17 ounces or so. When it wakes in the spring nearly nine months later, its weight has fallen to only about four ounces. In some places, where the vegetation is particularly rich and the climatic conditions less severe, susliks hibernate for shorter periods, lose less weight, and are active on the surface for a larger part of the summer season.

Where susliks are numerous, their energetic burrowing is an important factor in modifying the surface of the grassy steppes. They break up the soil very easily and it has been calculated that one individual may turn up about 95 cubic feet of soil every year. About 200 holes, dug by a single suslik, have been counted in one acre of land. For some reason, these little rodents do not thrive in well-managed grasslands—which is just as well, because they might become pests. Various species can be found in rough pastures, derelict ground, roadside verges, and railroad embankments in parts of America and western Europe, as well as in the Eurasian steppelands.

It is easy to recognize a grassy area where great numbers of rodents have been living. Wherever it is—in uplands or lowlands, in Arctic regions or temperate climates—it has a derelict appearance; large areas of grass appear dead, and the turf can be rolled back quite easily with the foot. If you examine the ground closely, you immediately notice enormous numbers of burrows and tunnels: in fact, the grass is honeycombed with them. It is at this high-population-density stage that predators begin to collect. Foxes, stoats, weasels, cats, owls, hawks—all will have rich pickings for a short time, or even for a whole season, during which they too may rear several broods. But when the predators' food supply dwindles, they must emigrate or starve.

A few rodents are generally able to survive the crash, and they begin to breed again as the grassland recovers and new tender shoots appear. At first, the females are likely to produce only two litters in a season, and so the population grows slowly, but gradually the pace increases.

71

Young females from the first of the season's litters may have families of their own before the summer ends; in the second year after the crash the production machine goes into top gear, with almost continuous breeding. During this highly fertile period, many females reach sexual maturity at the age of three weeks, and can become pregnant again while still suckling their young.

Perhaps the best-known grassland animal almost everywhere—technically not a rodent at all, but very much like a rodent—is associated in the minds of most people with extremely swift breeding: the rabbit. Most people do not dis-

tinguish between true rabbits and other members of the vast family of hares. The distinction is worth making, however. There are many species of hare that are native to both North America and Eurasia. The jackrabbits of America's western plains, for instance, are technically not true rabbits but hares. The true rabbits are native to Europe only, although they have been introduced into other continents, as we shall see. They are burrowing creatures that live together in colonies and are consequently able to build up enormous populations. Because of their numbers and insatiable appetite for vegetation, they become a very serious pest to

agriculture. Hares can become a nuisance, too; the jackrabbit is hardly popular among American farmers. But they do not form warrens and are not burrow breeders. So although they are often numerous, they are less of a menace to crops than are the European rabbits.

The original home of the rabbit seems to have been the Iberian peninsula and the islands of the western Mediterranean. At an early stage in human history, however, rabbits began to take up residence in other places, and they were brought across the channel to the British Isles as long ago as the 12th century. Since then the true rabbit has spread or been introduced into many parts of the world, including North and South America, Australia, and New Zealand. It seems to be able to flourish anywhere, for its original habitat was open grassland of a semi-desert nature, quite different from the wide variety of situations to which it has since become adapted.

During the period of world exploration by the Europeans in the 15th through 17th centuries, explorers took the rabbit with them in order to provide a ready supply of meat. In some of the places where it now found a new home, it eventually achieved some sort of balance with its environment, possibly because its numbers were kept in check by numerous local carnivores. In other places, however, it has been responsible for considerable destruction of plants.

One of the most dramatic events in the history of the rabbit, and the beginning of perhaps the foremost "success" story for any animal transported to a new environment, was its introduction into Australia. Twenty-four wild rabbits were imported from England in 1859, and these few multiplied to the millions that soon colonized some two thirds of this vast continent, becoming adapted to all kinds of ecological conditions, including the semidesert. This pattern was later repeated, almost as dramatically, in New Zealand and in South America.

The success of the rabbit in colonizing so many different areas, in spite of predation by man and wild animals, is undoubtedly due to its remarkable reproductive capacity. The female is able to breed very early and very fast; within three weeks of being born, the young are weaned and beginning to look after themselves; and a mother can become pregnant again within a few hours of giving birth. In mild climates, breeding can take place at almost any time of the year, although the most favored months are January through June. Litters vary according to the conditions of grazing, but about three to seven young are produced every time.

In fact, people have always been so much impressed by the ability of rabbits to multiply that some curious theories used to be accepted as fact by even the fairly well informed. Some thought that both male and female rabbits could bear young. In the middle of the 19th century, a number of letters appeared in a British nature magazine from people who seriously believed that female rabbits could simultaneously carry two litters of different ages. Fortunately for the earth's vegetation, even the most fertile rabbits cannot work such wonders. Indeed, there are a great many factors that militate against fantastic breeding rate. Some young do not even survive to birth, but are reabsorbed as embryos by the females, either because of shortage of food or for some other environmental factor. In addition, young rabbits are a favorite food for large numbers of predators, including hawks, eagles, weasels, stoats, and polecats.

But where food is plentiful and predators are not too numerous, the rabbits have often become seemingly indestructible pests. Because they are mainly grassland feeders, they are important competitors on rangeland where

Below left: the black-tailed jackrabbit (which is in fact a species of hare) of western North America has enormous ears, a longish drooping tail, and a colossal appetite. Damage of the kind pictured below, right, has not endeared the members of the vast hare family to the farmers of the world. Hares feed on the bark of trees and on many other kinds of plant food.

Above: the European weasel is a common predator of grassland animals. Mice, rats, moles, frogs, and rabbits—particularly the young—are all eaten as prey by this slim hunter.

flocks of sheep are kept. It has been estimated that some seven to 10 rabbits will eat as much as one sheep. Thus, when, back in the 1940s, New Zealand exported nearly 18 million rabbit skins (for use as fur or felting), this equaled about 2 million sheep in terms of the amount of vegetation needed to rear them! Today New Zealand no longer exports rabbits; sheep are a far more valuable product. In spite of the fact that wild rabbits are edible and have other commercial uses, many governments take strict control measures or even try to exterminate them.

Such methods of control as traps, snares, shooting, gassing, and poisoning have all proved either to be inadequate or to have harmful side effects: gases and poisons, for instance, may endanger the lives of other creatures (including human beings) for whom they are not intended. A breakthrough in rabbit control came a few years ago as a result of earlier experiments with a natural virus that attacks Brazilian cottontail rabbits (actually hares, not true rabbits of the European type), causing tumorous swellings and loss of energy. The South American animals survive the viral attacks pretty well, but it was discovered that the rabbit populations of Europe and Australia were extremely susceptible to the disease—now known as *myxomatosis*—and that nearly all infected rabbits died. Myxomatosis is spread from rabbit to rabbit by either mosquitoes or fleas, which transmit the virus through their bite. The effects of an artificially induced epidemic of the disease were spectacular. When the rabbit population of Australia was infected, back in 1950–57, something like 99 out of every 100 rabbits soon died. The removal of this tremendous grazing pressure on the continent's grassland areas had an immediate dramatic effect. Desertlike regions turned green, and agricultural production increased at a remarkable rate. By 1952 myxomatosis had reached France, and then a year later spread to England —nobody is quite sure whether by accident or by design—and again with striking results. In parts of England where rabbits had been abundant, the change within two to three years from wasteland with more bare ground than vegetation to greensward was an ecological event without precedent. Not only did agricultural production increase, but also rare plants that had not been seen in flower for many years suddenly blossomed. In particular, the chalk grassland of southern England, once renowned for its many species of

Above: a short-eared owl with its kill. Above right: small herbivores such as the field vole live in great numbers wherever there is cover. The animals that prey on them, such as the owl, are less numerous, because it takes many voles to feed one predator.

attractive orchids, showed a remarkable recovery; for the first two or three years after the near-disappearance of the rabbit, it was one of the most attractive grassland areas anywhere in the country. Later on, as the ungrazed vegetation grew taller and thicker, the more vigorous species dominated, and the orchids, and many other colorful plants, declined in number.

In France—especially in areas where the rabbit density was six or more to the acre—the vegetational landscape changed even more drastically. Before myxomatosis, regeneration of young trees in the forests had been rare, and intensive grazing had maintained green lawns in once-wooded spots. Almost immediately afterward, crowds of seedling oaks and beeches appeared in places where they had not been seen

for years. In the limestone country of Bouches-du-Rhône, thyme and rosemary grew again on the hillsides, and natural seedlings of the Aleppo pine also appeared. In the Camargue there was a sudden regeneration of junipers, and more junipers, lichens, and other plants began to cover the bare sandy soils of chalky wastelands in other parts of France.

But a steep drop in the number of rabbits inevitably affects other wildlife, particularly the predatory animals that depend on the rabbit for food. The stoat (or brown ermine), for example, immediately declined in numbers over a wide area of the Continent after the great myxomatosis epidemic. Its smaller relative, the weasel, declined less dramatically only because it could replace its diet of young rabbits by other small

mammals such as voles and mice. Fortunately for the weasels, the growth of vegetation favored the spread of voles, and this source of food increased as the rabbit declined. There is some evidence, too, that the rabbit's old enemy, the fox, went hungry in France and Britain and was forced to seek out alternative foods, such as mice and voles. Buzzards, tawny owls, and other rabbit-hungry birds, bred less successfully than before in areas to which myxomatosis had penetrated.

Today the very high mortality recorded in the early years of the Australian and European myxomatosis epidemic has declined. There is no doubt that more and more rabbits have developed an immunity to the disease. Nevertheless, it is still widespread and partially effective. So the sort of balance now being maintained will perhaps endure, and the wild rabbit will be no worse a pest in other parts of the world than the jackrabbit now is in America.

In Russia the small rodent that does most damage to crops is the field vole. In the open steppe country of European and Asiatic Russia, swarms of voles may infest hundreds of thousands, or even millions, of acres. In 1932, for instance, some 25 million acres appear to have been affected by a plague of these rodents. Another famous outbreak occurred in California in 1926, when voles and house mice invaded 11,000 acres of a dried-up lake that had been planted with corn and barley. In a short time the rodents virtually destroyed the crops and had to move out in search of other food. It is said that along 17 miles of highway observers counted a dead rodent almost every yard, and that at the height of the plague the mice and voles reached 80,000 to the acre (which works out at 17 to the square yard)!

Even in normal times, grassland rodent populations are enormous. The vast difference in numbers between the lone eagle soaring over

Above: the abandoned burrows of North American prairie dogs are often used by rattlesnakes as breeding places.

Right: from its vantage point on a stem of wheat, a European harvest mouse keeps a sharp lookout for predators.

several thousand acres and the hundreds of voles that may live on a single acre of grassland serve as a good example of what ecologists call the "pyramid of numbers" among living creatures. This is a characteristic feature of almost all ecosystems: the largest populations are at the bottom of food chains, the smallest at the top. Thus, because small herbivorous animals live in a continuous cover of green vegetation, they are able to make the most of the tremendous food supply and to build up very high numbers; but at each successive level of the pyramid there are fewer predators, because there are fewer creatures for them to prey upon. For this reason, there must always be fewer carnivores than herbivores in a given habitat.

As you might expect, the species of grassland rodents differ from one continent to another, but their functions in the ecosystem are very similar. For example, in temperate North American grassland regions the niche of the larger European rodents is occupied by ground squirrels, prairie dogs, rats, and jackrabbits. South American rodents include the very big Patagonian cavy, which we have discussed in a preceding chapter; the common cavy, which is a close relative of the guinea pig; the viscacha; and the chinchilla, which, when reared in fur farms, provides expensive fur coats for American and European ladies of fashion. On the other side of the world, in Australia, there is the native wombat, and, of course, the introduced European rabbit and rodent-sized (and rodentlike) marsupials. And the field voles of the eastern European steppes share their habitat with still another group of rodent species, the hamsters.

Burrowing rodents in most major grassland areas also create habitats for other animals, many of which make use of their excavations. Even birds sometimes move into empty burrows. One example is the pygmy owl that uses the hole dug by the viscacha in South America. Because of the scarcity of trees and other natural shelters, such sharing of underground quarters is a quite common feature of grassland communities. In the American plains, rattlesnakes and burrowing owls are often found breeding in prairie-dog "towns." Some observers believe that these three very dissimilar creatures live together harmoniously. If so, there must be at least an occasional sour note, because we know that owls kill young prairie dogs, and rattlesnakes eat both young prairie dogs and owls' eggs.

The prairie dog probably acquired its name because of its barking call, although it is related to ground squirrels such as the marmots (rabbit-sized grazers of Alpine meadows), and not to dogs. Prairie dogs are large, plump rodents, with

flattened heads and short legs, and are a familiar sight on the American prairie. They have developed a high level of social organization, with up to several thousand individuals living in "towns" and "governed" by a hierarchy of dominant males. The several species now living in the grasslands of North America used to be extremely abundant. As cattlemen moved into the prairies during the 19th century, they regarded the enormous colonies of prairie dogs as potential competitors for pasture, and destroyed vast numbers by poisoning, hunting, and shooting. Today, although only one species seems to be threatened with extinction, prairie dogs are much less in evidence than they were.

Each group, or family, in a prairie-dog colony has its own small territory to live in and to guard, and it depends for its grass diet on the resources of this limited area—perhaps only a few yards' radius from the entrance of the burrow. The prairie dogs are great diggers; they construct complex mazes of passages, with side chambers and numerous exits and entrances, these apparently providing them with an alternative avenue of escape from possible enemies. During the course of thousands of years, these digging activities have constituted a sort of deep-plowing of the wide expanse of the prairies. In addition to digging under the surface, these busy little animals build *on* the surface, for they construct moulds around the burrow entrances. The rim of each such mound may be two feet higher than the surrounding land, and the whole elevation measures about four feet in diameter.

The purpose of these strange structures is probably to protect the burrows from flooding in wet weather. The depressions between the mounds tend to be a good deal wetter than the

Predator and prey. Left: a prairie dog keeping sentry at the entrance to its burrow. These plump little grass-eating rodents, a species of ground squirrel, live in large colonies excavating vast networks of underground tunnels. They are prolific breeders, but their numbers are kept in check by predators, such as this prairie falcon (right), feeding a ground squirrel to its nestlings.

mounds themselves, and the grass grows more luxuriantly in these places. In earlier times, intensive grazing by the prairie dogs also kept scrub growth of all types out of the plains. But as an aftermath of the ranchers' systematic destruction of the "towns," other plants—such as sagebrush, and in places even cactus—were able to invade.

The great numbers of prairie dogs were an abundant source of food for a large group of predators. One of the most efficient of these was— and still is—the prairie falcon, which is a specialist in taking the prairie dog unawares and swooping down on it as it grazes the grassland near its burrow. The American badger attacks

the tasty little rodent from the opposite direction A competent burrower, it easily digs out the prairie-dog families.

Another very interesting predator of the prairie dog is the black-footed ferret, a large weasel now almost on the verge of extinction. This animal was first described by the great American naturalists John Audubon and John Bachman when they saw a specimen from Nebraska in 1849. Very few specimens have been seen by naturalists since then. It is a beautifully marked animal, which seems to have evolved quite naturally along with the prairie dogs, and it lives almost exclusively with, and on, them. One of the few facts we know about it is that it

used to be distributed across the North American prairies to the east of the Rocky Mountains, extending from Alberta in Canada through Montana southward to central New Mexico. As far as we can tell, it has ceased to exist in all but a very few localities in South Dakota, Montana, Nebraska and Colorado. Its present range is, in fact, almost identical with that of the prairie dog, and it is thought to depend on the burrows of its prey for shelter and for rearing its young, as well as for food. The reason for its extreme rarity has never been fully understood.

We have been dealing mainly with small animals and some birds of the cold or temperate regions of the earth. Now let us turn once again, as in earlier chapters, to that most prolific and varied of continents, Africa.

The savannas of northern Africa, from Senegal to the western Sudan, are drained by a few great rivers, among them the Senegal, the Niger, and the Volta. The seasonal rains bring a rise in the water level during April and May, with a corresponding fall during the winter months (December through March). In this winter dry season the flow is usually reduced to a few shallow streams, which connect huge fish-filled pools; everywhere else, enormous banks of yellow sand that look rather like small deserts are exposed. When the rains come, the water level may rise as much as 20 or 30 feet and cover all the sandbanks, so that the rivers spill out of their channels over vast expanses of flat land known as floodplains. These floodplains, occurring along the banks of all West African rivers, enable a distinct type of animal community to live in what is essentially savanna grassland.

Some of the floodplains are covered by a special sort of forest, but in other areas we find a typical savanna landscape of very tall, stiff

tive bird of the sandbanks is the gray pratincole, which lays its eggs in depressions in the sand. While the parent bird incubates the eggs, it takes on a beautifully cryptic coloring, which blends so well with the surroundings that enemies need keen eyes to see it. There are other species of pratincole, too.

Some of the most beautiful birds found in the river valleys are the bee eaters. Some species of bee eater—all of which eat other insects as well as bees—breed in holes that they excavate in

grass, with a scattering of small trees. The flood-plain forests provide shelter for such large animals as buffaloes, bushbucks, and red duikers, and in the grass swamp there are water bucks and kobs (both of which, like the bushbucks and duikers, are kinds of antelope). The bird life along the rivers is extremely rich, especially during the dry season, when many species are able to breed in and on the high sandbanks.

Egyptian plovers, spur-winged and Senegal wattle plovers, and tiny white-fronted sand plovers are just a few of the great variety of birds that have become adapted to life in the river valleys of the savannas. There are also skim-mers and terns—particularly white-winged black terns, gull-billed terns, and little terns. Most of the terns are migrants, but the little terns breed right on the sandbanks in the dry season. Then in the swampland there are storks, ibises, jacanas, ducks, and geese. An especially attrac-

Left: seasonal flooding of the Niger River has a considerable effect on the surrounding wildlife. Right: white-winged black terns, which have adapted to this inland freshwater habitat.

vertical banks, and they live in colonies that often consist of thousands of pairs of birds. Among these are the carmine bee eater and the red-throated bee eater, whose names give an idea of their brilliant coloration. The effect of so many brightly colored birds flying in and out of the nest holes is a remarkable one. During the migration period, they are joined by the single European species of this group of lovely birds. The European species, however, breeds in Europe and merely overwinters in Africa. Another species, the rosy bee eater, nests in a different habitat: the slopes of the low sandbanks, where large colonies excavate nesting holes rather like a rabbit warren.

The erratic rainfall in most African grasslands

influences the behavior and breeding habits of birds, just as it does of the larger herbivores. All these animals must be either nomadic, searching out food where it occurs, or able to withstand prolonged periods of drought. Among the birds, the onset of the rainy season is a signal for tremendous breeding activity. The sudden flush of greenery and flowers and the bursting into leaf of the thorn bushes have an especially immediate effect on the weaver birds, whose nests festoon the branches of acacia trees. During the short rainy period, when food is abundant, the parent birds can be seen working very energetically to rear their broods.

The bishop bird is also a widespread species in savanna country. In the dry season it looks rather like a small, dull sparrow; but when the rains begin, it acquires a glamorous breeding plumage. The male of the orange bishop bird is a brilliant orange-red, with a black crown and belly and brown wings. Breeding usually takes place in the long grass, and each male defends a territory into which he entices a female, who lays her eggs in a small nest low in the grass.

Other common savanna birds include the glossy starlings, rollers, hoopoes, hornbills, and doves and small pigeons of many different species. In much drier grassland—which abounds in Africa, of course—we find guinea fowls, francolins, and bustards. With their strong, well-developed legs, they are active runners and can therefore thrive in the open savanna country. They are more numerous in Africa than anywhere else in the world.

Also numerous are birds of prey. They abound almost everywhere in Africa, and the dry savannas are no exception. There we find the pygmy falcon and the gigantic nine-foot-wingspan lappet-faced vulture. In addition to such resident birds, tremendous numbers of migrants travel down to the savannas through the Nile valley and along the line of the Red Sea Hills, where, in the November and December rains, they are likely to find abundant food. There are hawks, also, and eagles, and other vultures, which feed upon all forms of life from live insects to the dead bodies of large animals.

Very often there is a marked specialization in the food taken by these predators. Vultures, of course, normally eat carrion. Verreaux's eagle eats the rock hyrax; lanner falcons are primarily hunters of other birds; the chanting goshawk feeds mainly on lizards. On the other hand, when

termites are dispersing from their nests, even the larger birds of prey—vultures and eagles, for instance—immediately collect around the termite mounds, to seize the insects before they can take wing. Swarming of the termites usually occurs just after the first showers of rain; and for a short period not only the big predators but hawks and falcons, as well as swallows, rollers, bee eaters, and other birds, are provided with an excellent food supply.

A further source of bird food is the large number of annual grasses and plants that survive the dry season as seeds. These attract such seed-eating birds as game birds, weaver birds, doves,

bustards, larks, and pipits, all of which are sometimes very numerous in Africa's semiarid regions. One species of the weaver birds, in fact, almost rivals the locusts as a pest. In the dry season, this species may assemble in flocks of several millions, which migrate from place to place and may destroy far more grain on farmland by damaging it than by eating it up. They have done increasing damage in recent years, partly because of the spread of agriculture, which provides a uniquely reliable dry-season food supply. They roost together in their huge swarms in reed beds or clumps of bushes, which they often smash by sheer weight of numbers.

Carmine bee eaters, a few of a vast colony that inhabits a sandbank near Botswana's Okovango Marshes. Bee eaters specialize in catching many other kinds of flying insects, as well as bees.

They also nest in colonies of millions of pairs covering areas of from 50 to 500 acres. The onset of a wet season stimulates them to breed, but they cannot build nests unless the rains have been plentiful enough to produce a good supply of leafy grass. If this is not available, breeding does not take place.

The African dry savannas are also a habitat for the largest of all living birds, the ostrich. A full-grown male ostrich stands about seven feet tall

The strong legs of the vulturine guinea fowls are well adapted for running through their East African savanna homeland.

Contrary to popular belief, ostriches do not bury their heads in the sand. When nesting, they lie flat on the ground at the approach of danger. This is an effective method of concealment, and the female is completely inconspicuous when she is incubating her eggs. The more strikingly colored male helps out with the incubation, but he is less in need of visual camouflage because he generally sits on the eggs only at night. Several females are likely to lay eggs in the same nest, which may hold as many as 20 or 30 eggs at once. But only one bird at a time incubates, and so it is not unusual for a sitting ostrich to be surrounded by a number of eggs that it is unable to cover. Some of the eggs may therefore be wasted. Occasionally, however, the female will remove some of the eggs from underneath her body and place them around the nest in small depressions, and by alternating these with the ones under her, help to ensure simultaneous hatching. The young appear after a month or so of incubation and can run as soon as they are dry, but they stay close to the parents for some time before striking off on their own.

Considering the large number of potential predators that live in the same area as the breeding ostrich, it is surprising that eggs are ever hatched. There is no doubt that hyenas eat a great number of ostrich eggs, and lions may actually use them as playthings, if they can manage to drive off the adult birds. We also know that some vultures have learned how to break open an ostrich egg by dropping a stone onto it. In spite of all such dangers, however, the ostrich has managed to survive, although in recent years human predation has reduced the numbers of these fascinating creatures.

Africa is used as a winter refuge by huge numbers of birds from Europe, Asia Minor, and Siberia—swallows, wheatears, spoonbills, white storks, kestrels, black kites, short-eared and scops owls, and many others. One regular migrant is the very attractive demoiselle crane, a well-known bird of the steppes and damper grassy valleys. Of an ashy bluish gray color, with a black head and a tuft of white feathers behind the eyes, it lives on insects, snails, lizards, and snakes, and nests in open grassland. These cranes arrive at their nesting place in the Crimea and other parts of eastern Europe and northern Asia in March. They stay there until some time in September, when they fly back to northeastern Africa for the winter.

and is black with white wings and tail. Females are grayish in color. All of them have bare-skinned, pinkish necks and thighs. The young birds are speckled and striped—a coloring that helps to conceal them when they are lying in the grass. Ostriches travel in small parties and are usually very shy and difficult to approach. They cannot fly, but are capable of running at a speed of 45 miles an hour, and this enables them to out-distance most of their potential predators.

Although concentrated largely in Africa, larks are familiar—if not nearly ubiquitous—throughout the world's open grasslands. The horned lark, or shore lark, is particularly remarkable for its widespread distribution. You can see horned larks high in the barren mountain areas of Alaska and northern Europe. You can find them wintering along the shorelines of the British coasts, where they feed on seeds of salt-marsh and sand-dune plants. You can spot them in the dry, hot steppes of southern Europe and eastward to Siberia. And they also turn up far off in the northern Andes of South America and in the Atlas Mountains of northern Africa. There are many other species of lark found throughout the transitional zones from dry to grass-covered steppeland—the short-toed and calandra larks, the lesser short-toed lark, the black lark, and so on. Other birds that have become adapted to dry steppes and semidesert regions, where they live on seeds and the young shoots of plants, include Pallas's sand grouse and the blackbellied sand grouse, both of which are related to the dove family. Pallas's sand grouse is unusual in that it occasionally makes enormous migrations, far out of its normal range. Scientists have not been able to discover the reason for these long trips.

Of all the birds mentioned so far, however, perhaps the most interesting are the bustards. This group of birds is nearly worldwide in distribution, being found not only in the dry grasslands of Africa but once also throughout the grassy plains of Europe and Asia, and again in the open country of Australia, though not in either North or South America. There are several species of very large bustards. A really big male bustard easily qualifies as heavyweight champion among the world's flying birds. (The ostrich remember, does not fly.) One species of these very large birds, the great bustard, used to abound throughout the Eurasian steppes, but their numbers have declined in recent years because of such human activities as hunting and appropriation of the great bustard's habitat for agricultural and other uses. One of its disadvantages, from the standpoint of survival of the species, is its size and weight (normally up to 30 pounds), which make it a coveted prize for hunters. Nevertheless, it is still found here and there in central and western Europe as well as in Africa and Asia.

The little bustard, a very much smaller game bird, also nests in grassland, and remains rather

Weaverbirds' nests adorn acacia trees during the rainy season; in dry weather these birds become seed-hunting nomads.

more widely distributed throughout central Europe and Asia. The houbara bustard breeds in southeastern Europe, Asia Minor, and southwest Asia, and is really more a bird of the desert or semidesert than of steppe grassland. Until recently, for instance, thousands of houbaras lived in the semidesert regions of Jordan, but today they have become extremely rare there because of hunting and the destruction of the nest sites. They are still to be found in northern

Among the many birds that migrate to African grassland areas for the cool winter months is the lovely demoiselle crane (above). It spends the spring and summer in Eurasia, where it breeds, then flies to India and northern Africa in September. Unlike the demoiselle crane, however, some birds thrive in any climate. Horned — or shore — larks (above, right) can be found simultaneously in the hot steppes of southern Europe, in the frigid mountain peaks of Alaska, and in northern Africa. But the yellow-billed hornbill (left) avoids cold climates and is chiefly at home in the warm thornbush-scattered African savanna.

Africa, however. Bustards in general are particularly well represented in the African savanna; there are some 11 known species, ranging in size from the great kori bustard, the male of which can stand as much as five feet high, to the one-foot-high little brown bustard.

The courtship display of the males of the larger species of bustards is a remarkable sight. The male great bustard—certainly an early bird, for he does his courting only in the early morning—twists his wings to show the white underside to the female, inflates the air pouches in his neck, and fluffs out his attractive breast feathers, so that he appears to swell and grow as you watch him. Unfortunately, few people have had a chance to watch him, and his display has seldom been photographed, because the birds are extremely shy and difficult to approach.

The Australian bustard, which lives only in

that continent and New Guinea, is second in size to the African kori. An outstandingly large Australian male bustard can stand 3 to 4 feet tall, with a wingspan of over 7 feet, and may weigh more than 30 pounds. This is not quite so heavy as the recorded weight of one enormous great bustard: 37 pounds. Typical weights, of course, are much less. The average male Australian bustard weighs no more than 15 to 18 pounds, and the females are about a third smaller.

The male's courtship display is even more resplendent than that of the great bustard. In the early morning or late evening, perched on a small raised mound, he inflates his breast sac so that the whitish feathers of the underparts reach down to the ground, creating a vision of dazzling white that can be seen from a considerable distance. At the same time, he throws his head backwards, fans his tail forward, and utters

Bustards are well adapted for running in their grassland habitat, having sturdy legs and three front toes on their feet. Depending on the species, the males have a variety of adornments—collars, crests, ruffs, inflatable pouches—for display during the mating season. Far left is the African male great kori bustard and, near left, a rare picture of the great kori bustard with raised neck feathers in a dawn courtship display.

Below: the venomous European viper is recognizable by the dark zigzag line down its back. This grassland and heathland predator is widely distributed in Europe and parts of Asia.

Above: the North American garter snake. There are many species of garter snake, whose habitats range from open countryside to woodland and the banks of streams.

sounds described by some who have heard them as resembling a roar of a lion.

As with related species in Africa and Eurasia, the Australian bustard adjusts its breeding cycle to the short rainy season of the dry grassland—where the rainfall averages less than 15 inches a year. Often it rains only sporadically. The first rains bring new growth of vegetation, and that means a supply of food and shelter for the bustard. Therefore it is important for breeding and the rains to be synchronized. The Australian bustard was once widely distributed throughout the dry central part of the continent, but the European settlers found it an excellent bird for the pot—they even called it "turkey"—and so its numbers declined rapidly. Then, in the middle of the 19th century the European red fox was introduced into Australia and soon became a well-established predator of the bustard. Today it is extinct over very large areas, and legislation to protect it has not proved very effective in safeguarding the populations that still survive.

We should perhaps mention briefly the reptile and amphibian life to be found in the grassland ecosystems, although on the whole the reptile fauna of the world's grasslands, though numerous, is not particularly rich in species.

Unlike the forest-dwelling or the desert snakes, many of the temperate-zone snakes are difficult to classify according to a specific habitat—the European viper, or adder, for instance, generally prefers dry heathlands and moorland, but has also been found in marshes. In Scandinavia, its range extends well into the Arctic Circle. It preys on rodents, birds, lizards, amphibians, earthworms, and slugs. Commonest of the snakes in North America is the garter snake, which is found in a wide variety of habitats from open grassland to woodland as well as on the banks of streams and lakes. Its diet usually consists of earthworms, but the slender, three-foot-long snake will tackle a number of other small creatures that it can cope with. The grass snake, which has probably the widest distribution of all snakes, is found in places as far apart as North Africa, central Asia, southern Europe, England and Wales, and Scandinavia. It is not, as its name suggests, exclusively a grassland dweller, for it is also a good swimmer, and is frequently referred to as a water snake. It preys mainly on mice, fish, frogs, and newts, and like all temperate-zone snakes, it hibernates from fall to spring, usually in burrows, in manure, or under straw. Other snakes with a wide range of habitats are the king snakes, some 30 species of which are found throughout the United States. They devour large quantities of other snakes, including venomous rattlesnakes.

Lizards, too, are plentiful in the temperate zone, and, like the snakes, they have become adapted to a wide variety of habitats. The European green lizard, which grows to a length of 16 inches, prefers grassy plains but is also found in hedges and at the edges of woods. It is just one of the 150 species of lacertids, which are to be found throughout Europe, Africa, and Asia. A common lizard with a wide distribution in the United States is the race runner, which is also found in Central America and southward as far as Argentina. And a close relative, the sixlined race runner, or fieldstreak, hunts insects in the open, well-drained areas of southeastern and midwestern United States.

In the dry plains and deserts of north, central, and western Africa, live the spiny-tailed agamid lizards. These fierce-looking but really harmless creatures, with their tail ringed with plates of large, hard, pointed scales, feed on grass, fruit, flowers, and leaves. The toad-headed agamid lizards of the steppes and deserts of central Asia have a similar diet, but supplemented by insects. Another inhabitant of steppeland and desert is the African savanna monitor, which measures

from 30 inches to six feet long; it eats eggs, insects, birds, and small mammals.

Not surprisingly, amphibians are far from common on the world's grasslands. The thin-skinned frogs spend most of their lives in or around water to avoid drying out. One family of frogs is terrestrial, however. They are known as creeping frogs. Unlike most frogs and toads, which have longer back legs than forelegs, the creepers (found only in South and Central America) have unusually long forelegs, for "creeping" along the ground rather than for leaping and swimming.

Toads are generally terrestrial animals, their

thick skins allowing them to remain away from water once they have passed the larval stage, returning only to breed. The most widespread of the toads, the common or true toad, with its thick, dry, warty, skin, is typical of the toad family as a whole. They are found throughout Europe, Asia, and northwest Africa in gardens, fields, and plains wherever they can shelter from the sun's rays. There they wait patiently for a wide variety of small grassland animals and insects that form their diet, such as flies, spiders, snails, slugs, frogs, and worms.

A common toad of grasslands in the eastern United States is the greenish brown American toad, whereas farther south in the scrublands and savanna of coastal South America lives the small Mexican burrowing toad. On the pampas of South America is the large, poisonous escuerzo toad, a highly camouflaged predator of other toads, frogs, birds, and small mammals.

Thus reptile and amphibian life, too, are part of the diverse and—because largely made up of small animals—mainly hidden wildlife to be found on the world's grasslands.

The shy green lizard, common throughout Europe and Asia Minor is at home on the plains or in the woodland fringes.

Grassland Insects

When we speak of animal life, we are normally thinking about the large animals, mainly mammals and birds, but there are many thousands of other animals in grassland. Most of these are tiny creatures, and there are sometimes enormous numbers of them. The great majority are insects, but the phylum Arthropoda, to which the insects belong, also includes such interesting creatures as the millipedes, centipedes, mites, spiders, and crustaceans. And grasslands are also favorite habitats for terrestrial mollusks such as slugs and snails.

Some arthropods have very ancient pedigrees; when we examine fossil specimens millions of years old, we find that they are quite similar to present-day forms. Others have evolved more recently. No phylum of many-celled creatures is more durable or more widespread. Insects and other types of arthropod are found from the poles to the equator. They live under the snow, in hot springs, in salt lakes, along the sea coast, and within all kinds of living and dead matter. We can say with certainty that virtually every kind of flowering plant—and there are many thousands throughout the world—is used as food by one or more species of insect. In addition, a very large number of insects live as parasites, whether externally or internally, on the bodies of other animals (including other insects).

Many substances on earth are left severely alone by even the most ravenous of animals, but not by insects. There are, for instance, some insects that feed on corks in wine bottles, or on paint brushes; there are species whose larvae feed on carpets, eat stuffed natural-history specimens in museums, or even manage to make a meal out of an Egyptian mummy. Perhaps the most enterprising such creature is a small fly whose immature stages live in the natural pools of petroleum that collect around the oil wells of southern California. It is not surprising therefore, to find that the insect fauna of grasslands is exceedingly varied. But most of the grassland species are relatively small, inconspicuous

An orange-tip butterfly searches for nectar among delicately tinted forget-me-nots. Still found in the tropics, these butterflies are an increasingly rare sight in temperate-zone gardens.

Only the invisible microbes are more widespread and varied in feeding habits than the small invertebrate animals. Above, left: the red spots on the body of this marbled white butterfly are not part of its coloration; they are arachnids—parasitic mites. Above, right: a nearly white American tree cricket, one of many species, feeds on an evening primrose; like some other crickets, it will eat just about anything. Moths flourish nearly everywhere in the world, and are incredibly varied in coloration and food preference. This attractively marked caterpillar (left) is the larva of the burnet, one of the many thousand varieties of moth—and there are numerous different kinds of burnet!

creatures that you must search for energetically if you want to learn to know them.

On the other hand, there are some strikingly beautiful species that you cannot fail to notice: butterflies and moths, for instance. Grasshoppers and crickets belong to another group that you are sure to see or hear during a summer walk through a meadow. In the great plains of North America there are about 100 different species of grasshopper, some of which can do a vast amount of damage to crops. It seems probable that about half the species live on grasses, whereas the other half specialize on different types of broad-leaved plants that grow in grasslands. Thus, practically the entire vegetation could be gobbled up by grasshoppers alone if they were not kept under control. Biologists have estimated that when members of this insect group are really abundant—that is, about 30 to a square yard—they are capable of eating as much vegetation in a season as a buffalo would. Fortunately for farmers, this sort of situation seldom develops, because so many birds and small mammals eat the adults, the young stages, and the eggs. Still, in spite of the predators, the grasshopper population can maintain itself at more or less the same level from year to year as long as only one pair survives out of 200 eggs!

The most destructive member of the grasshopper family is, of course, the locust. Locusts thrive on every continent, and many areas have suffered from their depredations for thousands of years. In many parts of Africa, for instance, the appearance of a swarm is dreaded by local tribes because of the effectiveness with which they can devastate crops and pastures. Modern

97

research and efficient methods of control have substantially reduced the damage caused by this insect in most of the Western world. But a firsthand knowledge of its power to destroy crops on a vast scale is still retained in the memory of many agricultural communities.

Not only man is affected. Some of the larger mammals and birds may be forced to move away from the devastation following a locust invasion. And from time to time some smaller sedentary animals may well die of starvation because the locusts have taken all their food.

A large swarm of locusts probably contains 1000 million insects, which can, if unchecked, consume about 3000 tons of green food daily. Nowadays we can achieve a good measure of control by spraying insecticides from aircraft onto the flying swarms or onto the nonflying "hoppers" on the ground. Nevertheless, although a less terrible plague than it used to be, the locust is still a widespread, fairly common, and very hungry insect. One must bear in mind that the potential for rapid increase is still there, particularly in Africa and Asia, if we ever slacken our efforts to keep down its numbers. And a few voices *have* been raised against too stringent control. After all, the locusts do provide certain animals— particularly birds and some rodents—with a valuable food supply. It has been known since biblical times, for example, that the common stork consumes large numbers of locusts in

Below: South African brown locusts feeding. For centuries migrating plagues of locusts have been synonymous with famine, because they devour all green vegetation in their path. Right: an antilocust vehicle approaches an infested area in Ethiopia.

Above: a hover fly searches for nectar. Many species of hover fly are important as pollinators. Below: warm mammalian blood provides a meal for this tsetse fly of Africa. The encroachment of wildlife habitats by man and his cattle is held in check largely by the disease-transmitting tsetse fly. Insect numbers are kept down by a host of predators, such as the tiger beetle (right).

Africa. Some ornithologists have expressed concern that anti-locust operations might deprive this desirable bird of much-needed food.

Herbivorous insects, like other animals that feed on vegetation (which is a *primary producer*), are known as *primary consumers*. The predators that feed on the plant-eaters are termed *secondary consumers*. Many of these insect predators are very familiar to us; there are wasps, hornets, ants, ladybugs, dragonflies, robber flies, ant lions, ground beetles, tiger beetles, and very many more. Together with such larger predators as birds, shrews, and hedgehogs, they help to regulate the numbers of grass-feeders. Otherwise, populations of such insects as the grasshoppers and others capable of becoming pests would increase tremendously, and much of the earth's valuable grassland might become dry desert.

Among the many insects that are injurious to agricultural crops, especially cereals, there are some that are less widespread than the locusts but that may be particularly harmful in certain specific localities. Europe's farmers, for example, must constantly battle against such a creature—the frit fly. This small insect is one of the most serious spoilers of European crops of oats and wheat; and it is very hard to control, because it can produce several generations in one year. In a natural grassland habitat, predators and parasites act as checks to sudden increases in the number of frit flies, but there are not many predators in a field of grain. Instead, there is an abundance of food material, so that the frit-fly population can multiply without difficulty. Frit-fly larvae burrow into the stems of young wheat and oat plants, which soon collapse and die. And both larvae and adults have a special liking for the new shoots, or tillers, in a young crop, much preferring this artificial environment to the mature grassland that is their natural home.

Some grassland insects have a more immediate effect on larger animals than on plant life. Perhaps the most spectacular example of such creatures is the tsetse fly, whose habits have profoundly affected the lives of both domestic and wild animals of Africa. The tsetse fly, an inhabitant of west African savannas and elsewhere on the continent, has sometimes been called the "protector of nature" in Africa. This may seem a strangely flattering phrase to apply to an insect that spreads disease to man and his domestic animals. But it is a fact that fear of the tsetse has kept man from overexploiting marginal land and thus destroying wildlife.

Some species of tsetse carry the parasite of sleeping sickness in their salivary glands, and other species carry parasites causing sickness in domestic stock. In both cases the diseases are passed on through the insect bite. The cycle is continued by other tsetses, which become infected when they feed on the blood of diseased animals or people. The parasites pass through the various stages of their life cycle within the body of the fly; when they are ready to be passed on to the next host, they move to the fly's salivary glands.

Consequently, a tsetse that takes a blood meal from a disease-carrying warthog one day may transmit the disease to a cow or a human being a few days later. The warthog does not suffer from the sickness, though, for wild animals are generally immune or at least resistant to it, host and parasite having developed a tolerance of each other during the long course of evolution. and so it can truly be said that the tsetse fly protects nature by discouraging man from encroaching on the long-established territory of grassland wild animals. Methods of controlling the tsetse can be drastic. A method still widely practiced is the wholesale removal of savanna bushes and trees, for a certain amount of shade is essential to the life cycle of the fly. But this is a very costly procedure; furthermore, it can never be completely effective, because total eradication is impossible. Another method was the indiscriminate destruction of the wild animals that act as principal hosts of the fly and of the parasites it transmits. Though also ineffective (because some small mammals are always sure to escape destruction), such massacres were actually carried out until quite recently.

As a matter of fact, little has ever been gained that way, because once a cow has the disease, infection can be spread through the herd by other biting flies, even in the absence of the tsetse. Many ecologists believe that the most sensible procedure in tsetse-infected areas would be to protect wild game and crop it as a source of meat instead of trying to rear domestic cattle, which have no natural immunity.

It is a long way from the humid savannas of Africa where the tsetse fly lives to the soft

101

A Simple Food Web in a Temperate Grassland

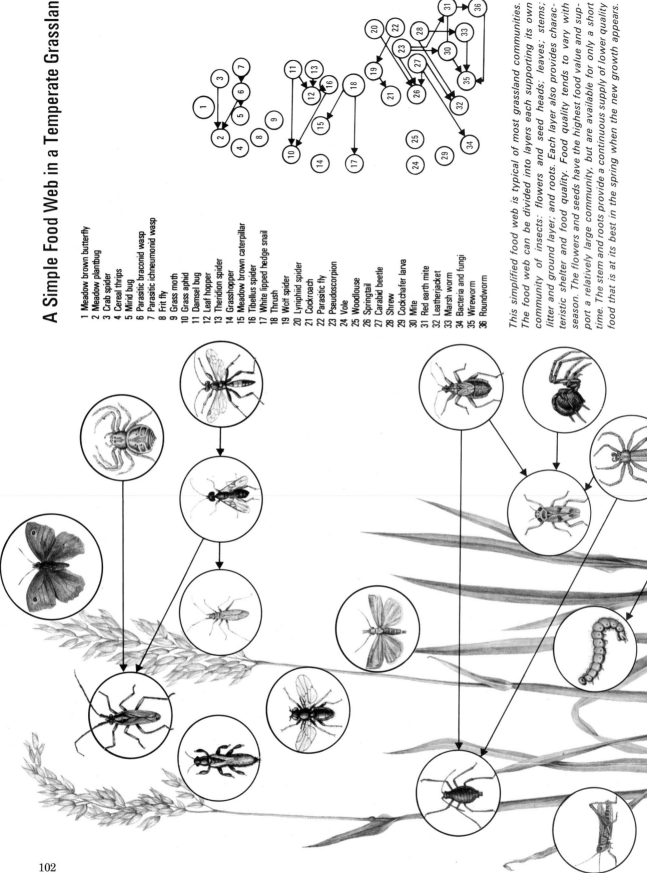

1 Meadow brown butterfly
2 Meadow plantbug
3 Crab spider
4 Cereal thrips
5 Mirid bug
6 Parasitic braconid wasp
7 Parasitic ichneumonid wasp
8 Frit fly
9 Grass moth
10 Grass aphid
11 Damsel bug
12 Leaf hopper
13 Theridion spider
14 Grasshopper
15 Meadow brown caterpillar
16 Tibellus spider
17 White lipped hedge snail
18 Thrush
19 Wolf spider
20 Lyniphiid spider
21 Cockroach
22 Parasitic fly
23 Pseudoscorpion
24 Vole
25 Woodlouse
26 Springtail
27 Carabid beetle
28 Shrew
29 Cockchafer larva
30 Mite
31 Red earth mite
32 Leatherjacket
33 Marsh worm
34 Bacteria and fungi
35 Wireworm
36 Roundworm

This simplified food web is typical of most grassland communities. The food web can be divided into layers each supporting its own community of insects: flowers and seed heads; leaves; stems; litter and ground layer; and roots. Each layer also provides characteristic shelter and food quality. Food quality tends to vary with season. The flowers and seeds have the highest food value and support a relatively large community, but are available for only a short time. The stem and roots provide a continuous supply of lower quality food that is at its best in the spring when the new growth appears.

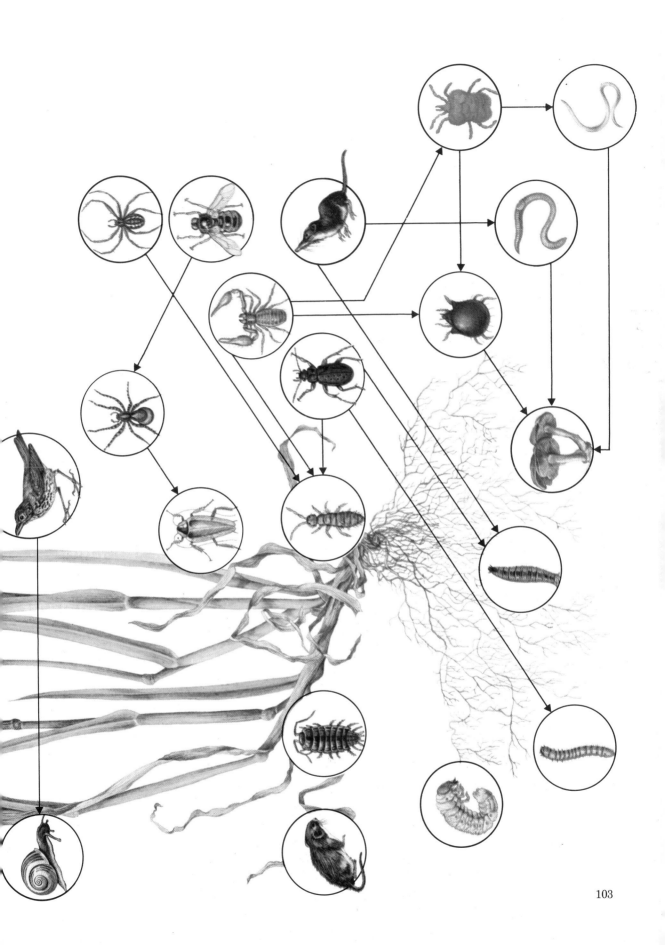

Above: a cardinal beetle searching for its insect prey. These colorful beetles, predators among grasses and flowers, also search under loose bark for the larvae of bark beetles. Left: a mating pair of burnet moths. These day-active moths exude an oil that protects them from their predators.

Golden rod infested with aphids. Normally inhabitants of grasslands, aphids do enormous damage when they invade cultivated areas, as generations of farmers and gardeners know!

meadows of the temperate zone. And the tsetse fly itself is a very different creature from the invertebrate fauna of other types of grassland. Even within a relatively small area, the fauna of one place is likely to be considerably different from that of another. A grassland on a dry chalk hill will have an arthropod community quite unlike the inhabitants of a grassland in a wet meadow, or one on coastal sand dunes, or in the South American pampas. Each community has its own distinctive species, just as each kind of grassland could hardly be mistaken for one of the others. And yet, although the differences are striking, the similarities are equally so.

We can generalize about the characteristic features of the insect life in grassland everywhere, even though somewhat different species are found in different places. Thus, it is evident to the close observer that the *structure* of grassland at least partly determines the type of fauna within it. For instance, where the vegetation is tall and dense, you will find a series of vertical layers, or *microhabitats,* where insects with different food requirements are able to live. This grassland insect world is like that found in a forest, differing only in scale; there are miniature layers corresponding to the forest canopy, the shrub layer, field layer vegetation, and the ground zone. And each small layer has its own range of microhabitats.

When we look at the insect inhabitants of a grass plant or of a broad-leaved plant growing in a grassland, we find several kinds of community.

At the top of the plant are certain species whose life cycle is linked to the seeds that are produced there. Other insects depend on the flowers, either as larvae living within the bud or as adults feeding on pollen, nectar, or other parts of the living flower. As we go lower down in the vegetation, we discover the larvae of small flies and beetles, which burrow into the grass stems, where they complete their development. And within the leaves there are galleries formed by many different species, such as small moths, flies, and beetles; these creatures, known as leaf miners, produce characteristic patterns of tunnels or galleries in the leaves, so that we can often identify the leaf miner just by looking at its handiwork. Yet other insects prefer the lower parts of the stem, close to the ground.

One of the most common groups that feed on the stems and leaves of plants—particularly on those that have soft tissues—is the aphid family. There are many species of aphid whose natural habitat includes grassland plants, and some of these have also adapted themselves to agricultural crops. Aphids are able to increase in numbers very rapidly because during part of their life cycle they reproduce *asexually*—that is, without the need for males. This quick multiplication is one reason why they can do so much damage to growing things. Many of us have seen aphid-infested bean crops in our gardens; and sugar-beet farmers know only too well what a serious problem these insects can prove to their crops, where aphids may spread the virus of a crippling disease.

Finally, there are insects capable of living on vegetation below the soil surface. There are many kinds of specialized feeders on roots of grasses and other plants. In fact, some of the most persistant enemies of the farmers are insects that are primarily grassland root feeders.

The vertical zonation of microhabitats in tall grasslands that we have just considered is immediately affected when the grassland is cut

microclimate within the grass; this means that the animals that were confined to the moist shady zone close to the ground suddenly find themselves exposed to bright light, drying winds, and the attentions of even more predators than usual. Therefore, life for the animals in that particular area cannot continue, and they must either move or die. Grazing thus has an immediate impact on the fauna, even though the same grassland plants still continue to grow.

When a meadow is no longer used for grazing or haymaking, the parts of the plants that were previously removed are able to grow again, so that flowers and seeds flourish once more. For a short period the effect is dramatic. Young

The loss of protective cover, whether through crop-cutting, such as this Austrian haymaking scene (right), grazing, or during fall, means that some small creatures will starve through lack of food, and others, such as the edible snail (above), are exposed to even more predators than usual.

or grazed. The reduction in the height of the grass does two things. First, in removing the upper parts of plants—that is, most of the stems, flowers, and seeds, together with a good many leaves—it kills all but the basal foliage of grasses and the ground-hugging rosettes of other plants. This, of course, diminishes potential food material for the insect community. Secondly, the change in vegetation structure alters the

106

seedlings appear in places where they have not been for years; rare plants that have not been permitted to grow to maturity come into flower at last; vigorous vegetation quickly grows tall and thick. And the insects that have been living in the roadside and field verges, or in other fields with uncut grass, immediately spread into the new area and multiply.

In countries with a modern and efficient agriculture, however, grassland is seldom allowed to rest unused, and so it is often only a temporary habitat for invertebrate life. Farmers are always looking for new ways to increase productivity, and one very efficient way is to plow the land every few years and replant it with fast-growing strains of grasses. Another is to use fertilizers, herbicides, and irrigation in an effort to encourage the kinds of vegetation that provide the most food for domestic animals. This means that undisturbed and unmodified permanent pasture, which is far richer in wild life than artificial grassland, is becoming increasingly scarce in the developed parts of the world.

Most meadowland today has a sparse fauna associated with temporary swards that provide only a limited variety of grasses, along with a very few other plants apart from agricultural weeds. There is one small compensation for the zoologist, however. New crops on cultivated land provide a type of habitat that occasional rare

and interesting animals are able to colonize for a short time before the crops are cut, grazed, or harvested. A curious example is a small, dark money spider *(Milleriana inerrans)*, a rare species that is normally found only in European sand dunes and other dry places, but that sometimes finds its way to available land that has been newly sown with grass or a cereal crop. Nobody yet knows exactly how it gets there. Such species breed rapidly and are likely to disperse elsewhere immediately afterward. But most grassland invertebrates cannot adapt themselves to such conditions and are not found in temporary leys.

Certain butterflies, for instance, will not thrive in areas where the type of vegetation does not remain constant. An example is the European species called the chalk-hill blue. This attractive insect is found only in grasslands on chalky soils in the European mainland and southern England. The larva feeds on the flower heads of the horseshoe vetch, a pretty plant with brilliant yellow blossoms, which grows abundantly only in places where the vegetation has been undisturbed for a long period. And so the chalk-hill butterfly is also localized.

Another example is the large blue butterfly, which is also European. This handsome insect has a remarkable life cycle, and this is probably why the species is becoming increasingly rare in some areas, particularly in Britain. It lays its eggs on the wild thyme, a low-growing plant found in quantity primarily in grassland where the vegetation is very short. When the eggs hatch (in June and July) the young larvae feed on the flowers and leaves of the wild thyme. Then, in the fall, a strange event takes place. Certain species of ant collect the larvae and take them underground into their nests. At this stage in their life cycle the caterpillars produce a sugary secretion that the ants relish. Throughout the winter months, each larva continues to grow in the ants' nest, but it becomes carnivorous and feeds on the developing ant larvae. In the spring it pupates, and in the summer it emerges above ground as a perfect blue butterfly.

In this case, the butterfly is dependent on a particular plant growing in a certain habitat, and also the presence of the species of ant that give the caterpillars their underground hospitality at just the right stage in the butterflies' development. Thus, the number of large blue butterflies has declined for two reasons: first, the delicate balance between wild thyme and the presence of the necessary species of ant is easily upset; and, secondly, agricultural "improvement" of pasture has decreased the extent of the butterfly's natural habitat.

Although such large, attractive insects as grasshoppers, crickets, butterflies, and a few kinds of beetle are the ones we can most easily spot in dry open grasslands, there are many other little creatures of considerable interest. For example, the famous 19th-century French naturalist Jean Henri Fabre was attracted by the behavior of a certain species of burrowing wasp. You can recognize these creatures by the beautiful colors—yellow, black, red, and orange in a variety of combinations—and if you are patient enough to sit still for a little while, you can watch their behavior without difficulty. Soon, if you wait long enough, you will discover that they are parasitic on spiders, which are essential to the development of the young wasp. The female

Opposite: the male adonis butterfly is just one of many of the blue butterflies of Europe that are becoming rare because agricultural land use inhibits the growth of the specific plants on which they feed. Below: the chalk-hill blue is utterly dependent on the yellow blossomed horseshoe vetch (right), a soil-enriching legume that is found only on the more stony soils.

wasp selects her victim and slowly approaches it. After a few moments of paying no apparent attention, the spider seems to become mesmerized and allows the wasp to sting it, injecting just enough poison in it to induce paralysis.

Now the wasp drags her victim away to a burrow that she has dug in a patch of bare ground, and there she stores the inert but still living body. Before leaving the burrow, the wasp lays an egg on the surface of the spider's body and plugs the burrow's entrance hole with earth, so that there is no trace of its existence. The wasp then seeks out the next victim to begin the process again until, like many insects, she either dies with the oncoming winter or hibernates. When the wasp's egg has hatched, the larva feeds on the paralyzed spider until only a shriveled skin remains. The larva then spins a cocoon. Eventually, the adult emerges, digs away the entrance, and begins the life cycle again.

Perhaps the most interesting and beautiful insects found in open sandy places, and especially on heaths and in dune grassland, are the tiger beetles. They constitute a very distinctive group of beetles, widespread in North America and in Europe, and particularly numerous in the tropics. One of the more common tiger beetles is a lovely green color and has large, prominent eyes. The larva, which lives in a burrow excavated in soft soil, is remarkable for its powerful head and strong jaws. It waits at the entrance of its burrow until some unwary insect passes by, then seizes the prey with a sudden lunge.

You may not find tiger beetles anywhere near your home unless you live in the right sort of countryside, but you can certainly find any number of interesting spiders that live in open short-tufted grasslands. In many parts of the world, for instance—especially in the warmer countries—there are a number of species of brilliantly colored jumping spiders, which you can recognize by their rather sturdy bodies, short legs, and large eyes situated at the front of the carapace. These eyes look a bit like the headlights of a car; if you watch closely, you will see that the jumping spiders actually have a total of eight such "headlights," but only the two that point forward are well developed for vision. Good sight is necessary for these spiders because they hunt by stalking and making sudden leaps at insects. It is probable that the six extra eyes help the spider to maintain its orientation through their sensitivity to different intensities of light.

Spiders are classed as arachnids, not insects. For one thing, they have eight legs, whereas insects have six. Interestingly enough, though, a number of spider species *look* like insects—a physical adaptation that may either protect them from predators or trick their prey into not recognizing them as dangerous enemies. To the inexperienced eye, some spiders mimic ants so successfully that they seem immediately identifiable as such. Their bodies are shaped like those of ants, they run with the same rapid motion, and they hold their foremost pair of legs in front of the head to give the appearance of antennae—which, of course, spiders do not possess. Thus they resemble six-legged ants instead of eight-legged arachnids. What they probably derive from this disguise is the protection gained from seeming to be more formidable creatures than they really are.

Another spider worth looking for in almost any dry grassland area is the fascinating *Theridion saxatile,* about whose life history we know a good deal, thanks to the work of Edwin Nørgaard, a modern Danish biologist who has spent many hours studying its behavior. This arachnid spins a small web under an overhanging bank or in vegetation, and you will know you have found its lair if you see the remains of insect prey outside its silken retreat, which is a cocoon-shaped structure, situated in the upper part of the web, within which the spider normally lives. If the spider has had a number of meals in its current hideaway, the web is covered with small brown fragments that look rather like pieces of dead vegetation suspended in mid-air. On closer examination, you will find that the insect fragments are nearly all ants, for this spider is a specialist feeder on ants, and the web that it constructs is a simple but effective ant trap.

Vertical strands of silk are attached from some sort of overhang to the ground, and there is a drop of sticky fluid on the lower part of every strand. When an ant blunders into these inconspicuous silk threads, perhaps touching one with a leg or antenna, it is immediately stuck and unable to pull itself free. Because the spider's retreat is connected to the web, the spider becomes rapidly aware of the ant's struggle and hurries out to capture its prey. It is, however, much smaller than some large ants, and so it must approach the prey warily or run the risk of being destroyed by the powerful jaws.

It now tries to bite the trapped ant between the joints of an antenna or leg, whichever happens to be nearest. Because ants have very hard bodies, it is likely that the delicate jaws of the little spider can penetrate only the softer membrane at the joints. Even that amount of penetration suffices, however, because the spider secretes a powerful poison, and the tiny quantity it is able to inject is enough to subdue the ant. When the poison has taken effect, the spider rushes down upon the ant, wraps it up in silk, and carries its prey back to the lair, to eat it in peace.

Another interesting feature of this spider's behavior is the care it takes of its eggs during their development. Normally, it keeps the egg sac inside the retreat, where the sac is safe from detection. But when the weather is very sunny, the enclosed space may become too hot; the spider then carries the egg sac outside, where the air temperature is lower. Knowing that the objective is to keep the eggs cool, you might be surprised to see the sac hanging in the web outside the retreat in full sunshine, but you can be sure that the egg sac is better off there. The reason, of course, is that the movement of air has a cooling effect in spite of the hot sun, whereas there is no ventilation inside the retreat.

So far, we have been glancing at some of the insects and other invertebrates associated with the living parts of a grassland ecosystem. But there is more to such an ecosystem than merely its living parts. When winter comes, the upper

Above: although the green grasshopper feeds on plants in its early stages, when fully grown it joins the huge army of predatory creatures and hunts for small grassland insects. Left: a jumping spider, which hunts its insect prey by stalking until close enough to leap upon it. Right: the potter wasp is a solitary creature that builds a vase-shaped nest for its larvae. Here we see the potter wasp provisioning its nest with a paralyzed bollworm.

111

portions of vegetation (in particular the flowering stems and their leaves) gradually fall to the ground. There they form what we call the *leaf-litter layer*. Anyone who walks through tall grassland that has not been grazed or cut for several years will have no trouble finding the soft mat of dead vegetation—sometimes as much as three or four inches deep—that lies on the ground surface.

Generally, this leaf-litter layer is a light, open structure, full of air spaces and little crevices where ground-living animals can shelter and find food. The dense shade and the protection from heat and drying winds provided by the leaves and stems that grow above the litter enable this microhabitat to remain cool and moist for most of the year. This makes it a very stable environment for a number of creatures that could not survive in more open, drier situations.

As the leaf litter gets older, it breaks into smaller pieces. If it is relatively moist, many species of algae, fungi, and mosses are able to live in it. Together with bacteria, they also serve as important food plants for small leaf-litter animals, especially the mites. Other animals feed on both the dead litter and the living fungi.

Many litter feeders—which we call *saprophagous* because they eat decaying rather than

A common early-morning sight on grasslands almost anywhere is the dew-spangled webs of spiders, such as the one shown here. Beside the web are a pair of mating grass spiders.

living vegetation—need the fungi and bacteria along with the leaf litter because they cannot digest plant material without the aid of these primitive forms of life. The reason for this is that the cellulose in plant cells can be broken down to digestible substances only by special enzymes, which few animals possess. Bacteria and fungi, however, do have these enzymes, and so they can break down the cellulose in the leaf litter to simpler substances that the saprophagous arthropods can more readily digest.

If you spread a handful of moist leaf litter over a pale-colored sheet of paper, you will probably find that you have captured several very small living creatures. At least two kinds of invertebrate are almost certain to be among them,

standing out against the pale background: the tiny, wingless insects known as springtails (because of special organs on their tails that enable them to leap about) and the very slow-moving mites. Springtails live almost entirely on decomposing leaf litter—or, perhaps more accurately, on the fungi, algae, or mosses that grow on the litter. The eight-legged mites are related to spiders, but the body of a mite is a single unit, not divided into two parts as those of spiders are. The mites include a vast number of different species: some are herbivorous, some saprophagous, and some either predatory or parasitic on other grassland invertebrates.

Predators are remarkably common in leaf litter, and among them are several species of very small spider no more than a tenth of an inch long. In rather rich, turfy grassland, which is not intensively cut or grazed, such spiders may occur in numbers of up to 800 to the square yard during the fall months, when with the arrival of the season's last generation, the population density usually reaches its highest point. It may appear improbable that such great numbers of spiders find enough to eat. But there is no doubt that their main source of food is the even more numerous springtails, which are only about half as long as the tiny spiders.

It is the little grassland spiders that create something that delights most people on sunny days in the fall: gossamer. In the late months of the year the litter spider leaves its moist, dark home and climbs up the nearest plant stem. When sufficiently far off the ground to feel the upward movement of air warmed by the morning sun, the spider combs out a strand of silk, which floats away like a balloon or parachute. As the silk strand lengthens and is caught more strongly by the breeze, the spider drifts away to find a new home. The urge to move to new places exists among most animals at some stage in their life cycle; it is basically a natural insurance against extinction—to start up new colonies that might balance the possible loss of older ones.

Sometimes, however, when millions of spiders have emerged from the litter ready to balloon away, a slight change in weather may make conditions unsuitable. When this happens, the little creatures continue for a time to search actively in the vegetation for a taking-off place; and as they move about, they leave trailing silken lines behind them. Because these threads are so numerous, they cover all the vegetation thickly

enough to form a fragile, shimmering white film. This extensive covering soon breaks up in the breeze, and we call the pieces that float away *gossamer*—a name probably derived from "Goose-summer," when people ate their geese, because it was the end of the season when they could be fattened with grass.

Although bacteria and fungi are probably the most important decomposers of the leaf litter, other creatures play their part in breaking up the material and changing its chemical nature by eating it and passing out the undigested parts as fecal pellets. The arthropods that probably do most of the decomposing are certain kinds of wood lice and millipedes.

Wood lice are crustaceans. Often abundant in tall grassland, they feed on a variety of different plants, but they also make a significant contribution to the mechanical breakdown of leaf litter. Some scientists believe that they cannot digest the cellulose and that it is only

the fungal material that grows on the litter that provides them with energy. Even so, simply by being passed through their guts, the leaf matter becomes available to other forms of life, especially to bacteria. And the bacteria finish the process of decomposition and return the organic material to the soil.

The pill millipede—a robust and tough animal about half an inch long—seems to be of particular importance in the process of litter breakdown. It is widespread in grasslands throughout the temperate regions of both the Old and New Worlds. In a recent experiment, naturalists studied the activities of the pill millipede in an area dominated by a vigorous, fast-growing grass; and they concluded that practically all the leaf litter produced there was being consumed

The dead plant material of the leaf litter is broken down and returned to the soil not only by microorganisms but also by many somewhat larger creatures—among them the millipedes (left) and the red mites (center). One very important litter feeder is the pillworm (right), a type of millipede that curls up in order to protect itself from predators.

by the large numbers of pill millipedes! In this particular case a single species was fulfilling a valuable role by breaking down the tough dead plant material, which would otherwise have been very slow to disappear.

However, even pill millipedes cannot eat dead grass until it has lain on the ground for about a year, because, as we have seen, certain chemical changes must take place before the cellulose in dead vegetable matter becomes digestible for insects. The digestive system of the millipede does not have the enzymes required for breaking down the cellulose that is the main constituent of plant cell walls. And so the litter goes through a year or so of attack by fungi, algae, and bacteria before it is "ripe" enough for the hungry pill millipedes.

It is interesting to note that leaf litter accumulates much more readily in the grasslands of cool temperate regions than in the tropics. This is because the heat and high relative humidity of wet tropical areas induce a rapid oxidation of organic material, so that it never piles up into a

permanent layer. For instance, in the extensive African savanna grasslands the occasional accumulation of litter is a very short-lived phenomenon and is likely to be of little importance to the ground fauna.

From the leaf-litter layer it is a short step downward to another grassland habitat: the soil itself. Here we find large numbers of the two most common leaf-litter groups—the small mites and the springtails—but they are joined in grassland soils by those all-important creatures, the earthworms. The upper layers of the soil usually have a fairly high proportion of humus. Humus is organic matter consisting of decomposed plant material into which are incorporated a quantity of soil particles. Most of the soil fauna is concentrated in this narrow upper zone, although the earth worms and a few other animals do go much deeper. The number of soil-dwelling animals is a good deal larger than you might think. It has been estimated that there may be as many as 60 million springtails and

3 million earthworms in an acre of grassland.

The extreme importance of the earthworm population arises, of course, from the fact that earthworms eat humus, and the fine soil that passes through their guts is deposited on the ground surface and acts as a fertilizer. Charles Darwin was the first biologist to point out that earthworms move an astonishing amount of soil by this means. He estimated that in an ordinary meadow the earthworms bring about 11 tons of soil per acre to the surface every year. They are the largest of soil invertebrates, and in a good pasture their underground population may be equal in weight to that of the grazing population on the surface. And so the balance of nature is maintained, with surface creatures depending on the living vegetation for food, while those below the surface consume the dead plants and humus.

It has been estimated that when a particular species of earthworm that was not indigenous to New Zealand was introduced into one grassland area of the country, plant productivity there increased by as much as 77 per cent. The worms' activities evidently benefit the vegetation in two vital ways: by incorporating fertilizers, such as dung and plant material, into the soil; and by aerating and improving the soil surface to a point where it provides the plants with better water-holding capacity and considerably easier root penetration.

Among the other soil animals that normally thrive in grassland regions are the larvae of flies and beetles. They feed on plant roots (as well as—to the constant anguish of farmers—on cereal and vegetable crops and on pastures sown for cattle grazing). The grubs familiarly called "wireworms," which are actually the larvae of click beetles, are probably the most notorious and widely dispersed of all root eaters. The wireworm is light brown in color and half an inch to three quarters of an inch long, and it feels hard to the touch. Click beetles themselves do very little harm to crops, but the wireworms in the soil will voraciously eat into any roots they can find. In particular, unfortunately for some farmers, they are fond of potatoes. And sometimes as many as a million or more of these hungry root-eaters will crowd into a single acre of farmland.

Another widespread inhabitant of the grassland soil is the large, fat, legless grub of the crane fly (or, more popularly, "daddy longlegs," a name it shares with harvestman spiders). These juicy grubs may be as much as one inch long and are apparently a favorite food for ground-feeding birds, particularly for starlings and crows. Studies have shown that in some areas starlings spend much of their time searching for larvae as food for their nestlings. Although the crane flies are most common in natural grasslands, they do find their way into cultivated fields. If you ever do any gardening, you will almost surely notice that your newly dug soil has some special attraction for the neighborhood blackbirds and, in Britain, robins. These and other birds will have come to prospect the turned-up soil for food. What they are looking for are the wireworms and crane-fly larvae that you have almost certainly brought to the surface while turning the soil.

It is not generally realized that the caterpillars of a number of common moths are also root-eaters that live in the soil. Several different species have this habit. On the other hand, although spiders are such common animals, found in almost every situation from the tops of mountains to coastal sand dunes and salt marshes, very few of them actually live in the soil. There are one or two very tiny species that thrive in the surface layers among the soil crumbs or under stones, but it is unusual for a spider to penetrate below the surface unless it lives in a burrow.

One such burrow-living spider is sometimes present in abundance in grassland areas, although you will not find it easy to catch a glimpse of it. This is the trapdoor spider, a large and sturdy predator, which constructs a silk-lined tube some nine inches or more deep into the soil. Trapdoor spiders are particularly common in the semidesert grasslands of the world's tropics, but many species live in America, Africa, and Australia. A closely related European spider (which the British call the "purse-web" spider) differs from the others only in that it does not close the entrance to its tube with the hinged lid (or trapdoor) of the related nonEuropean species.

The purse-web spider normally lurks down low in its tube, but the silk that lines the tube is spun right up above the surface and along the ground for three inches or so; and this extension of the lining is shaped rather like the finger of a glove. Even the experienced observer may have trouble finding it because it is covered with dead leaves and other litter fragments—a very effective camouflage for deceiving the spider's prey.

Beetles that wander through the grassland and stumble into this curious web structure either get their feet tangled in it and cannot move or

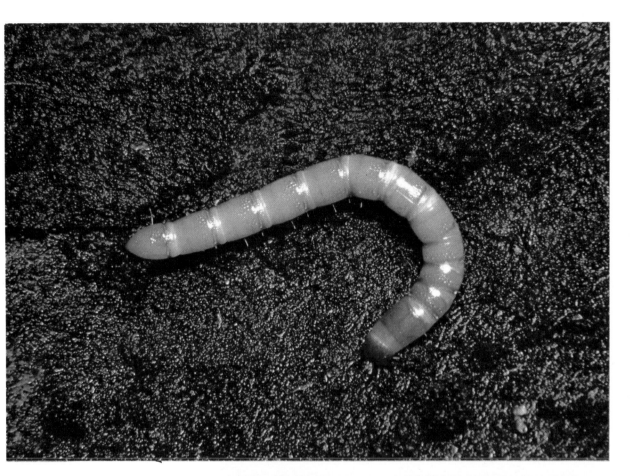

Above: this wireworm (to give it the name by which such grubs are generally known) is the larva of a click beetle, and sometimes as many as a million of these destructive root-eaters live in a single acre of farmland. Unfortunately, they are especially fond of potatoes and carrots.

In the lowest of grassland habitats, the soil itself, live a number of very useful animals, as well as some that can do a great deal of harm to plant life. Perhaps the most valuable such soil creatures are the common earthworms (left), which aerate and help to fertilize the earth. More of a nuisance are slugs (right), the relatives of land snails; both slugs and snails eat green vegetables and can severely damage soft fruits.

The juicy larvae (known as leatherjackets) of this crane fly live in the grassland soil. Hungry birds dig many of them out.

else create a disturbance in the silk that arouses the spider waiting below ground. The alert predator rushes to the surface and seizes the prey with its powerful jaws, which can slice their way through the silk tube into the body of the insect. The spider then makes a neat cut in the tube wall, pulls its prey through, and mends the tear expertly before taking the victim down below to consume it at leisure. As you can see, although the tube of the trapdoor spider is difficult to find, it is well worth studying, once the keen naturalist has searched one out.

Such spiders are good examples of the species that utilize both the soil and the leaf litter in the world's grasslands. The tube in the soil provides the spider with a safe retreat, and the part on the ground surface traps its prey. Like this spider, very many other interesting invertebrate species depend on the permanence of leaf litter, and they are all adversely affected by treading and grazing. Sheep and cattle eat the green vegetation and expose the litter, which is also broken up when these large mammals tread on it. People trampling about a great deal on grassland—the picnicking public, for instance—have the same sort of effect.

Most litter animals dwell in this habitat because they prefer the shaded and moist conditions characteristic of undisturbed grassland. When the vegetation is removed by cutting or grazing, the sun dries out the litter, which is scattered by high winds and the hooves of the big animals. And the action of treading breaks up dead stems and leaves, many of which may be compressed into the soil surface, thus depriving the litter-layer creatures of their benefits.

Experiments have shown that, in general, undisturbed grassland that reaches perhaps 10 or 12 inches in height has a larger number both of species and of individual animals living in it than the shorter cut or grazed grassland. Other investigations also indicate that undisturbed leaf litter may be as much as four inches deep and is full of spaces and crevices where small animals can live, hunt, and feed. When treading takes place, the fauna immediately declines in variety and individual numbers.

The vegetation itself (apart from its inhabi-

tants) is for the most part much more resistant to such treatment, so that it is quite possible for a grassland to remain pleasant and green even though subjected to heavy use. This is because many grasses and other plants can live for a very long period—several years, in fact—without having to produce flowers and seed. They grow by vegetative means, spreading their roots and rhizomes through the soil, and they can produce lots of fresh new leaves even though the upper portions of the plants are removed. Insect life is much less resilient.

This spider outside its silk-lined burrow is not, as it would appear, a trapdoor spider, but a wolf spider. Many wolf spiders both look and act like other kinds of spider and all live either directly by hunting or by lying in wait for their prey.

Grassland Conservation

We have taken a look at some of the different types of grassland in the world and have learned that only a few of them can be called truly "natural." Most of the grassland areas with which we are familiar are artificial or have been much modified by man. This is because during the course of human history men have destroyed forests in order to create rangelands, have drained marshes to form meadows, and have constructed large recreational areas of grassland for sports and other leisure activities. And so, with very little natural grassland still remaining to us, it seems obvious that the best such areas must be protected from further exploitation if the characteristic wildlife is to survive.

One objective of nature conservation is the preservation of interesting or rare animals and plants, but this is only *one* objective. Conservation has another important goal: to protect the future of our own species. All living things in nature form the environment in which we live. They contribute to our food supply and to the pleasure we get from attractive landscapes and they also help to heal erosion damage and the dereliction caused by industrial activities. Grassland plants play a vital role in all our lives because, in addition to including species important as food crops, many of them are extremely well adapted to colonizing disturbed ground and renewing its vigor. It is shortsighted folly on our part to allow the extinction of any living thing through unwise use of the land, for the impoverishment of wildlife communities means the inevitable loss of material that could contribute to the well-being of mankind.

As we have seen in the preceding chapters, natural grasslands are generally much richer in animal life than those modified or made by man. As natural grasslands decline in area, the larger and more striking animals tend to be the first to disappear, because they need much more space than smaller creatures, and also because they are

Twenty minutes from London's crowded center, the slopes of Hampstead Heath preserve a refreshing "country park," where Londoners and their dogs can stroll in peace. London has managed to retain more green spots than most other cities.

especially vulnerable to predation by man. Intelligently handled conservation programs, however, can reverse this trend. Just to take a few examples of what such programs can achieve, let us take a brief look at the bison, the great birds of prey, and the bontebok, all of which have been brought close to extinction during the last 150 years.

The American bison, which used to roam the prairies in great herds, was almost eliminated during the 19th century. Had it not been for the efforts of a few public-spirited persons, including the noted American naturalist William Temple Hornaday, the species might well have been lost forever. These people banded together to form a society dedicated to the bison's protection, and they managed to find shelter for some of the surviving animals in Yellowstone National Park, which the United States government had created in 1872. It was, incidentally, the first national park in the world. The government itself took over the effort to save the bison after the winter of 1893–4, when the remaining animals were nearly destroyed by poachers who had penetrated into the most inaccessible areas of Yellowstone Park.

In 1895 Congress made it illegal to hunt buffalo in a national park; and during the first

wo decades of the 20th century, small additional herds were established in four national refuges. Meanwhile, Canada had also passed laws against killing bison, and she acquired her first protected herd from the United States in 1906. By 1912 a newly formed Buffalo National Park in Alberta had become a major center for the restoration of this animal as part of the Canadian fauna. North America's bison multiplied rapidly under such protection; today they are increasing in numbers in a very healthy way throughout millions of acres of government-controlled grassy plains.

As an indication of how the existence or non-existence of one type of creature affects the well-being of others (an object lesson in ecology, in fact), consider what happened as the bison came close to extermination. With its decline, and with the consequent removal of competition for food, the prairie-dog population soared for a time, and this prompted a vigorous attempt by farmers to exterminate it. Their campaign nearly succeeded—and one of its side effects seems to have been that the population of black-footed ferrets, which prey on prairie dogs, was also reduced. This may have been partly due, too, to the destruction of the original grassland and the plowing up of the prairie-dog burrows.

An attempt is now being made by the United States National Parks Service and the Fish and Wildlife Service to live-trap any black-footed ferrets found in areas where rodent control operations are going on. The live animals are then transported to national parks where prairie-dog colonies are being allowed to exist undisturbed by man. Thus, the near-extinction of the bison ultimately meant the near-extinction of other creatures that inhabit the same kind of ecosystem as the bison. But nature conservation has, we hope, saved them all.

A less dramatic but perhaps more sinister story is that of the large birds of prey. It is a highly significant story for our time, because the villain is a modern invention: the chemical pesticide. The big predatory birds are especially vulnerable to the dangers of pesticides because they are at the end of the *food chain*. (That is, a chain of organisms in which each link in the chain feeds on the one before and is eaten by the one after. The chain starts with the vegetational primary producers and ends with the carnivores.) We can best understand what this means by considering an example. The osprey is a fish-eating hawk widespread in North America and northern parts of the Old World. The large fish that it catches in freshwater lakes have eaten smaller fish, and these in turn have preyed on even smaller invertebrate life. If a pesticide is present in the water, greater concentrations of it are to be found at each successive link in the food chain, so that the strongest dose is eaten by the largest "top" predators.

With large vertebrates such as birds of prey,

A bison grazing in Yellowstone National Park. Such scenes might have been mere memories today, had not the United States government taken conservation measures in the 1890s.

125

Above: a young fish-catching osprey exercising its wings before flight. Right: carrion-eating vultures at rest. Carnivorous birds are increasingly endangered by the large amounts of chemical pesticides that tend to become concentrated in their food.

the pesticide is seldom taken in big enough doses to cause death. But such poisons as DDT tend to accumulate in the tissues, affecting bodily functions and perhaps diminishing breeding success. It was this accumulation of pesticides in the tissues that reduced the ospreys breeding on the Connecticut River from 200 pairs in 1938 to 12 pairs in 1965. By this time the ospreys' eggs contained 51 parts per million of DDT residues, and the average clutch produced only 0.5 young. This contrasts with a normal production of 2.2 to 2.5 young per nest. A similar situation applies to both the bald eagle and the peregrine falcon, which temporarily disappeared from the United States in the days just before the use of DDT came under government control.

The golden eagle has been affected in a slightly different way. In Europe and, to a lesser extent, North America, this eagle frequently feeds on carrion during the winter. In the mountain pastures where it lives, the commonest source of carrion is sheep, some of which generally die during periods of either food shortage or severe weather. Until quite recently, most sheep used to be treated once a year with a very persistent insecticide, dieldrin, to kill skin parasites; and the dieldrin gradually accumulated in the bodies of the carrion-eating eagles. The greater the accumulation, the fewer the offspring, and the eagle populations of America and Europe were reduced at a spectacular rate.

In recent years, however, there has been a great deal of legal action to reduce or even ban the use of the more persistent chemical poisons.

As a result, there has been a noticeable rise in the eagle population of the Western world during the 1970s. In less developed parts of the world, however, pesticides are still used freely, and the wildlife suffers.

The bontebok of southwestern Cape Province, South Africa, is another threatened creature, and its contrasting markings of black, white, and brown make it also an especially attractive one. Even before the arrival of Europeans its distribution appears to have been restricted to a total area of only about 170 miles by 35 miles. And the population has now declined to such a degree that bontebok can be found solely in a number of relatively small protected areas. As far back as 1830, the species was thought to be in danger of extinction, and it survived primarily through the interest of a few land-owners who attempted to preserve the animal on their property. By 1931, when South Africa established the first bontebok national park, it

was stocked with only 17 animals—the last surviving members of the species.

Fortunately, these few survivors bred successfully, and they continued to increase, though slowly. The original protected area proved to be too poor in vegetation to sustain a viable population. There was some evidence that the soil lacked certain elements essential for proper nutrition. And so the stock was moved to a completely new park in 1960, by which date there were 61 bonteboks in the area. Now they began to flourish: by 1965 the herd had increased to 150, and by 1970 it numbered about 250.

Meanwhile, the original herd had been split from time to time, with the intention of giving the bontebok a somewhat wider distribution. It seems likely that as many as 800 bonteboks now inhabit a variety of protected areas in southern Africa. Even 800, however, is a small number; the bontebok must still be one of the rarest antelopes in Africa. Perhaps the easiest place to catch a glimpse of one is the University of Cape Town, where a small herd—fewer than 20—graze peacefully on the green slopes of Table Mountain, below the memorial to Cecil Rhodes, founder of the university.

Although uncontrolled hunting can do a great deal of harm to wildlife, so also can too much protection, and it can be argued that disciplined hunting is by no means an unmitigated danger to

example, hunting eliminated the red deer in the Swiss Engadine, and the red deer's natural predators, the wolf, bear, and lynx, were also shot. Soon afterward, when the area was protected from hunting and set aside as a national park, the red deer began to return, drifting in from the mountains of Austria. Today the population is about 1350—which, in the opinion of the park managers, is about twice as many as the natural pastures can support. In the absence of

Among the rarest of African antelopes are these handsome bonteboks, which live in only a few protected areas of South Africa. Less than half a century ago, fewer than 20 members of this threatened species survived. Today, thanks to conservation measures, there are several hundreds of them.

Right: a safari camp near Nairobi. Camps such as this do not merely provide fun for the tourists; they are ideal for the detailed observations of many kinds of grassland animals in their natural surroundings.

wild animals. Granted that hunting almost brought about the extinction of the bison and must take much of the blame for the disappearance of several other species in other parts of the world, the fact remains that it has ancient and honorable traditions and is self-defeating only if practiced unwisely. Most of the big herbivorous animals in the wilder regions of the world can withstand a certain amount of hunting if their rangelands are maintained in good condition and cover a large enough area. A healthy population has a great capacity for increasing its numbers, and so the controlled taking of a "crop" does no harm.

Too much protection, on the other hand, can result in part of the herd being lost through starvation. When there are no natural predators to regulate populations, hunting may be necessary in order to prevent overexploitation of natural food supplies. Half a century ago, for

natural predators, this population could withstand considerable cropping by hunting, but park regulations do not permit this. As a consequence, the mountain pastures suffer from overgrazing, and there is a heavy mortality of deer during the winter, when food is short.

What, then, are the function and purpose of national parks? And what are some of the problems that develop when the national-park method of conservation is adopted? To answer these questions, let us take a look once more at the situation in Africa, where a number of such parks now exist—mainly because they provide Africa's developing nations with a rich source of tourist revenue. Although the chief function of these parks from the standpoint of local governments is, no doubt, to make money by putting wild animals on public display, they are certainly of the greatest ecological importance, because they are helping to preserve some of the world's finest aggregations of animals.

We must remember that the wide open spaces of Africa have a particularly rich wildlife, including very many birds and large numbers of species of reptiles, fish, plants, and invertebrate animals. Some 2000 species of fish have been identified in Africa, for instance, as compared with about 50 in Europe, and the abundance of species of birds is second only to that of South America. The birds include the largest living species—the ostrich—and the 3 million flamingos of the Rift Valley of east Africa have been acclaimed as one of the most remarkable spectacles that naturalists can see anywhere. This rich wildlife provides an unrivaled field for study, and that is why foreign biologists, as well as the Africans themselves, have begun to use protected wildlife areas for ecological research.

As we have seen, however, too much protection can mean too many animals for the land to

support, and overpopulation has become a problem in some of these areas. Consider the savannas of Uganda, where a relatively high rainfall produces a lusher growth of grass and probably supports a greater *biomass* (that is, weight of living animals) than anywhere else in the world. A number of the animals in this superb big-game country are species that reach a considerable size: notably elephants, hippos, and buffaloes. An average adult elephant may weigh 4 tons, a hippo 2 to 3 tons, and a buffalo 1 ton. So if we compare an elephant with a small antelope such as the hartebeest (300 to 400

pounds), we see that a single elephant represents a biomass equal to that of about 25 hartebeests. Similarly, a herd of 15 kob antelopes equal only one bull buffalo. So it is the preponderance of very big animals that accounts for the greater part of the high biomass supported by the Uganda savannas.

In some sections of the region, one square mile has to support more than 100,000 pounds of living animals—twice the biomass of the famous wild-game populations in places such as the plains of Tanzania's Serengeti National Park. In addition to the big animals, of course, there

Crater Lodge, overlooking the Ngorongoro Crater in Tanzania, provides a splendid starting point from which to embark on a serious study of the area's abundant wildlife.

are many of medium size, including a species of hartebeest, the topi, the waterbuck, and the Uganda kob. It is the large herbivores, however —particularly elephants and hippos—that may seriously degrade their environment when there are too many of them. The result can be seen in Uganda's Kabelega (formerly Murchison) Falls Park, where the protected populations of large animals have been steadily increasing. There are now about 9000 elephants, 8000 hippos, and 10,000 buffaloes in the park. Corresponding figures for another Uganda reserve, the Ruwenzori National Park, are equally startling: 2500

elephants, 12,000 hippos, and 12,000 buffaloes.

In recent years the elephant herds of Kabelega Falls Park have destroyed almost all the tree growth over vast areas. In the absence of trees, the grass grows tall and lush, but fires easily break out during the dry season, and so the young trees that might have replaced those killed by elephants are always destroyed. Thus the countryside is being changed from a fairly dense woodland to open tall grassland—a process that cannot be reversed unless the number of elephants is significantly reduced.

Although elephants prefer the bark and foliage of trees, they can live almost entirely on grass if no other food is available. We know, however, that they need a large amount of calcium to keep their bones healthy, and some experts believe that they get much of their calcium from eating bark. Whether they can remain in good health and continue to breed and rear their young on a diet of grass alone has yet to be seen.

The new grassland environment created by the elephant is, to be sure, a boon to grazing animals.

If there are too many large herbivores in a limited area, the environment may suffer severe damage from the depredations caused by their enormous appetites. Left: a giraffe browses in the Masai steppelands of Tanzania. Above: a baobab tree, whose edible fruit and ropy bark are highly valued by Africa's human populations, can look like this after hungry elephants have browsed upon it.

Giraffes and black rhinos, which are browsers, are scarce in Kabelega Falls Park, and there are no kudu or impala; but the square-lipped—or "white"—rhinoceros does well in this new-made habitat. The white rhino is grayish in color; possibly it gets its misleading name from the Afrikaans word *weit*, which means "broad" and is a reference to the beast's huge, square muzzle, which is adapted for grazing, not browsing. Formerly widespread, but much less common in recent years, the white rhino is the third largest land mammal in Africa. It is only slightly smaller than the hippo, and about twice the weight of its nearest relation, the black rhino.

Most of the continent's remaining white rhinos—perhaps not more than 1000 or so—are confined to an area on the left bank of the Nile. In recent years, however, a few have been transferred to Kabelega Falls Park, to give them security from predation, to which they have been peculiarly susceptible. This may be partly because they do not apparently see very well, having small eyes for an animal of that size, and they may have to depend on an acute sense of smell for detecting danger. They should certainly thrive in the grassland savanna where they are protected from all but illegal hunters. Some illegal killing of the white rhino

is inevitable, though, for many poachers export the rhinos' horns to Asia, where it is believed they have aphrodisiac powers.

Kabelega Falls National Park is of particular interest to the conservationist because we know something about the landscape changes that have taken place over more than half a century. In the early 1900s, young Winston Churchill walked and cycled through what is today the national park, and he described the area as woodland, with broad corridors of forest along the river valleys. Today that same area is a sea of grass, relieved here and there by a few stretches of derelict forest and scattered bush. This illustrates the sort of problem that can arise when animal populations, relatively safe from the hunter's gun, are confined within a limited area bounded by such man-made barriers as roads, towns, and agricultural land. Unable to wander elsewhere if the habitat becomes unsuitable, protected from most forms of predation, the growing numbers of herbivores are soon forced to compete for too little food.

One of the clear symptoms of habitat over-exploitation is a general trend toward simplification; as the vegetation is destroyed, other types of variety within the habitat are also lost. Thus, the disappearance of trees and bushes means not only the spread of grassland but also the loss of hundreds of species of birds and such small mammals as squirrels and monkeys, and of thousands of insects, along with large browsing animals such as the giraffe and the black rhinoceros. We all know how a lemming population rises to a peak and then falls with a crash following the destruction of its arctic habitat. A similar fate may await the large herbivores if they are permitted to eat out their food supply. When their food becomes scarce, animals lose weight and vigor, and populations tend to go into a decline as breeding stops.

This is one all-important reason why Africa's large national parks need to look seriously into alternatives to a policy of strict noninterference with nature. Some people in authority still fail to realize that animal populations should be

Left: Central Park in the heart of New York's Manhattan and (below) the Hajenbeek Zoo at Hamburg, Germany, are outstanding examples of "nature parks," carefully planned to serve as temporary retreats from busy sidewalks.

controlled by regular cropping in order to prevent them from degrading the environment—which means eventual starvation for many of the animals. Many naturalists feel that it is not unethical to cull some of the animal population before the habitat is damaged. Tourism compounds the problem, of course, for park authorities know that the public visit national parks mainly to see wild animals at close quarters; if the numbers are reduced, even though it is ecologically necessary, the chances of their being sighted by tourists will be so small that tourists will be discouraged, and, in many cases, a profitable source of revenue will be lost.

A number of densely populated countries, particularly in Europe, have established "nature parks" or "country parks" as a special type of amenity land. Such a park is likely to be set up in an attractive part of a larger area, and the aim is to maintain diversity as a public benefit for local people to enjoy. The park is often situated close to a large town, and it may be equipped with camping grounds, boating lakes, swimming pools, and artificial grasslands, sown and maintained for outdoor activities of all types. In more rural areas, enlightened planners try to preserve a landscape in harmony with the history of the region, and perhaps to provide interesting walks through meadows and pastures, where wildlife is one of the special pleasures to be enjoyed.

This type of amenity can also be created out of virtually nothing. In industrialized countries there are an increasing number of sites that have been abandoned because of devastation caused by industry. Some of these are areas where minerals such as gravel, iron ore, sand, chalk, or coal have been worked out or where once-active factories have fallen into disuse; others consist of ugly heaps of industrial waste. Such places used to be thought of as useless deserts, but modern knowledge about soil and plants enables us to create completely new landscapes in them. Trees can be planted, the land can be contoured to make hills and valleys, lakes can be excavated, and grasslands for leisure activities can be formed. When such newly made grasslands include flowering plants as well as grasses, they soon attract many common insects, particularly butterflies—and so what was until recently a lifeless desert may well become a fertile and pleasant oasis in an urban area where open rural land is scarce or non-existent.

136

Pennyhill Park, a former hunting park of Britain's Stuart kings at Bagshot, in southern England. The lawns at Pennyhill are typical of the many artificial or much modified grassy areas in parks and gardens throughout the industrialized West.

Although a grassland flora and fauna can survive in a wide variety of areas, from landscaped highways to former waste heaps, the only places that can be managed specifically for the preservation of wildlife are nature reserves and national parks. The question of *how* to manage them is by no means easy to answer. Some national parks, particularly in America, operate according to strict regulations. For instance, the public are not permitted to wander away from designated footpaths. Elsewhere, the large national parks may be mainly natural areas, where the object of management is primarily to protect the site from disturbance by limiting agriculture, forestry, and building development. The wild animals in such places maintain the grassland areas in their own way.

In still other parks, especially in the mountain pastures of Europe, a tradition of grazing persists and is, so to speak, "tolerated" by the wildlife. Such grassland is known as "seminatural." Large flocks of sheep attended by a shepherd, for example, remain a common sight in the Spanish

Pyrenees, where they have grazed for centuries, and many species of birds and mammals have become adapted to their presence in this seminatural grassland.

The nature reserves of lowland regions require a different kind of management from the rather easy type that works well in mountain country above the timberline. Whereas mountain grassland will remain grassland with or without human intervention, many kinds of low-lying grassland would, if permitted to develop naturally, change to some other type of vegetation. Ecologists are aware that, as a result of natural succession, grasslands below the natural timberline may gradually revert to forest if they are not cut, grazed, or burned. It may take a long time for bushes and trees to take over in places where the soil is poor and there is little rain, but it can happen quite rapidly under suitable conditions—in western Europe during the 1950s, when myxomatosis destroyed the rabbit population, open grassland became thick scrub in a few years.

In low-lying regions, therefore, conservation

Creative landscaping can reclaim disused industrial sites, as shown in these Scottish scenes: an old quarry, filled in, makes a lovely picnic spot (left); and the green path allowed to grow over a long-abandoned railroad has become a nature trail (above).

of grassland may require the kind of management that concentrates on halting the natural succession, so that the bush phase never develops. Or, alternatively, bushes may be allowed to develop, but only temporarily. They can be cleared away before the grass is smothered in order to restore the grass cover. The advantage of this latter procedure for nature conservation is that the rotation of grassland and scrub provides more variety for the habitat. As a result, a more varied selection of animals—particularly of insects—can live there.

An informed management of a nature reserve defines its objectives and then regulates the permitted amount of grazing according to those objectives. As a final example, if there is a particularly interesting insect fauna, grazing should be rather light, so that a mosaic of tall grass and short grass is developed. This provides a wider range of environmental conditions for various insect species—those that feed in the upper parts of grasses as well as those that live close to the ground in the humus. With comparatively light grazing, such patterns often occur quite naturally, because the more palatable grasses are cropped short, whereas the grasses that the grazing mammals avoid grow tall and dense.

Thus, in any one of a number of ways, man and nature can work together to provide benefits for both, with no losses for either. The idea of co-operation should be at the heart of any intelligent program for conserving the flora and fauna of a grassland area. The great British ecologist Charles S. Elton has pointed out that any environment fit to live in is one in which man is prepared to modify himself as well as nature. True conservation, he says, involves a search for "some wise principle of co-existence between man and nature, even if it has to be a modified kind of man and a modified kind of nature."

Index

Page numbers in *italics* refer to illustrations or captions to illustrations

robins, interest in newly turned soil, 118
Rocky Mountains, effect on North American prairies, 10, 38
rodents, 68–82; effect on grasslands, 71; species variation in different continents, 78
root system, of heavily grazed grassland, 16
root-feeding insects, 106
rotation, of grassland and scrub, 138–9
roundworm, *102–3*
Ruwenzori National Park, Uganda, 131
rye, 19, 20

Sable antelope, *54–5*, 57–8
safari camps, *128*
saiga antelopes, 29–30, 35, 63–7, *67*
salt marshes, consolidation with *Spartina anglica*, 19
sand dunes, stabilization with marram grass, *18*, 19
sand grouse, 87
saprophytes, 112–3
savanna, 14, 22, 30, *32*; birds of, 82–91; fauna, 43, 47
scavengers, *43*
scops owl, *44–5*
Scotland, reclaimed industrial sites, *139*
secondary consumers, 101
seed-eating birds, 84–5
"seminatural" grassland, 138
Serengeti National Park, Tanzania, 130
sheep, destroyers of woody plants, *13*
sheep-farming, in Australia, 63
sheep-grazing, New Zealand, *26*
shrew *102–3*
simplification, in habitat over-exploitation, 135
size, of grassland animals, 130
sky, of the prairies, 38
sleeping sickness, 101
slugs, *119*
snail, edible, *106*
snakes, grassland, 91–2
soil: amount moved by earthworms, 117; insects of, 116–21
sorghum, 19
South American grasslands (pampas), 25; animals of, 58–62
Spartina anglica, 19
speed, of grassland animals, 51–2

spiders, 110–1; burrow-living, 118; parasitized by burrowing wasp, 108–9; small, predatory, 113
springtails, *102–3*, 113, 116
steinbok, *54–5*
steppelands, 13, 27, *27*; large animals of, 63–7; vole infestation, 77
Stipa, of Eurasian steppes, 28
stork, as locust-eater, 98, 101
structure of grassland, effect on insect life, 105
susliks, 71, *73*
Swiss Engadine, red deer population, 128

Table Mountain, Cape Town, 128
tawny eagle, 68
temperate forest, reversion to grassland, *14–15*
temperate grassland: food web, *102–3*; world distribution, *14–15*
termites, *43*, *44–5*, 84; eaten by anteaters, 62, *63*; fungus, *44–5*
terns, 83, *83*
territory, of the prairie dog, 80
Tertiary period, 13
thatching, *18*, 19
theridion spider, *102–3*
Theridion saxatile, 110
Thomson's gazelle, *35*, *44–5*, *54–5*
thrush, *102–3*
thyme, wild, 108
tibellus spider, *102–3*
tick, *44–5*
tiger beetle, *100*, 110
tillers, 16–17
tine, 43
toads, 92–3
topi, *44–5*, 49, 51, *54–5*
trapdoor spider, 118
tree cricket, *96*
trees of savanna lands, *32*
tropical grassland: encroachment on to tropical forest, *14–15*; reversion to semidesert, *14–15*; world distribution, *14–15*
tsetse fly, *100*, 101
tundra, 27

Underground food stores, of rodents, 68
underground invertebrates, equal in weight to surface grazers, 117
undisturbed grassland, yield of

fauna, compared with grazed land, 121
ungulates, 61
upland grasslands, 12
Uzbekistan steppeland, *27*

Vegetation, re-appearance with rabbit depopulation, 75–6
vegetation–animal balance, 51
veldt, 25, 32
vertical layers of vegetation, and insect life, 105, 106
vicuna, 60
viper, European, *90*, 91–2
vole, *102–3*
vultures, *44–5*, 84
vulturine guinea fowl, *86*

Wallaby, 35, 63
wallaroo, 62
warthog, 35, *54–5*
wasp, burrowing, 108–9
water buffalo, *44–5*
water hole, Texas, cattle at, *13*
weasel European, *75*
weaver bird, *44–5*, 85, *87*
webs of spiders, *112*, *114*, 118, 120
weevil, *44–5*
wheat, 19, *20*
white rhino, 42, 132
white-lipped hedge snail, *102–3*
wildlife: of grasslands, diminishing, 12, preservation of, 67; richness of African, 129
wildebeest, *44–5*
wireworm, *102–3*, 117, *119*
wolf: maned, of pampas, 62; Russian attempt at extermination, 66
wolf spider, *102–3*, *121*
woodland bison, 40
woodlouse, *102–3*, 114
woody plants, destruction by sheep, *13*
worms, value to soil, 117

Yellow-billed hornbill, *88*
Yellowstone National Park, 124, *125*

Zebras, *36*, *44–5*, *54–5*, 57

143

Picture Credits

Key to position of picture on page: (B) bottom, (C) center, (L) left, (R) right, (T) top; hence (BR) bottom right, (CL) center left, etc.

Artist Credits